CHANGING LANES
Couples Redefining Retirement

By Beverly Battaglia, Ph.D.

Acknowledgments

Many people have helped me over the five years it has taken to research, interview and write this book. I now have the opportunity to express my gratitude, first, to my husband, who has lived with me through the many stages of writing and developing this book. To my sons, Dave and Ric, and my daughters-in-law, Julie and Shelly who have been supportive in giving me ideas and input. To my grandchildren, Alden, Roman, Kate and Chris who provide me the caring and love I need as we experience each other.

A special thank you is extended to the over 100 individuals and couples interviewed for this book. *Changing Lanes: Couples Redefining Retirement* couldn't have been written without their candor in sharing their ideas, thoughts, and experiences, which became an integral part of this book.

I'd like to acknowledge Gail Kolsky, who was my champion and advisor through the various iterations of the manuscript. Thank you to another dear friend, Sherene Zolno, who encouraged me, read parts of the manuscript, and put me in touch with my editor, Heidi Stahl. A big thank you to Heidi for not only editing, but for her support, guidance, and ideas.

Thank you to my "Brain Trust" group of retirees, who initially encouraged me to write this book. And thank you as well to those members of my Vashon Island book club and my First Tuesday book club, who took time to read some of the early chapters of this book and provide me with their comments.

Table of Contents

PREFACE

As a forward thinking, pre-baby-boomer, with retirement looming on the horizon, I viewed it as a future "next chapter in my life." My husband and I had planned for an active retirement life in two locations in order to fulfill our dreams. My husband, Steve, is older than me. At 64, he was ready to retire. Although I had known for some time that retirement was approaching, now that it had arrived, I wasn't sure that I was really ready to retire at 60. I was reaching a peak in my career and part of me wanted to continue my work as a consultant and instructor. Another part wanted to share the dream life we had envisioned and for which we worked so hard. But how could I do both?

I faced a fork in the road of life—a change dilemma. As a consultant, I had assisted people and organizations to change. I had helped clients embrace change, or at least imagine that change could lead to positive results for all concerned. Now I faced a major challenge to change before I'd fully prepared myself. How could I creatively make this a win-win situation? What could I do to achieve a positive outcome?

Despite my quandary, a plan to slide gradually into retirement evolved. I realized that in this high-tech age, I could have a virtual office anywhere, whether in the desert or on an island. For the first two years of my husband's retirement, I continued consulting and training at about 50 percent of my original level of work. My plan was to continue working until I was 62 and retire. I would continue to do a few consulting and training projects, plus write and publish into my retirement years. I won't pretend that I didn't feel a sense of loss for what I could have accomplished had I continued working full-time. But, from the vantage point of several years later, I also see that my decision to transition gradually was a wise one. While I sacrificed some of my individual dreams, I gained something in terms of shared dreams. We both had spent years working and planning. Now we are living out our retirement dreams. Since retiring, these have been happy and productive years with my husband and I've discovered new doors open when old ones close. I gave up some of the joy of working with clients, but discovered new joys in adventures with my husband.

I came to write this book because, as I was navigating this unfamiliar terrain, I discovered that there were few resources that addressed our particular situation. How do couples success-fully retire together? There were workshops and books dealing with the financial preparation for retirement and even some that addressed the intellectual challenges. But I found few, if any, on how couples can deal with the emotional changes that retire-ment brings. The lack of information, and our own transition experiences from professional careers to partial or full retire-ment inspired me to research and write. This book is for cou-ples who have the courage of their convictions to forge a shared retirement that is satisfying and successful for both members, individually and collectively. I hope that it will help you learn to create a retirement that reflects both your personal and your shared dreams.

INTRODUCTION

Prepare for the unknown by studying how others in the past have coped with the unforeseeable and the unpredictable.

— *General George S. Patton*

Perhaps you envision driving together into the sunset of your lives, while leading the good life and achieving your dreams. This is a wonderful dream that takes planning, effort, and commitment to achieve. However, no matter how well you plan and how good your roadmap is, unexpected changes and events occur. Wouldn't you like to know what has helped other retirees adapt and adjust to these life changes? The information in this book can help. It is about how men and women are successfully navigating the challenges, curves, and roadblocks of active retirement.

Changing Lanes: Couples Redefining Retirement is written for couples who are planning retirement, beginning retirement, are semi-retired, or have already retired. The purpose of *Changing Lanes* is to develop for yourselves a rewarding time of life and to prepare yourselves for the changes the future has in store for you. The information in this book can't prevent a change from happening nor cure all your retirement problems. But it can help you navigate the change process. Reading about ideas, strategies and skills, which others have found useful, can help you reach your personal destination.

While researching this book, I spoke with over 100 active men and women, ages 51 to 81, about their experience of retirement. I interviewed people already retired, partially retired, still working or involved in a new field of endeavor. They shared what it's like living in a busy retirement community, a summer resort community, or in their traditional family home, as well as sharing the benefits and drawbacks of these retirement decisions, such as living in two locations.

Whether you continue to work in some way, retire to a life of leisure and hobbies, or begin a new type of endeavor, you will be going through changes. Change involves a transition of some kind. Change can be positive or negative but your life will be different. Educate yourself about what can happen so that you can effectively better handle transition dilemmas within your own retirement.

WHY "CHANGING LANES?"

Even though adjusting to change is not a mechanical process, a driving analogy is useful for thinking about retirement. The more I thought about the language of cars and driving, I began to connect the changes that retirement presents to the ideas of roadmaps, curves, detours, closed roads, speeding, fender benders, crashes and so on.

I titled the book *Changing Lanes* because retirees, myself included, have had to change our speed, direction, avert accidents and detour for roadblocks. All of these possibilities can cause us to change lanes, and in some cases even change highways. Sometimes during retirement we can operate at top speed in the fast lane. We might appear to zoom down the highway of life in a red convertible, without a care in the world. And yet, there are times when we have had to slow down and move to a slower lane, or stop on the shoulder of the highway because we've experienced unexpected change such as a sports injury, accident, or reduction in retirement funds. We are then temporarily or permanently sidelined into a slow lane.

There is no set formula for when you'll need to change lanes during retirement. When driving, you tend to change lanes depending on where you want to go, how quickly you want to get there, and what the traffic is like. The same is true, as you journey through retirement. However, you and your spouse or partner are driving together on this journey and you will need to make travel decisions together. If you want to change lanes and he or she doesn't, you both can encounter a temporary roadblock, which needs to be resolved.

Fast Lane

Retirees in the fast lane continue to lead busy and active lives by continuing to work, combining work and play, or keeping busy with various pursuits. Their days are full of activity and they feel energized. The fast lane often characterizes the early years of retirement. If new retirees are working full or part-time, they are usually juggling a social life and a work life. At some point, some change usually occurs causing them to transfer to a middle lane or slower lane. This might be a change in income or, in health, or they may just want to slow down or stop what they are doing in order to pursue other interests or devote more time to family.

Middle Lane

Some retirees might move into a middle lane in order to slow down from a busy work-life and ease into retirement. People who want to keep one foot in the workplace as they move into retirement often find a way to cut back to part-time work, consult, work seasonally or do special projects. Middle "laners" tend to want to be somewhat busy, but also want time to enjoy their retirement, spend time with family, and cut back from their busy work pace. Moving to a middle lane can occur early on in retirement—upon leaving their paid employment or it can happen in the middle years of retirement. If a person initially enters retirement with great enthusiasm and tries to do everything in the first few years, he or she may actually "burn out" on retirement. At that point he or she may want to change to a slower lane. Or the opposite might be true, that the person is bored with retirement and is looking to be more involved and busier. He or she will then swerve into a faster lane of traffic.

Right Lane/Slow Lane

This is a lane where people can experience a slower pace of life. They might initially start their retirement in the slow lane, especially if they are leaving high-stress, high-powered work lives. They dreamed of a leisurely life style where they can see the country in an RV, or live on a boat in Florida. Some retirees may want to relax and enjoy the desert of Arizona or California. They picture themselves sitting around a pool or on a beach with a drink in their hand soaking in the sun. Perhaps they envision playing tennis or golf everyday. It may be hard to believe, but after a period of time some retirees have actually experienced boredom with play, play, play. They then needed to change lanes into a faster lane, one that will provide them with more interesting and productive activities.

Changing lanes can happen for a variety of reasons, which I will explore in more detail throughout the book. The idea is not to get stuck in one lane. Don't be fearful of changing or switching lanes when you change your mind about what you are doing or are forced to change by life's circumstances. The worst thing you can do is nothing. When you are behind the wheel and you do nothing, you end up going nowhere.

ROAD MAP

The twelve chapters of this book address the challenges; issues and information that can help you define and live a more fruitful retirement. Each chapter focuses on the various areas that have challenged retirees in their retirement. You will read about how the challenges of change are being creatively dealt with by those retirees who are one step ahead of you, as well as advice from retirees who not only have been "there and done that"; they "are there and are doing it."

Each of the first eleven chapters contains a Tool Kit. Answering the Tool Kit questions will better prepare you and your partner for your retirement experience. You will then be "revved up" to develop your personalized Road Map from the guidelines in Chapter twelve.

CHANGING COURSE

Whether beginning or continuing your retirement journey,
You are altering your life's course.

Maintain an open mind to new thoughts and ideas,
Which can enhance and enrich your experience.

These can be the "best years of your lives together."

B. Battaglia

CHAPTER I –
CHANGING COURSE
Change - Past and Future

*Change in life is a given, but successful change needs
time, understanding and is a process of learning.*

— *Betty D*

CHALLENGE:

To acknowledge, accept, and make the most out of the
changes you encounter in retirement utilizing experience and
knowledge from past changes in your life.

UNDERSTANDING CHANGE

As you and your spouse approach retirement age you may
know that a change is coming. You may want the change to occur. However, even if you're mentally prepared for a change, you
can be unexpectedly and emotionally affected when it happens.
This chapter explores how change affects us. You'll read how
others have looked to the past in order to deal with the changes

they will encounter in retirement. Reading their stories will help you recall your own experiences with change—what you may already know about change but perhaps have forgotten. In turn, this will help you to develop strategies to deal with what lies ahead.

As we encounter a need to change lanes, it helps you and your partner to have a common understanding of change. Although we've all experienced change at one time or another, we may not understand the process we're going through. We have a hard time recognizing the stages that characterize change.

In the past it was thought if you could carefully analyze the situation you could see the benefits of a change and implement it. Change was perceived as a simple process of unfreezing the old way of doing something; moving to a newly defined way of doing it; and then refreezing in the new state of operating and thinking. However, people don't change as easily as this. This approach didn't take into account the common emotional response of resistance. People tend to resist change in their lives, especially if it is forced on them from outside sources. People resist change in an effort to hold on to the familiar, what is known and understood.

William Bridges, an expert on change, said, *"It isn't the changes that do you in, it's the transitions."* Bridges suggests that change and transition is not the same thing. Change is a "situational" event, such as retiring, moving to a new area, or starting a new career. Transition, on the other hand, is a three-part psychological process you must go through in order to understand and integrate the facts of the new situation within your experience. In other words, transition requires internalizing and accepting the change. According to Bridges, transition comprises three stages:

I. Endings – releasing the old situation or the old identity

I. The Neutral Zone – allowing yourself to live in the unknown between the old reality and new reality

I. New Beginnings – starting anew

Endings

You can't begin a new role or purpose without letting go of the old role or purpose. During a process of change, you have to release attachment to old ways of doing things and begin doing them in new ways. Much of the resistance to change comes from the difficulty in "letting go" of the way things were.

At first, when a change occurs, you may feel a sense of loss— a longing for what is familiar. In retirement you might feel that you have lost your professional identity and all that came with it. Perhaps you were highly skilled and enjoyed great respect for your work. You may have had an important position in an organization, with all of the attendant power and choice, and find yourself asking "Who am I now?" You may experience loss of friendships—professional and/or personal and say to yourself, "I don't know anyone in this new retirement community. I miss my old friends and acquaintances." Although you need to acknowledge your feelings of loss, it's best not to dwell on it for a long time.

One day as I was walking through my development, I stopped and said good morning to a lady who was gardening outside her house. We began to talk and she told me how unhappy she was in this new community. She missed her former home, on a hillside, in another state and the longtime friends she had there. She said her husband wanted to move to a warmer climate and was happy here with his golf and his hobbies. Perhaps this lady had not closed the book on what she perceived was lost and felt powerless to change her situation. You can go through your retirement as a victim or as an empowered participant. You have to get behind the wheel and take charge of your retirement experience. In the case of our sad gardener, she should have a serious talk with her husband and share her feelings. She might seek a retirement counselor who could help her consider plausible positive actions that she could take to build a better life for herself. If you get stuck in a similar rut after a change, you need to "shift gears" and act, as no one will do it for you.

Neutral Zone

In the middle phase of transition people have left behind the familiar and can't yet see the new reality. They may find themselves in neutral gear, unable to move forward or back. It can be a time of loss and confusion, a time when hope can vary from despair to joy. Some people feel lost. The neutral zone is a time of reorientation. While in this state, the best you can do is to just go through the motions of changing.

The best lesson I learned when younger was "Don't panic.
Just pretend everything will be fine and usually it will be."
So I go ahead and make a change and I'm fine with it once

it is made, but at first I do have to overcome my inertia to act.

Marge G

So often when faced with a change, we either resist it by holding on to what we know, or we accept the inevitability of change, and we want to jump right into the new situation. We feel uncomfortable in the neutral zone because we feel like we are "spinning our wheels" and going nowhere. Because of the discomfort of being in an "unknowing" or neutral zone, we want something else to begin immediately. We react impulsively.

We previously lived in an 1898 vintage home in New Jersey. As we neared retirement, we wanted to be closer to our daughter and family in California. So, we sold our home with all its antiques and moved west. On first sight we fell in love with the Malibu area and impulsively bought a mobile home with a spectacular view of the mountains and ocean. Our daughter was about one hour away, but to go see her, shop, or anything else I had to drive over windy canyon roads and a very busy Pacific Coast Highway. We had a gorgeous view, but it didn't mean much as I was miserable, lonely and depressed. If we had rented first, I would have known it was a mistake without putting out a lot of money.

Barbara W

Perhaps you've acted quickly in the past in order to get through the discomfort of the unknown. You had a sense of urgency to do something about your situation and acted impulsively. When we're living in the unknown of the neutral zone, it's easy to be tempted to act on impulse, to do anything to ease our anxiety. Despite these temptations, we need to take precautions to check our blind spots not only when we drive, but also as we live our lives. Without serious research and a shared decision with your partner, if you act impulsively about when to retire or where to retire to, you too may discover a blind spot you hadn't anticipated.

It's easy to be impetuous when stuck in the neutral zone. You might furiously pump the gas pedal to try to restart your car, but all that happens is that you flood the carburetor. Just as you have to wait for the car to settle down before it is ready to run, you need to give yourself some time in the neutral zone to recover, to get to know the territory in which you find yourself and move cautiously when responding to a major change.

The time each person takes to rebound from a change is different. Some of us recover fairly quickly from change. We may spend a short time—possibly a few hours or minutes—mourning what we've lost. Others may take longer, recover more slowly—they need to "come around" to the change. Because each of us views change differently, we tend to react at a different pace, and it helps if our partners understand and sympathize with this.

New Beginnings

When you've adjusted to the necessary changes, you're ready for a new beginning. The new beginning may involve developing new competencies, establishing new relationships, becoming comfortable with the new situation, or learning to think in a new way.

When poised on the brink of a new beginning, you may feel energized by your willingness to take action, ready to move out of the stagnation of the neutral zone. When working with people in the throes of organizational change, I used to say the new beginning is that moment when you have flipped a trigger in your mind, stopped stalling, and decided to move forward.

> *At first I was somewhat pessimistic about moving to Toronto, Canada. I certainly was not excited about it because we would move much further away from our daughters and grandchildren. Now, I've adjusted to the thought of moving and am looking forward to it. After discussing it with my husband, I began to see the possibilities and what the job could lead to in the future. I think it will be an interesting two years living out of the country in a new environment before we retire.*
>
> *Pat D*

When you begin to see the positive reasons for a change and you look for clear and conscious steps that you can begin to take, you're entering the third phase of transition. You've restarted the car, shifted gears, and accelerated forward into traffic.

By following Bridges's formula of first ending, being patient within the neutral zone, and then moving with change, couples can more effectively handle the changes they encounter in retirement.

LEARNING FROM PAST CHANGE EXPERIENCES

One of the things I most wanted to know when I interviewed retired couples for this book was how their earlier experience of change affected their ability to navigate the changes brought on by retirement. I had an idea that people's earlier positive experience of change had contributed to developing skills and a "can do" attitude for dealing with change in one's retirement years.

My idea turned out to be true. People who experienced lots of personal and family changes while they were growing up reported that they view change as a way of life. These people seem to continue to deal effectively with changes later in life. The following examples come from people who learned about change early in their lives.

I am a rolling stone. I'm from a traveling family as my father was in international business and I spent one year with them in South America. I became a flight attendant and worked in guest relations. Later, I acquired a position of assistant to the Deputy U.S. Trade Representative in Geneva, Switzerland and worked in Europe for a number of years. Because of these experiences it was fairly easy for me to make a home in a new community when I retired. I was already used to change.

Deryl C

My father was a role model for adjusting to change. He was ill with diabetes when I was growing up. First he lost his sight and he resorted to listening to recorded books and talking to people to gain information. He then lost the use of his legs and found a way to get around in a wheelchair. He was one of those special kinds of people. I'm trying to be as resourceful and courageous in my life as he was.

Lynne S

People with stable childhoods usually developed their capacity for dealing with change later in their professional careers through job changes or transfers around the country or the world.

I experienced a lot of change in the organization where I worked. As a manager I had to implement a lot of changes in the company. What I learned is that I first had to manage the change in myself before I could influence my employees about the benefits of the change. This experience with change has actually helped me to adjust to the changes I'm encountering in retirement.

Carol B

Sometimes you have to root yourself out of your drudgery. When you are doing something you don't want to do or are unhappy in a particular situation, you have to force yourself to make your own change. You have to believe that you can change. I've changed careers three times because I wanted something different and may change again before I retire.

Jerry G

You learn by doing. I think each one of us has to learn things in our own way. Some of us can learn from school, but most people ultimately have to take what they have heard and learn it for themselves later in life. We get ideas that we can grasp onto or believe are applicable for us and we make them our own.

Richard H

Individuals within a couple find that they developed their change skills at different times in their lives. John experienced change as he grew up and had no trouble with working in various parts of the world and adjusting to a new retirement community.

I credit the fact, that because my family moved so many times while I was growing up, I'm comfortable with meeting strangers and I'm not afraid of going into new situations. It was easy for me to go out and get acquainted with people in this new community.

John L

John's wife, Shirley experienced personal changes in her family, but grew up in one place, a dairy farm in the Midwest. She had to learn more about change during her marriage.

What do I draw from to respond to difficult change? I believe there is a force within us that helps us do what we must do. Because of my husband's job, I have had to move all around the United States and lived a number of years in Brazil. I learned that the world isn't waiting for me. I had to go out and locate things and make connections with each move. This experience helped me to meet people and make a life in our new retirement community.

Shirley L

Some individuals are quicker to respond to change in their lives than others. When a husband or wife reacts more quickly than the other, this can cause friction and difficulties in the relationship. Jon and Mary had differing experiences of change and thus, they responded differently. He was a change agent in his work and tended to pro-actively prepare for change.

> *I guess change is an important aspect of life for me. Every time I am faced with a new change or new project, I bone up on it to get ready to do it. I thought about how to design a process for our living situation that would make sense to get away from the cold and weather up north and move to a warmer climate.*
>
> *Jon B*

Mary, on the other hand, is slower to change and wasn't ready to make a move.

> *I grew up and lived in one city most of my life. When my husband thought of moving to another city while we were still working, it took me a year to just agree to think of it. I learned that I don't like change all that much. I'm not ready for a retirement community.*
>
> *Mary B*

Often the partner who was more experienced with change assisted his or her spouse to adjust to the changes they were encountering. If a person couldn't handle it alone, he or she wisely found additional outside counseling support in dealing with change.

One theme generally ran through the interview data—that some experience with change appears to help a person better handle it later in life. This doesn't mean that you must have a lot of experience with change to be successful. It just means that if you don't, you may have to work harder to change your mindset, especially if unexpected change occurs.

Let's return to our changing lanes analogy. Have you ever made a turn when driving and found that you were on the wrong road? How far did you go before you checked it out or back tracked? Was the unexpected experience an adventure or a cause for anxiety? The realization that you were on the wrong road and needed to change course to rectify the mistake is what changing your mindset is about.

SUMMARY

Change is an ongoing, never ending process. Nothing ever stays the same. It helps to view change as part of the cycle of life. A cycle is actually a circle and thus holistic. Robert Marshak, Ph.D., tells of discussing transformational change with a Korean host. The host said that there was no Korean word for change. Marshak asked: "How do you say the caterpillar changed into the butterfly?" The Korean host replied, "In Korean, we say the caterpillar becomes a butterfly." Utilizing Confucian "holistic" philosophy, you might see that you aren't "changing," but "becoming" or "evolving." Assessing who you are, what you've done in the past, and how you've reacted to changes in your lives can help you create a more balanced retirement life as you both experience future changes.

CHANGE TOOL KIT

Questions:

The following questions can help you identify how you feel about change. Both you and your spouse or partner can take a sheet of paper and answer these questions separately. Then meet and discuss your answers. Talk about how ready each of you is for the coming changes in your lives. (If you have already retired, these questions can help you identify what you've successfully done, or why you may still have some change issues.)

1. What are some of the changes I've experienced in my life? Was I able to deal with the change? What was the result?

2. What can I learn from the way I handled past change experiences that will allow me to handle future retirement changes more effectively?

3. How do I now view change? How do I react to: Planned change? Unexpected change?

4. Do I tend to resist change and try to hold on to what is familiar and comfortable to me? How long?

5. What am I afraid of losing if I retire? If I continue working?

6. What do I want from this anticipated job or retirement change?

7.   What do I have to gain by embracing change?

8.   How would my spouse (or partner) and my family be affected if I make this change?

9.   What is the first positive step I can take to help me move forward into embracing this change?

10.   Each of you ask yourself: "Given my partner's life experience with change, what do we need to do now to prepare for changes in our lives together?"

CHAPTER 2 –
"BRAKING" AWAY
Transitioning to a Redefined Retirement

Not everything that is faced can be changed, but
nothing can be changed until it is faced.

— *James Baldwin*

CHALLENGE:

To have a focus and meaning to your retirement life, while being able to enjoy activities and relationships with each other, family and friends

Most likely you anticipate "changing lanes" at least once in your planned retirement—from a busy work life to either an active or leisurely retirement life. You see yourself making the change and arriving at your planned destination. However, you might be surprised to find that in retirement you continue to "change lanes" throughout the years. Just as you negotiated the twists and turns on the road of life, you will continue to negotiate a few more curves during retirement.

One way to navigate this part of your life is to maneuver through the various stages of retirement as you moved through the earlier stages of your life, if you were successful in doing so. For example, retiring from the workplace is one part of this stage of life and that alone could encompass considerable change and stress on your lifestyle and your relationships with spouse, family, or friendships. However, throughout your lifetime, the skills, knowledge, and expertise that you have acquired can be utilized to handle whatever you want to do or whatever comes at you in retirement. You have the tools within you to make the transition and adjust to a new life style, new environment, new acquaintances, or new community. This chapter focuses on the transition process from working full-time to other retirement options available to you and your spouse or partner.

If you already plan to retire or are in the process of retiring, you most likely have assessed where you are financially and emotionally as you relate to your job and life. If you work for a company, you may have attended a retirement seminar. Many seminars today cover not only the financial aspects of retiring, but touch on the personal/emotional aspects as well. However, when retirement comes, even financially prepared individuals can experience a downturn in their portfolio or have problems with the personal and emotional aspects of change. This chapter provides you with a "heads up" as to what can happen so you are better prepared. Since each couple's situation is different, you won't find specific guidelines. There isn't one retirement that fits all people. However, you will find a discussion of the issues related to change and transition from your career or work life and a variety of successful retirement experiences that can help you develop your plans or understand what you are going through as you retire.

COUPLES RETIREMENT

Are you Ready to Leave Your Job? Is your spouse ready?

Perhaps you've found it difficult to determine if you are ready for the next chapter in your lives. A large percentage of baby boomers fully intend to continue working, and depending upon the job market, they most likely will be able to do just that. Some individuals will have to continue working because they need the income and the insurance benefits. Others might determine that they want to change to a slower lane and either cut back to part-time in their present field or retire and get involved with other activities that interest them.

Making a decision to retire or not to retire is often seen as a personal one based on an individual's specific circumstances. However, if you are part of a couple, the decision to retire will not just affect you but your spouse as well. If he or she has a career, you both will have to jointly work out a retirement plan that meets both of your needs. This can be one of the more difficult decisions you, as a couple, make in your married life, especially if you aren't both ready to retire at the same time. This has to be a joint decision, because it can come back and haunt you later in retirement if one person is unhappy with his or her situation. I know of situations where the husband or wife was ready to retire and their spouse really didn't want to leave their job. This can cause conflict when one partner is much younger than the other or when one is at the peak of his or her own career and not ready to retire.

> *It's not like I came into the retirement over time with my peers. I'm now in retirement before any of them. I don't feel ready for this as I am just 51. I was 48 when my husband retired. I have such a wealth of skills and knowledge. Now what? I'm not really comfortable living in a retirement community right now. I am searching for the next step for me. I have some anger and frustration about the retirement move because I'm not happy with where I've landed. I don't know what the next thing is.*
>
> Miriam L

I believe that Miriam is in the neutral zone of this transition. She had a professional career in training and organization development and felt that she had to leave it because of her husband's wish to move to a warmer climate in the winter months. With a six-month stay in each area, and not being a citizen of the U.S., she is unable to work full time. She is searching for a way to meet her own needs in the context of her husband's desire to retire. Perhaps she should have had a greater say in the retirement decision or at least in the decision to spend retirement in two locations.

> *It's very difficult to plan now. Part of the reason is my wife's work. She teaches adults and has a very intense schedule. I've got ultimate flexibility now because I've retired while she's still tied down to schedules and production work. So she is not available to go when I am. I was hoping that the two of us would have time together to go on trips.*
>
> Rick S

In this case the husband has, in essence, retired and wishes his wife would cut back her professional activities to spend more time with him. He has some serious health problems and is concerned that time when they could be together is being lost. Yet she is somewhat younger and has hit her prime as a leader in her field. What they need to do is sit down and discuss this whole matter and come to some compromise as to how much time they each can delineate to spend together. He has to share with her his concerns and begin to understand her situation. She needs to assess the importance of her work and their need to spend time together.

> *My husband decided to retire at the end of the year. I was an ESL teacher and I just wasn't ready to retire. I loved what I was doing. I was teaching English as a second language to adults and I had wonderful experiences and fun with students from all over the world. It was a great job and I hated to leave it.*
>
> *Phyllis W*

In Phyllis's case, although she loved her job, she was able to adapt to change and move to a retirement community when her husband decided to retire. Since her skills are greatly needed in schools, she could easily find a job or volunteer work in her area of expertise.

As we learned in chapter 1 on change, we each tend to go through a process of letting go when faced with a major life modification. The decision to transition from long-term employment can be a difficult one, if we don't recognize possible new beginnings for ourselves.

Loss: Letting Go

In order to accelerate your transition process you might first look at what advantages you get from your work. What might be initially lost? You most likely will think of income first, but there are other factors that you may lose that now provide you with a sense of accomplishment and satisfaction. As you move toward retirement, letting go of these parts of your life may be more difficult than you anticipated. Many retired people, especially those who have had interesting work careers, tend to talk about what they were and what they did. Initially this is acceptable because it provides others a context within which to assess your background. However, it can get pretty boring if you continue to only talk about your previous career over the succeeding retirement years. People will think you are dwelling on the past when they want to know who you are today: they want to connect with the "you of today." At some point in retirement you will have to let go of who you were in your career, so that you can transition and evolve into the "new you."

> *I was happy with my nursing job and my association with my professional social group for fourteen years. Although I have moved away, I am still attached to it. I drive back to work per diem or by contract several days a month and I don't really feel that I have to let go of it yet. I am clinging to that tie.*
>
> *April P*

In April's case she utilized her nursing skills to continue to work part-time and keep her connections. Her retirement was just a step in her transition process. However, some people lose the connection that they had in their work life. Their work gave them status, a place in our society, and a cohort group of which they were a part. Sometimes you don't realize how much your career identity is part of your persona until you retire.

As a professional woman, my job was really important to me. I was the top dog at the job. I had a staff and my staff had a staff and they all catered to me. What I did to ease into retirement was to take a part-time job in finance. However, as part-time I was low on the totem pole in a much smaller environment. A large corporation affords you a lot more luxury than a small mom-and-pop company. This transition into part-time meant a longer commute and a lot less money.

Judith A

Judith held an important position in a large company; she had status. When her husband became ill, she took early retirement to care for him. Later she was ready to reenter the job market as a part-timer and accepted a position in a smaller company. However, soon she became disillusioned with the job and realized that without the perks of her former position, the drawbacks of the new job outweighed the benefits.

My husband has worked as a public insurance adjuster. He can't quite give it up in his retirement. I can tell he's still interested in the field because every time he sees something on the TV news he is ready to follow it up. Although he sometimes complains about the calls he gets from his old company, I can see that he can't wait for the phone to ring.

Jeanne E

Jeanne's husband is still drawn to his previous field while looking for a new career, post-retirement. Although he hadn't found that new career at the time of our interview, he has recently gone back to school and is going into a completely new area of work.

> *I realized that as I retired, I had to turn over my clientele of individuals and institutions for whom I managed assets to younger partners. If you are still available and convenient, the ties will never be severed and the young partners will never become the principle person to whom clients turn. By moving I became less available and was able to actually begin to experience my retirement life.*
>
> *Patrick S*

Patrick had a healthy view of his retirement and knew enough about his clients and former partners to make him self less available so they would begin to handle situations on their own. This allowed him the freedom to do what he and his wife wished in retirement.

> *I find that some people living here in this retirement community are angry. I think it's because they've lost some of their identity. Before they may have been a captains of industry and now they feel like they're nobody. It's probably hard to take.*
>
> *John A*

Some retirees never come to grips over their lost career and identity. Perhaps what happens is that they lose their sense of self. They are in unfamiliar territory and experience a loss of competence, confidence, and sense of who they are. Losing your work-related identity can show itself as sulking, anger, reminiscing or dwelling on the past, and resisting adaptation to a new life.

Whether or not you believe that work identity and career satisfaction are important in your life, work will have occupied many of your productive waking hours up to the time of your retirement. If you get clear about what motivated you in your work, you may have a much better understanding of what to look for in your planned transition to retirement. Besides the financial income, did you get intangible psychological rewards from your work such as status, influence, satisfaction, or close relationships? If these were important, you have to discover ways to recreate some of these intangible rewards in retirement. Also, while you may not think these were important to you, their value may increase in retrospect as you experience a lessening or loss of identity, self-esteem, prestige, or power.

Developing a New Persona

Today both men and women can experience what is called disidentification upon leaving their life's work. Our American society emphasizes who you are and what you do. When you go to a party and meet someone new you may first get asked your name, but then you get asked, "Well, what do you do?" If you previously identified with your career work, you may need to create a new identity in retirement. "Identity loss" doesn't just relate to how you picture yourself, but is related to how the world sees you now that you're retired. Do they see you as old and "out of it" when you retire? How can you instill some of the respect you may have previously derived from your work?

> *I noticed that when I retired people would ask me "what do you do?" When I would say I'm retired, I'd see a blank stare in their eyes. It was as if they were looking through me like I was a pane of glass—like I wasn't there. I didn't have an identity anymore. To them I was just an old person who's able to retire and have no life anymore. So when I was asked what do I do, I started responding, "I'm a photographer." They all love photography and immediately there is an opening to discuss something with me. They lose sight of the fact that I'm retired and we then have a common interest.*

> *John A*

One of the dilemmas of retirement is that unless you can transition your skills and talents from the work arena to the retirement environment your status may be perceived as zero. Past professional achievements generally don't mean much to your new acquaintances.

In retirement you have to develop a whole new persona. Who are you today? Who do you think you want to be in retirement? How can you replace the positive rewards you enjoyed in your work life? I became acutely aware of this within the first year of retirement. I went for coffee with tennis players after we got off the court. Someone asked me, "What do you do besides playing tennis?" For some reason this jolted me into thinking about, "Who am I now and what is my role in life?" It made me think about the importance I had placed in my past career role. Even though I was in the process of transitioning out of consulting to writing, I realized that in retirement I had to carve out a new role for myself. Would writing give me the same satisfaction as my work had done? How would I feel about being in a more solitary kind of environment where I had been out in the public, training and consulting with corporations and universities?

Continuing Work

We only have to watch television, go to the movies, and read magazines to notice that the United States tends to be youth oriented. Most people don't want to age or be perceived as elderly. Those adults in their 50s or 60s may say, "That older person in the TV commercial isn't me. That's the other guy or gal!" Where in other parts of the world age and senior status in life are respected, in the U.S. elders are generally not revered as valuable.

Mature adults detest being seen as not having value to society. This may be what motivates some individuals to continue to work because they maintain their status in society and retain their sense of contribution to the world. Others are motivated to remain productive and creative in their field, while some individuals basically need the income or insurance benefits the workplace provides.

I think some people can't stop working. I have one friend like that, who can't ever envision not working.

Jane S

At first I found retirement very difficult. I was an engineer with an electrical utility and once we made the decision to retire, it was like driving 80 miles an hour and coming up to a brick wall. I thought I could perhaps do some consult-

ing, but given the tax bracket we were in, working wasn't a viable path.

Bob G

I retired from an educational administration position, but after we moved into a retirement community, I decided to look for a part-time job with the local school district. After two years, they asked me to go full-time so, now I teach, write curriculum, supervise teachers, and do in-service training. When you have been teaching for so many years, it's very difficult to pull back. I hope there will come a time when I won't even want to work part-time.

Marge S

If you go on working, you need to think about how long you will continue to work and what are your retirement plans for after you stop working. How old do you expect to be and what do you hope to do at that time in your life? Working in a full-time position requires a lot of stamina as you age. You will need to assess if you have sufficient time and energy for it. The longer you work, the fewer years and less vitality you may have later to follow other dreams. This is a time to assess the relative importance of work versus your other dreams.

If you continue to work, and still plan to retire to a retirement community, you will be delaying your transition to a later time and at an older age—a period of life when you may have less energy to make new friends or invest in new dreams. You especially need to weigh this if you still have dreams about specific activities you want to do. Will you be physically able to do them at a later date? You have to think through and discuss with your spouse the idea of a later retirement and how it might affect your plans and your future activities. Although it may not matter to you if you can't travel later in retirement or play certain sports, what affect will it have on your spouse and your marital relationship?

Neutral Zone

Sometimes we don't have the option of leaving a position as we near the end of our careers. The decision is made for us by an unexpected lay-off or an offer of a retirement package. This is a surprise turn of events for some people and it may happen to you. That is why it is so important to begin planning and saving for your retirement in advance. (For more information about managing finances in retirement, see chapter 9.)

> *I was the key financial officer of a privately owned company in Connecticut. When I was 58 the company was put up for sale. Upon a possible sale I asked my boss what kind of package could I get and he said, "None—that's the way it goes." So my wife and I started talking about early retirement and moving to the west coast to be near one of our sons. When I left my job I said to myself, "Thank God that I am out of here because I may live longer."*
>
> *Larry M*

Larry and Lorraine moved to California and after a period of time he started looking for a finance position. He found that at his age and previous salary, no one was beating the door down to hire him. He said that his interviews went well until he was asked how much he had been making at this previous position. He said:

When I told one owner how much I previously earned, he was in complete shock; he didn't think I would stay with the company at the salary he could pay. I saw that obtaining a job where I could utilize my past skills in the new area would be difficult. After experiencing some rejection and dejection, I was encouraged by a friend to go into the house repair business. I always liked to fix things and scored high on all the trade tests in high school. So, as it happens I ended up in the handyman business. I have control of my time and projects and it feels satisfying to put a natural talent to work.

Larry M

Larry went through what would be called the neutral zone of his change during the time he was job hunting in the financial field. The interesting point here is that he wasn't closed to considering other options and because he was open, he found a new career.

When I retired I thought I would enjoy not having to do anything but after awhile it drove me crazy. Before that I worked all my life, from when I was a little kid. So I decided to do something about it and started to look for a sales job. I couldn't get one because I was too old, not to mention I had been a vice president. I guess they couldn't fathom me selling again. I finally got a job as a customer service representative at a famous golf course. I really enjoyed my job, met famous people, and finally retired after ten years.

Bob D

What Bob ultimately did was to transfer his skill in meeting and engaging prospective clients into a new area of work that fulfilled his need for connection, stimulation, and sense of accomplishment.

You have to determine what, other than income, gave you the energy and stimulation in your work life. Did you get mental stimulation and a chance to utilize your talents and be creative in your work? And then ask how you can replicate these opportunities in your retirement. Once you determine what is still important to you, look for ways that you can fulfill these needs in your new life.

> *I have a friend who recently retired from teaching and she was one of those folks that came early and stayed late, constantly working on new projects. Because of health issues she had to retire. She hasn't found something that will make her feel useful yet. Friends have counseled her not to rush into anything. They say, "you will hear about something or something will make itself known to you and you will find your niche." Maybe that is the key—finding something useful.*
>
> *April P*

I realize that some of you may not have the foggiest idea of exactly what you want to do when you retire. You just want to get there. During the "honeymoon" period of retirement—the first year or so, you might feel a sense of freedom and elation because you can do what you want, live where you want, travel when you want, and start a new life if you want to. What I have experienced and what I have heard from a great many of the people I interviewed for this book is that after the honeymoon, one is likely to go through a phase of "disenchantment" with retirement.

After a while I became tired of just playing in retirement. I gave up some of the clubs I belonged to and don't go anymore. I believe that you have to discover and create meaning in your life. That is why I went back to counseling and leading my groups because I know that I make a difference in peoples' lives.

Gail K

I think you have to ask yourself, "Is this what I am meant to do with the rest of my life?" There has to be something with more meaning to fill your time.

Lorraine W

Peggy Lee's song line, "Is that all there is," seems to sum it up. Those people that felt this way began to search for what would have meaning for them—whether it's through work, volunteerism, personal development, or new creative pursuits. Many significant transitions start first with a feeling of disenchantment. If this happens to you, see it as a sign that you need to make a change.

You have to be able to appreciate yourself in a different context after you retire. In our careers we see ourselves as what we do. Now we each need to realize that we are worth more than the context from which we've come.

Miriam L

New Beginnings

Just as when you decide to drive to a destination on a map, you have a variety of possible routes to take in your transition to retirement. Whatever you do—work full or part-time, find a new avocation, a new field of work, or get involved in volunteering, it's important for you to discover satisfying and personally productive activities in retirement, to give meaning to your life. A pledge recited at Junior Woman's Club meetings years ago comes back to me, "to live each day trying to accomplish something, not merely to exist." This pledge has become an affirmation in my life—whether it relates to family, friends, or community. In retirement we have the option to select from many different routes. What route do you plan to take?

ROUTE I: *Building On Past Experience*

Some of us utilize our past experience and training to transition our skills into a different arena or a new career in retirement. In my case, I maintained my consulting and training business for the first two years of my husband's retirement. However, this became much more challenging once we began living in two locations. I felt that I needed to settle on something that was energizing, would assist others, and would fit with this back and forth life we were now leading. I turned to writing as the way I could contribute and feel actualized during retirement. As I age, I will need to adjust and change still again as I meet new challenges or opportunities.

If there is a dilemma for an active retiree, it lies in being pulled in two directions—one to work for the greater good and the other to spend time with family, friends, and personal activities.

> *We want to live our lives, take cruises, spend time at our beach house, and visit friends around the country. I don't want to be constrained by a job, so I need to find a balance*

*between having a sense of accomplishment while meeting my
needs for social interaction.*

Art D

Art is not yet retired and would like to continue his present
management consulting work on his own terms in a convenient
retirement location. He feels that his skills and knowledge can
form the basis for his new phase of life.

Other retirees have done just that. They have utilized their
past experience in new situations and environments and are
leading positive, productive lives.

*I retired after working in the school district as a librar-
ian for 23 years. Because I wanted to stay in touch with
children, I readily accepted an offer to do weekly puppet
presentations and art lessons for a pre-school class. I have
been doing this for eleven years. I also have taught puppetry
in a local summer program for children and I'm writing a
series of children's books. This gives me a chance to be with
children and to use my creative skills.*

Dorothy N

*I was with a major business copy firm for 34 years and
had several careers with them. In my last position before
retiring I managed and ran the west coast site management organization for the real estate division. After the first
year or so, I wanted more from retirement, so I teamed up
with my wife and became a real estate agent specializing in
retirement property.*

Rick J

> *I have a background in nursing and was the nursing director of a senior care apartment facility in New Mexico. After we moved to a retirement community, I initially got involved in all the interest groups and began volunteering. Then due to a financial drop in our income, instead of volunteering, I got a part-time job as an intake nurse for the local hospice organization. I feel positive about the contribution I am making and also have some income coming in.*
>
> *Lorraine W*

These individuals drew on their backgrounds to transition their skills and experience to a new venue. Don't be afraid to try new activities and pursuits. You even might wish to start your own business.

> *My background has been in working in medical practice offices, mostly psychiatrists and psychologists. When we moved from Nevada to California, I continued working part-time for a neurologist. Since I retired, I have a home secretarial practice where I transcribe psychologist patient reports. I utilize the e-mails and Internet to transfer work, plus I do extra projects for others needing my services. This works well for me because I fit the work in and still have time off to take a vacation.*
>
> *Harriet S*

If starting a new business involves a large cash outlay, you need to think this through and look at your financial condition and how much you are willing to risk. However, there are many ways that you can transition your skills into a new field.

ROUTE 2: New Interest and Endeavors

The secret to success in retirement for some individuals is to create a new snapshot of themselves, which is new, exciting, and of value to themselves and others. This may require you to leave your comfort zone and search out and learn about something new and different. These people have done it and so can you.

> *Since I retired early I wanted to find something to get involved with. So a friend and I teamed up with a third partner to form an agency to sell a high-caliber clothing line. It is basically a trunk show, which moves from house to house seasonally four times a year. When I got involved in it, I thought it would require four to six weeks of my time per year, but it's not turning out to be that way. It is much more of a commitment. I market wherever I go, the nail salon, clubs, and organizations. It has been good for me because I have been a shy person and I can't be shy anymore.*
>
> *Judith A*

> *I retired at 57 and did not expect to be working in retirement. I changed my mind for two reasons. One is an economic need due to a change in income and the other was I wanted to be more constructively engaged. After I retired from hospital administration and moved to a retirement community I took a few courses in order to teach. Now I receive joy from watching kids flourish in the process of learning. That's really powerful because it is immediate feedback. I walk down the hallway at the end of the day high-fiving some of the students. Twenty first-graders move*

*on next year and maybe they will remember me. That is
rewarding.*

Ken W

Ken and Judith pursued new areas of interest and created
opportunities for themselves. Ken renewed an interest in education
when he remembered back to when he was thirteen and was
impressed with the value of teaching shared by a colleague of his
father. New endeavors come to people in many different ways.

*Prior to my second marriage, I worked in a laboratory as a
biochemist. After a short sabbatical, I realized I did not want
to go back. I considered going for a medical degree, but after
some thought I realized that by the time I finished the degree,
my new husband, who is twelve years older than I, would be
ready for retirement. It didn't make much sense to start a career at the time he would retire. That first year of retirement,
I took up mountain climbing and then I got involved in community service and fund raising projects. Another woman
and I began a walking group of a dozen women and now
have 40-plus members of various ages and professions. They
have become a support group as well as an exercise group.
Walking marathons has been a life changing experience for
some of the women. They never dreamed that they could do
it. We are now saving our money and traveling to Italy and
Spain to take longer treks. One woman said, "I've always
wanted to travel, but my husband wouldn't go. Now I have
the walking group to go with."*

Susan S

These people have reinvented themselves and are involved in pursuits that excite them, give them meaning and help others at the same time.

ROUTE 3: Attempt a New Field of Work

Many of the retirees I talked with were not afraid to go into new types of fields and to make a change when they found it necessary.

I had been an administrative assistant to the president of a company, but when we moved to a retirement community I wanted a job that was stimulating, but with a little less commitment than that full-time position. I couldn't find anything part-time and finally accepted a full-time position with an accounting firm. But, I found pretty quickly that this was not something I enjoyed doing. After six months, when I was asked what I thought, I said, "This isn't working out for me." I shocked myself in being that outspoken, because normally I would just deal with it. But, I didn't have to now that I retired. I then signed up with an employment agency and I found a temporary position at the foundation of a major drug rehabilitation clinic. I enjoyed working with the people and the job was a good fit, which has turned into an ongoing, part-time position.

Lorraine M

I was a children's librarian in the public library before I retired and really loved it. I felt I needed to do something in my retirement and took a job working part time in a bookshop. I thought it would keep me involved in the area of books and get me out to connect with people, and it did. However, I didn't like having to work at night and I found it just wasn't a good fit for me with the owner. I have since found a creative job at a crafts store and teach classes.

Jean M

When I first retired I made a list of retirement activities I wanted to do. I have tried a number of volunteer experiences and different jobs since retirement searching for what would satisfy me. At first my husband and I did volunteering at various sports events. I became a gallery assistant at a museum, but it meant long hours standing on my feet. I then parlayed a volunteer water aerobics instructor position into a part-time job, which provided health insurance coverage. After several years, I found an opportunity to buy a business contract for providing cakes to restaurants in our area and decided to purchase it. I bake and my husband delivers. This gives us additional money to spend while maintaining control of our time. If you are open, things come your way.

Jeanne E

If you try something new and it doesn't work out, don't be afraid to make a change and turn to something else. If you didn't try it you wouldn't know that it wasn't for you. These interviewees worked or volunteered and searched out various possibilities before they found something that works for them. You might have to search out what endeavor will satisfy you and function in your retirement.

In my gradual transition to retirement I was doing video production and editing in my home office. My husband and I then opened a bed and breakfast. I thought it would occupy a couple of weekends a month, but it was an immediate suc-

cess and it never ended from the day we opened. However, my husband and I separated and after another couple of years of operating the B & B on my own, I had knee problems and I had to have orthoscopic surgery. I don't think I ever really retired.

Gloria H

After many years living on an island in Washington state, Gloria decided to move back to her old stomping ground in the Portland, OR area to be near one of her daughters and grandchildren.

In a move to develop my knowledge of restaurants and how they are run, I changed jobs from being a regional manager for a wine distributor to managing a new restaurant. Although it is working long hours and having to cope with customers' requests and employees, I actually enjoy talking to people and picking out wine for them when they request it. The job has helped me to be a little more agile and stronger. I am 61 and am putting in 16- to 18-hour days. When I do retire I will use my restaurant and wine expertise to consult and write books and tapes on wine.

Jerry G

Jerry's situation did change within a year of this interview and he left the restaurant business. He now has begun his own wine consulting business. Resiliency is the key to making changes at any time in your life, but especially in your later years.

ROUTE 4: Finding a New Avocation
Retirement provides you with the freedom to develop your ideas and pursue them. If you are financially stable, you have the

opportunity to create what you want to do with your life. It isn't over by a long shot. Tap that creativity within you. Search out what is important to you. These people did.

In my career I was an engineer and often didn't feel a sense of satisfaction because a lot of what I designed never came to fruition. In retirement I am getting a lot of satisfaction from my new avocation—woodworking. It is a very creative thing. Right now I am building furniture for the house I designed. At the end of my work I have a product that you can see and enjoy. I have also made gifts for our family. Recently I built a wooden baby cradle for our first grandchild. I have always been a self-motivator and get pleasure from creating things. I can look at it and say I did a pretty decent job on this.

Bob G

When I retired I expected to play a lot of golf and do some volunteering. I never thought I would be presenting music programs to elementary school children. This opportunity came "out of the blue." I was volunteered by my granddaughter as a speaker to present a program on symphonies to her first grade class. Later I was telling a friend on the golf course about the program and he thought the local school district might be interested in my music program since many of the schools have had to cut music classes due to budget cuts. In the last five years, I have presented five different music programs to 35,000 elementary school children. They call me Mr. McSymphony. This has been a rewarding and gratifying experience to share my love of music with the children.

Steve B

Some of you may meticulously plan your retirement life down to the smallest detail, but once you are on the retirement road, changes happen, detours occur, and new possibilities open up. Be aware and take advantage of these "out of the blue" new opportunities.

ROUTE 5: Taking a Hiatus from Work or Retirement

Some individuals who work with universities, schools, or colleges can take a sabbatical to do research, travel, or involve themselves in new activities, but most workers don't have that kind of opportunity. That doesn't mean that you can't investigate new or creative pursuits or opportunities on your vacation time, and some companies may allow you to take a leave of absence during a slow business period. You can use these times to take a special program or explore new areas that interest you.

> *Last year I took advantage of the opportunity to go with a sponsored group to teach English as a Second Language (ESL) in China for six weeks. It was a wonderful experience. I was able to connect with the Chinese people in my classes and had the opportunity to tour China. This year I am going to teach ESL again on the island of Crete.*
>
> *Marge B*

You may want to take a break from your retirement routine. There is a dichotomy in retirement: we want the freedom to do as we please, but something inside of us seeks to establish a pattern to our days. As humans we tend to feel comfortable when our lives have a pattern. That is why it's important once in awhile to be aware of breaking the cycle to try something new in our retirement years.

SUMMARY

Given the number of years people will spend in the last third of their lives, it is important to make your retirement years count. Many retirees are finding that they need more than pleasure-oriented activities to make them happy and give them a sense of self-worth. Many others continue to work part-time or are going back to work in new ventures. Whether you continue to work or decide to leave the workplace to focus on personal activities and development, you should determine what is important to you, what gives you a reason to exist, and what will work for both you and your mate.

TRANSITION TOOL KIT

Questions:

Both you and your spouse take a sheet of paper and answer these questions. Then spend time discussing them with each other.

1. What are the elements in your work that are important to you?

2. Do you need to receive a sense of self-worth from what you do? Why?

3. How closely do you identify with your work? Your career?

4. Is having a purpose and challenge to your life important to you? Why?

5. How do you visualize your retirement years?

6. Do you still have unmet needs to contribute to society or do you feel that in retirement you can just enjoy yourself because you've earned it.

7. What skills do you see yourself transitioning into retirement? Into a new endeavor?

8. How do your retirement plans and dreams fit with your spouse's plans? Are there differences? How can you reconcile them?

9. How do you feel about your husband or wife retiring earlier than you? How do you see this affecting your life? Your relationship?

CHAPTER 3 –
DESTINATIONS
Quality of Life and Location

"When you change your address, you also change your life."

— *B. Bennett*

CHALLENGE:

To successfully decide together where you want to spend your retirement life.

When you select a place to live in your retirement, you not only select a residence, but you choose a quality of life as well. This chapter focuses on the destination decisions that retirees have made such as: moving to a retirement community, maintaining their pre-retirement home, having a vacation home, maintaining two seasonal homes, or moving into a condo. As you read about their experiences and about the benefits and drawbacks of these choices, you'll learn more about the process of making this decision, and how to do it successfully.

DREAMING ABOUT YOUR RETIREMENT

As you both sit down to plan your retirement you each may be dreaming of where you want to live and what you want to do when you retire. Many people have a dream to live in a foreign land or travel the world. When I read *Under the Tuscan Sun* it made me dream of buying a home in Italy, remodeling it, and discovering a new life there. You may have had the same dream if you read the book or saw the movie.

> *I always dreamed of having a second home someplace like France or Ireland. We could travel there a few months of the year and then come home, but we'll have to wait and see.*
>
> *Jerry G*

Although Jerry is still working, he and his wife are beginning to discuss possible dream retirement locations. He has an Irish heritage and they both love French wine and gourmet food. Some people dream of a life of sailing to different ports of call in retirement; others envision themselves playing golf or tennis at some famous resort. Some people want to attempt new endeavors or participate in new adventures, while others wish to continue to work in their chosen field. Whatever your dreams are, location will be important in enhancing those dreams or inhibiting them. Where you will live and what you will do are closely intertwined. Your retirement location can significantly influence your quality of life.

Within ten years of the time that you think you'll be retiring, you want, if possible, to begin planning your retirement. If you haven't already sat down with your spouse or partner and realistically assessed your plans, do so now. Given your retirement nest egg, pension, and financial situation, what is really possible? Make sure your windshield is clean so that you can clearly see what's ahead. Determine if you will be able to achieve your dreams with your present resources. Are your dreams similar or different? If different, can you find a way to weave them together? Here are some of the alternatives others considered and chose.

Living Out Your Dream in Two Locations

In order to realize their dream retirement many couples have turned to utilizing several locations. Perhaps it is a way of compromising that allows each person to have his or her dream fulfilled. Different couples have discovered a variety of ways to meet their objectives. Some retired people still live in their family home, but rent or lease a vacation home. Others, who wanted to experience several different locations, have actually purchased two separate residences. The more adventuresome rented or bought a home in a foreign country. Couples who decided on a two-location retirement shared their insights as to how this type of arrangement can work. What follows are stories about choosing a retirement, including the benefits and drawbacks of these options.

Original Home and Second Location - Some people decide to keep their family home for part of the year, and rent or lease in a more welcoming climate during less desirable months.

We live in western New York State and when my husband decided to retire, he wanted to rent a place out in California during the winter months. Years ago I really wanted to move to California, but my husband had his family and his busi-

ness back east and felt he couldn't move. So, when he said he was going, I was ready. We rented different places each time we came out and found some places wouldn't allow renters to use the facilities unless they joined the club to play tennis or golf. We found by renting at the Del Webb community we could use all the facilities at no extra charge. After several seasons we ended up buying a small house of our own. Now we can go back and forth when we please from one house to the other. Our plan is to keep our east coast home and use this small home during the winter months.

Phyllis W

Some people adjust to this approach more easily than others. Often it depends upon how long you have been in your own home, how adventuresome you are, and your openness to change.

We would drive down to spend time in the winter season in Southern California. My husband loves it down there. When we started going down there I could only handle being away from home for one month. The next year we tried two months away and then worked up to three months, by which time I was ready to go home. I would get on myself because I really didn't have anything I had to get back home for. I think I just change gradually by degrees. I don't know why I should be unhappy because we rent the same place each year and my husband always makes our driving trips interesting. When driving back we don't stop to sightsee because I just want to get back home.

Darlene L

Darlene tends to change slowly and likes the security of her home. She wanted to rush home, but said that once she got there, she wondered why she was in such a hurry. Upon returning home, she most likely experienced a let down after leading a different life style while away and found she now had to adjust to her same home life cycle.

Staying in Your Home and Renting a Second Location

Benefits	Drawbacks
Retain familiar home environment—doctors, dentists, shopping, friends, support systems.	Difficulty maintaining ongoing connection with family, friends, acquaintances while away at second location.
Continue to see family often if they live close by your original home.	Travel and rental expense on top of financially maintaining own home.
Luxury of being in a welcoming climate at a second location in appropriate seasons.	You are at the mercy of fluctuating or rising costs of rental property.
Have opportunity to expand interests, friendships, experiences, and knowledge of new area.	Changes in availability of property to rent can hamper acquiring the place you want.
Family can vacation at second location.	

Owning Two Homes in Two Locations — Couples who want to experience two different environments and are able to maintain more than one home purchase two residences. Having two homes allows a couple to spend part of each year in a different area or location. The following stories give some picture of what it's really like to have two homes.

> *I expected change in retirement because we moved to two places where we knew no one. We purposely chose two places to live that were totally new to us. We only knew two people in this desert community and two friends on Cape Cod. I think that when you decide to move to a new place, you have to be open enough to accept differences in people. My husband and I are not New Englanders and in Cape Cod we are known as the people from California. Since most of the people are from New England, we had to prove ourselves as good neighbors and friends. We spend six months at each home and each time we move, we have to reestablish liaisons and friendships. Upon returning, we make ourselves visible and spend a lot of energy renewing acquaintances. We do a lot of entertaining as we belong to two tennis clubs.*
>
> *Jo S*

Since maintaining two homes (and the different lives that come with those homes) does require physical and emotional energy, people considering this type of retirement generally need to be outgoing and involved in the community. However, your involvement may be limited to part-time participation rather than full-time leadership positions in either place. You need to carve out a niche in both environments.

Harold and I live in a rural Iowa town of about eight thousand people. This is a second marriage for us and I have two sons in Iowa. During our business years, we vacationed in different locations, one being the Southern California desert. Ten years ago we bought a home there while on vacation. At the time we were both working and we weren't thinking about retiring. We saw it as a place to vacation. However, it's turned into our second home during the winter months. As we travel back and forth to both communities, we are involved in the same type of groups and activities, but with different people. We have met some very nice people at our second place and still have our friends at home.

Dee H

There are a variety of ways that retiree couples are making a two-house situation function for them. They say that successfully maintaining this kind of lifestyle requires disciplined planning and teamwork.

We have our furniture and things we collected from a life of traveling at our main home. The second home is furnished with things from national chain stores (like Sears, Ikea, or Target). Maintaining two homes, if properly thought out, is not as difficult as people might think. We arranged to pay our bills directly from the bank accounts. Mail is transferred from point A to point B during specific periods of time. The computer is an absolute must as is a cell phone because it keeps us in instant contact with friends and family. Having a laptop computer is also useful as we drive from one home to the other. We just pack our bags, get in the van and proceed to the next destination.

Bob A

Bob said that when both he and Rita work as a team, everything generally works out fine. He has his jobs and she has hers. My husband and I have also defined jobs in closing one house, packing the car and opening the other house. We actually have check-off lists as to who does what. After a number of years, this process has gotten to be a regular routine chore.

We continue to live in our home of 35 years where we raised our family. We also have a summer home on the water. Although we do spend time at our summer home, in recent years we decided to provide each of our five children and their families with a week to use the home. The children figure out when each will use the house and this has worked very well. They are able to invite friends and enjoy themselves.

Judy D

Judy shared that she and her husband have also benefited from letting their children use their summer home. They get invited over to meet their kids' friends and are able to spend quality time with their family away from the daily routine of work and school. They find time to really talk with one another.

Owning Two Homes in Two Locations

Benefits	Drawbacks
Opportunity to lead two different lifestyles.	The burden of a second mortgage
Opportunity to explore and discover new venues, sights, attractions.	Cost of maintaining two homes—taxes, utilities, caretaker, gardener.
If both homes are near family members, have greater opportunity to see them.	Added tasks to open or close each house in season.
An expanded circle of friends and acquaintances.	Will need to expend effort to make new friends and maintain old ones while away.
Freedom to come and go as you please or lend home to family or friends.	

Owning or Renting a Home in a Foreign Country - Other adventurous souls who want to experience living abroad rent or buy in a foreign country. Still others choose to live outside the U.S. because they are able to save on cost of living expenses since it may be a cheaper place to live.

> For years we continued to own our own home, traveled, and rented places all around the world. We have rented homes, condos, or apartments for a month in such places as Sicily, Rome, Portofino, Paris, London, and Capetown, South Africa. We even lived on a ship for a round-the-world cruise. A month allowed us to really explore and

discover the best in each area. My wife never wanted us to buy a second home because she felt it would tie us down to just two places. Instead, we have spent time in 55 countries. This has worked well for us.

Jerry N

For many years we rented a vacation house in Mexico along the Baja coast and considered buying a place there. We talked to Americans who had an informal enclave south of Rosarita Beach. They found living below the border helped them stretch their retirement dollars, as the cost of living was so much less than the U.S. However, American citizens are not allowed to own property along the coast. The homes owned by Americans along the coast are on lease land. So we thought that this would not be a safe proposition for us. We also know that people living over the border on the Baja Peninsula come up to San Diego for their healthcare needs. In a medical emergency we didn't feel comfortable being in another country.

Barb A

Many U.S. retirees spend winter months in Mexico. I talked with a semi-retired schoolteacher in the northwest who owns a house in a small town in Mexico. He said there's a group of Americans who have bought there. According to the American Association of Retired Persons there is an enclave of retired Americans in San Miguel de Allende. (If you are interested in considering Mexico as a place to spend part of your retirement, go to http://www.aarp.org.)

After many years of living abroad, we decided to spend part of our retirement life in another country. We bought a home in a fishing village on Vancouver Island, Canada. When you own a second home in Canada, you need to establish a local Canadian bank. You also need your passports with you. If someone were interested in buying property in another country, we would advise them to investigate the laws with regard to paying taxes and issues around selling the property. Although it was not the main reason we bought on Vancouver Island, we appreciate being not too far from our daughter who lives in Oregon.

Rita and Bob A

Often people go on vacation and fall in love with a place. They think it is beautiful and would like to move there. However, what they initially saw on vacation may not be what they experience after spending more time there. When you are on vacation, you don't consider many of the necessities of day-to-day living. It's important to think about the kind of lifestyle you will have when you actually live in a place.

Owning or Renting a Home in a Foreign Country

Benefits	Drawbacks
Maintain benefits of original home plus opportunity to see new sights, new areas of interest.	Travel costs may prohibit number of visitors.
Expand circle of acquaintances, friends if fluent in language of country of second location.	If you live there permanently, you will need to become conversant in the language of the country.
Renting homes vs. buying limits your ongoing costs of maintaining two homes.	You will need to become knowledgeable in foreigner's property rights and legal requirements.

Moving into a Condominium Development - Some couples make a decision to move out of their family home and into a condominium development. This often occurs when the physical upkeep and maintenance of the home becomes too much for them. However, younger retirees are considering condominiums in exotic places or moving into condos as their main residence or vacation place. By living in a condo, you have the property maintenance taken care of and can feel secure that your place is being taken care of when you leave or travel on trips.

> *We had a two-year plan to sell our home, move into a condominium apartment in the suburbs of Toronto and refurbish the family summer cottage my husband inher-*

ited. We didn't want to be tied down doing a large amount of outdoor maintenance at two places. I wanted to keep a base in Toronto to maintain old friends, while my husband would have been happy living at the cottage. So we compromised and live part time at each place. We chose a condo on the 17th floor of a large building located within walking distance of stores and other venues. It's become a place we hang our hat when we are in Toronto, but I don't think we will make a lot of friends there because most tenants speak Chinese and are from a different social background.

Jane S

Fred and Jane were among the first of their friends to sell their family home and move to a condominium development. They felt that downsizing from a five-bedroom house into a smaller condo wasn't as easy as they anticipated, but they are now happy with their decision. They consider the summer cottage their main home and the condo is a place where they say they "hang their hat." Fred and Jane have been able to maintain their Toronto friends, while adjusting to an unexpected culturally different condominium environment.

Moving into a Condominium Development

Benefits	Drawbacks
Maintenance responsibility limited to own condo or apartment.	Generally smaller living quarters not sufficient for large family gatherings.
Use of grounds, pools, exercise facilities, etc. without having to maintain them.	Share building with other tenants, possibly from different cultures and social and economic backgrounds.
Security allows you to travel or be away without concern for your property.	May require participation in building association to be involved in decision-making process and pay association fees.

If you're thinking about relocating, do a lot of research about the area you're considering moving to. Your computer can be your best friend in doing research. Magazines, books, newspaper articles, and your local library are good sources for data. Assess how each area meets both your and your spouse's wants and needs in all your important criteria listed later in this chapter. Through this process, you will not only evaluate the area, you'll also assess what is most important to you and where you're willing to compromise. Planning is easy when both of you have similar ideas for your retirement life, but often this isn't the case and you may have to compromise or adjust your ideas to create a scenario that satisfies you both.

Our Story

When my husband and I sat down and thought seriously about the kind of life we wanted in retirement and what we could afford, he expressed a dream to be located on a golf course. My dream was to have a home on the water. If we were to realize both our dreams, we most likely would need to be in two different locations. Since both of our children live on the west coast, we felt that we should be located at a reasonable traveling distance from each of our children and grandchildren. As it is, we are approximately two to three hours from each family at either of our two locations. Initially, these were our most important factors for selecting a retirement location.

We began researching property up and down the west coast approximately seven years prior to my husband's forecasted retirement. About two years before his retirement, we finally found a piece of waterfront property that we could afford. We sold our income property and exchanged it for a rental house on the water. After several years of renting the house out, we renovated it and furnished it with excess furniture from our main house. For the two-years prior to retiring we visited the island for short periods of time to become more familiar with the area, the weather, and the people.

During the years leading up to retirement we also were checking out southwest desert property to fulfill my husband's dream to be on a golf course. We spent time in Tucson and Phoenix. We knew the areas because we had visited relatives living in both places. After doing our research, we concluded that these two areas, while providing affordable housing in retirement communities, were too far away from our immediate family. We thought Palm

Desert, California was not only close to our children, it offered us a warm climate, a sense of community, mountain scenery, good restaurants and entertainment possibilities. Since it was a more expensive area in which to buy a home, we opted to buy a smaller house that we could afford and be mortgage-free in retirement. Since we would be living in two locations for part of the year, we felt it made sense financially and maintenance wise to have smaller properties that we could afford and care for.

It may sound like an idyllic life to spend time in the best seasonal months at two locations and in many ways it is. However, there are always factors that you don't count on. Initially we tried to ask the right questions, but we couldn't think of everything and most likely neither will you. The following criteria may help you think creatively and critically about what questions to ask when doing your research.

CRITERIA FOR SELECTING A RETIREMENT LOCATION

Given the abundance of available options, discovering a suitable retirement location can be an intimidating task. So how do people make this decision? From my conversations with retirees about how they chose a retirement location, six general areas of interest and concern emerged.

- Climate and scenery
- Available activities
- Friendly and compatible neighbors
- Support systems

- Financial constraints
- Quality healthcare

Of course, these criteria factored differently for each couple. Depending upon the retired couple's particular wants and needs, some criteria were more important and carried more weight, while others had equal or lesser importance in the final decision as to where they retired.

Climate and Scenery - Frequently, retirees who wanted to relocate were looking for a more conducive climate for their retirement years than where they were living. Whether people wanted to move to a rustic cabin in the mountains, a beachfront cottage, or a retirement community in the desert, they valued the aesthetic aspects of the potential location.

> *One of the considerations in choosing a place to retire for us was weather. We had lived in the northeast and wanted to move to a warmer climate. In retirement you will have free time and if it is raining 99 percent of the time, you will sit home with nothing to do. I think that could be psychologically bad news. We settled into our retirement community and spent the first two years playing golf and enjoying ourselves. We went to different activities, got involved and met people. We had come across the country, knew no one, other than our son and family, and we found a life.*
>
> *Larry M*

> *When I retired I wanted great climate year round so we chose two locations to live. I didn't choose an ocean area in California because I worked in that coastal strip for years where the sun doesn't come out until noon a lot of the time.*

We live six months in the desert and six months in the mountains. Because I am interested in photography, great scenery, and hiking, we chose a place just outside Yosemite because it is so beautiful. My wife wasn't as into it as I was, but now she likes the lake and has made friends there. It is not a retirement community and I'd say the area is economically diverse and the people have a wide range of interests.

Bob G

When I retired I was divorced with two grown sons. After a number of years working abroad, I had a decision to make about where I was going to relocate. Although I grew up in Ohio and enjoyed the snow as a child, I wanted to go where it was warm in my retirement. Years earlier we had lived on the New Jersey shore and I learned that you have to know what the weather is like not only in summer but in winter as well. If you want to live up north or in the mountains, go up in the wintertime and see what it is like. I looked for a house in the desert in July and could feel the heat I would have to cope with if I moved there full time.

Deryl C

Although couples interviewed thought through many location factors, one climate factor that wasn't considered was allergies. The problem of allergies to native plants or environmental conditions in an area was found to be an unexpected change for a number of retirees.

We bought and moved into our pre-retirement house in New Mexico and established a large circle of friends.

Unfortunately, the weather really affected my allergies. I never had allergy problems before. I was allergic to juniper pollen and was practically bedridden during pollen season. I got tired of taking drugs and even acupuncture didn't work. That was a big impetus for moving to the California desert. I have occasional allergy problems here, but not as bad as I had in New Mexico.

Lorraine W

For the most part, the people who made decisions based on weather and climate expressed satisfaction with their choice. Those who failed to fully research the climate and weather changes of the new location expressed dissatisfaction with their choice.

Climate and Scenery

Benefits	Drawbacks	Compromises
Environment contributes to doing a variety of activities: golf, tennis, hiking, boating, swimming, bike riding, etc.	Unsatisfactory weather changes in various months or seasons such as wind, fog, rain, cold or hot days.	To have affordable waterfront property or top location, you may need to giveup year-round warm climate.
Beauty of area adds to retirement enjoyment.	Allergic reactions to environmental conditions.	Use RV parks, time-shares, renting or leasing homes to be able to afford best locations in the best seasons.

Activities - The availability of a variety of activities and recreational opportunities were high on the list of criteria for choosing a retirement location. People were interested in places where they could pursue playing sports, joining clubs and interest groups, learning and development opportunities, and entertainment venues. Individuals did not see their retirement as one dimensional, but wanted to engage in a variety of undertakings—recreational, educational and volunteerism.

When moving to a new community take a look at what's available—clubs you would like to get involved with as well as activities you don't like. Try different groups and drop those you don't enjoy. My wife and I found that between food (gourmet groups, wine groups) and financial (investment groups, men's discussion group), we discovered groups that support our interests and met a great number of friends this way.

John L

I was looking for golf, a house I could own with no mortgage, and a lifestyle. Boy, this retirement community fit like a tee. We stayed for three days at the Sun City villas. During this stay we drove around in a golf cart and talked to people on the street, rang doorbells and asked them how they liked living here. We made our minds up in three days, picked out a house model and told them we wanted to move in eight months. We then went back home and put our house on the market.

Bob D

Living in two locations, my husband and I appreciate the difference between both communities. Our desert retirement community has multiple activity opportunities including clubs for every possible sport or interest. If we tire of this, we have other entertainment venues in the Palm Springs area. During the summer months we live on a small island and are involved in golf and water sports. It's a slower pace of life that has provided us with time to relax, walk on the beach, and write. Although it is a small community, they have a community theatre and band concerts in the little park. We aren't far from a major city and can attend plays, concerts and special exhibitions. My husband and I feel we have the best of both worlds at this phase of our retirement.

Some people sought personal development along with recreational activities. Others found involvement and fulfillment by volunteering in the community or in the various interest groups in which they were involved.

I believe in getting involved. I first volunteered at the little post office in our retirement community because I thought that would be a good way to meet a lot of people. I also was very interested in volunteering as a docent at the local air museum because of my background in aviation. This volunteer opportunity provides me a chance to get to know people outside my retirement community.

Deryl C

What was important for us was that, wherever we retired, we would feel at home. That's why we came back to where we grew up. It provides a small town atmosphere where you can get involved in doing all kinds of volunteer projects. I am involved in a group that makes quilts for returning wounded soldiers. We've held a quilt-a-thon for two years and I'm in-

*volved in organizing it and doing public relations. My husband
and I also volunteer to help the Island Heritage Association
and were in charge of an island boat trip last year.*

Jean M

Although volunteering in areas in which you have an interest
can keep you busy and productive, your activities don't have to
be altruistic. You may want to develop yourself personally by
engaging in activities such as learning to paint or how to operate
a computer or how to salsa dance. More and more universities
and colleges are providing interesting programs for seniors. One
person I spoke to is signed up at a local community college and
will earn college credits while on a 21-day educational trip she
and her husband will take to Europe.

*My wife and I took four astronomy courses at the local
community college. It was something we both wanted to
learn about and never had the time.*

Stephen S

Each person finds his or her own means of self-fulfillment.
Some people find it in expanding their knowledge through
educational classes. Others look to a wide variety of sports in
which to be involved. Still others might wish to live near a large
city that can provide a variety of entertainment such as plays,
music, opera, science and art museums, and galleries.

One activity that is an added benefit in a retirement
community is a formal singles group. People, who are divorced,
widowed, or single can be involved in a variety of sponsored
social activities and not feel like a "fifth wheel."

Activities Available in Retirement Communities

Benefits	Drawbacks	Compromises
Sports: a variety of available venues and groups, i.e. golf, tennis, aerobics, hiking, and biking, swimming, exercising	Except for such activities as hiking, walking, exercising, playing cards, most activities require funding to use facilities.	On a fixed income, assess what you can afford to do and where you might have to cut back or look for alternative activities
Educational classes in computer, genealogy, photography, etc.	Whether it is sports equipment, art supplies, membership fees or travel it will cost you money.	Select activities and interests that meet your specific needs or goals in life. Don't get yourself over involved.
Health & Fitness groups, e.g. water aerobics, Tai Chi, Yoga, meditation. Pilates, exercising.	By joining a large number of activities, you can overextend yourself.	Find a balance of couple activities and single activities you both want to do.
Creative arts: painting, arts & crafts, sewing, ceramics, music, acting, woodcarving		

continued

Couples' Groups: putters, golf, tennis, gourmet dining, square & ballroom dancing, travel, etc.		
Entertainment: A variety events and shows are available: dances, dinners, wine tastings, and travel.		

Friendly and Compatible Residents - Whether people were looking for a vacation home or a home within a community, they wanted to locate in a place that had a friendly atmosphere, where they could make connections and new acquaintances. The importance of compatibility with regard to age, activities, and interests was an important consideration for many people who shared their stories for this book.

> *Although it was a little harder to move in to an established retirement community, we have found people here we enjoy. The boomers group was probably my favorite group because the people were younger. I think my husband and I forget that we are the age we are. We think we are younger because a lot of our friends are between our children's age and us. I'm not old and I don't think age is chronological; it's emotional. I think it is a matter of mindset, interests in the world, and what is going on.*
>
> Judith A

> *When we started looking for a place to retire I was the inspiration to move to a retirement community. My wife's reaction was, "no way do I want to go to an old folks home type of place." At the time I was 59 and she was 56. I said that the places I was looking at were communities with very active people of varying ages from 55 to 90. With all the activities we could be as active as we wished to be and this has proved to be true.*
>
> *Larry M*

Not just compatibility but the ability to assess the openness and receptivity of people in a community was important to many of the people I spoke with.

> *We looked at available houses with a real estate person before we retired. We stopped at the clubhouse to look it over and I wandered into the ballroom. There was a square dance club meeting going on. I wasn't in the doorway for 30 seconds when two different people came running over and said hello and invited me to join them. I said, "I don't live here yet." They said, "That's okay, come on." I liked the welcoming atmosphere in this community. That's why we settled here because it appeared to be the type of active community we were looking for.*
>
> *Jeanne E*

> *A client of mine recommended we look in the Northwest when we wanted to retire. We came up to look at various localities, but the day we came they had the worst snowstorm in 30 years and we were snowed in on an island. We stayed at a B & B for three nights and saw what it was like when the people reacted to a calamity. We loved*

the island in spite of the situation and came back the next
summer to find a house to buy. We figured out where we
wanted to go and once we found the place, that's when we
retired.

Richard H

Richard and Mona's experience was serendipitous, but it
points out that in researching retirement locations, you might
have to spend a little time in a place during different seasons to
get a clear picture of what life there might be like.

Friendly and Compatible Residents

Benefits	Drawbacks	Compromises
You expand your circle of acquaintances, neighbors, and friends	You have only the population within the new area to search for compatible connections.	You need to expend the energy to search out people with similar interests, age, and economic status, and forge connections.
You expand your knowledge of the history and culture of the local population.	You increase your responsibility to more individuals by increasing your acquaintances.	Weigh the amount of time you want to spend on friendships and your personal pursuits.
You learn and grow by interrelating with new and different people.		

Support Systems - Being reasonably close to family, relatives, or friends was a consideration for some retirees when choosing a retirement location. Some retirees want to see their children and grandchildren more often and thus move closer to where they live.

When we retired, we were living on the east coast and first looked in Florida and then Arizona. However, our son and daughter-in-law, who lived in California, said if we were looking as far west as Arizona, why not look near them. We would then be closer to our grandchildren. After a trip to look things over, my initial reaction was that it was too expensive to live there. But we really liked it and decided we could afford to build a house in a retirement community in Palm Desert. We sold our condo and made the move. It was very scary as we were in our 50s and we would both be out of work. If the stock market took a dive, we would lose a lot of the income and investments we were counting on. It's worked out for us, as we are close enough to help out by taking care of our grandchildren once in a while now that our son is divorced.

Larry C

I have come to realize in retirement that I need a community of people that I am a part of. I have to live in a community to be content. If we spent all our time traveling and being vagabonds, we would meet people along the way, but we wouldn't have those friends and close ties that we need. I see that in a retirement community you are thrown more together with your neighbors and get to be part of the community. I believe that if you take from a community,

you should also be giving back to it. That's why I chair the
emergency preparedness committee. It is my voluntary effort
to give back. You also get to know more people and feel more
a part of where you live.

Lorraine W

Other people may be farsighted and see that having a family support system or a friendship support system would be important to them now and in the future.

I can't sell the merits of the Sun City lifestyle enough. My
family was so blown away by what happened when my
husband died. During the time of the funeral, we were
provided with three meals per day for seven days. They took
in some of my family who came for the funeral. Friends
called to ask if I had anything on my "honeydo" list that
their husbands could do for me. My family could not get
over the generosity of the people here. They live here without
a career, without children, or grandchildren and are avail-
able to each other. I didn't experience this in my previous life
when I was working.

Sharon J

Sharon understood that during her working years she had less time to connect with friends. But, she also realized that if she and her husband had continued to live where they had been living nothing would have changed. She felt that the healthiest thing they did was to move to a retirement community where she found friendship and support when she needed it.

A sister of mine decided to move to Charlotte, North Carolina to be near her son. She lives in a regular neighborhood where most of the people go to work. She is quite a ways from the senior center. She doesn't drive at night so it has been hard for her to go to anything that is happening in the evening. We think she made a mistake. We told her to look around for a retirement community in different areas, but she won't move. She has refrozen and can't unfreeze to change. She can't be like water flowing back and forth.

Phyllis W

If you don't make many contacts outside of your family you can get pretty lonely, even if you live near them. If your children move again, you will be faced with the decision to move again or not. Do you move again with them, or just move back to your hometown? Keep in mind that the old adage often rings true, "you can't go home again" because you, your old friends, and/or your neighborhood have most likely changed.

Support Systems in Family or Retirement Community

Benefits	Drawbacks	Compromises
Living near children—you will see them more often and will share more in their life events.	May not see your children or grandchildren as much as expected due to their active lifestyles.	When one or the other of you want to follow your children, be sure to assess all your options.
You may have more opportunities for quality time with family and can attend functions for grandchildren.	Children may get divorced or transferred and move away.	Rather than moving your household, you might lease or rent a furnished apartment or home near family for part of the year.
Family who live close can help in time of illness.	When in a new community, you may need to expend the time and energy to make new contacts outside of the family.	Perhaps you can set up a schedule to visit family periodically rather than moving to be near them.
Living in a retirement community provides some assurance of support and assistance.		

Financial Constraints - Finances (which will be discussed in more detail in chapter 9) can be a major determinant of what you can afford, where you can move and what you can do. When looking at possible locations, you'll need to consider finances in order to determine whether you'll be buying, renting, or leasing. Sometimes couples had to change locations after experiencing a personal financial crisis. State and local taxes, as well as property taxes, are also a consideration when selecting a retirement location.

> *I think our planned change was our relocation. We wanted to get the equity out of our house and go somewhere that had less costly housing. I was actually very happy where I was because I had my social groups and a job I liked very much. We were 55 when we moved to this retirement community. I think that anytime you are looking at a problem, you should get all the information you can and then decide what is feasible at every stage of your life. You have to make compromises. I think being in a retirement community can make it easier to make a change because you have so many options available to you.*
>
> *April P*
>
> *We have been able to financially handle both small homes and still intersperse the kind of travel abroad that we wanted to do. We plan a big trip every eighteen months to two years. By owning two properties, there is always something to fix, replant or replace in one place or the other. There are ongoing costs in both places such as: utilities, security, gardening, homecare, upkeep, golf club fees, association fees and house taxes. Another financial consideration when owning two properties is the cost of insuring both properties for fire,*

*flood, earthquake, etc. These types of expenses have to be
included in forecasting our yearly costs of property.*

Barbara B

If you haven't saved enough, weren't able to forecast
your expenses over your retirement years, or if you tended
to over extend yourselves to buy a larger home in a more
prestigious area, you may find yourself in a financial
predicament.

*Because of illness my husband retired early and we spent
our first retirement years in Florida. We then made a decision to move cross-country at our daughter's request that we
live closer to her and her family. I had been out to visit them
several times and I really liked a retirement community
there, but felt it was too expensive to live in California.
We had low house taxes in Florida, but our house insurance was high because of hurricanes. Finally we convinced
ourselves to move. We've been here two and a half years. My
husband misses his life in Florida. We can't afford to move
again. It was terribly expensive to move here in the first
place. I feel we are stuck.*

Pat E

Pat's story demonstrates how important it is to make a
judicious decision about where to retire and the cost of change.
Perhaps if she and her husband had visited for three months or
six months and experienced being away from Florida, they might
have made a different decision.

Financial Constraints

Benefits	Drawbacks	Compromises
More savings equal more options in retirement.	Limited funds make for an untenable position if you need to change.	Monies saved for retirement will dictate when you both retire.
With funding you can travel and do what you want to do.	Rising costs of rents, taxes, utilities, food and healthcare require sufficient savings.	In order to do more in retirement, you might downsize and buy a smaller home.
With financial means you can buy and/or rent vacation homes where you want and when you want.		With limited funds, you might look at lowering living expenses, travel less, eat out less often and don't buy a new car as often.

Quality Healthcare - The availability of quality medical care and hospital facilities within a reasonable distance was also an important criterion in choosing a retirement location. Although medical support may not seem important in your first years of retirement, especially if you are retiring early, it can make an important difference in saving your life or the life of your spouse. As people age, they tend to make greater use of physicians, medical specialists, dentists, hospitals, physical rehabilitation centers, nursing homes and other healthcare facilities.

When we were selecting a retirement community, one thing we looked for was the degree of medical resources available for our later years. We didn't used to think about that particularly. We selected a desert area known for retirement, which has an unusual amount of medical resources, theaters and great restaurants. When we looked at various retirement communities, we always looked at the local city or town and what it offered.

John L

John and his wife live about fifteen minutes from a major hospital. The fire department medical team is located only minutes away outside their community front gate.

Our regular doctors and specialists are located near our main home. We get all our check-ups and operations done there. At our second home on the island we do have a health center to take care of non-urgent illnesses. However, the isolation of being on an island, only accessible by ferry, makes it more difficult to access professional hospital support systems. In an emergency we would call the fire department medical team and if seriously ill, be evacuated by helicopter to a hospital in Seattle. A friend was jogging last year, experienced a heart problem and called his wife on his cell phone. Help came, but he didn't live long enough to get taken off island to the hospital.

Ann B

Living on an island or other location remote from first-class medical facilities is a precarious position to be in when experiencing a life threatening attack or seizure. As you get older, you may need to reassess your risk factors and make a location change if you feel it is necessary.

> *Even though we live part of the year in Canada we, as U.S. citizens, cannot participate in their national health program. We can get treatment at small local medical facilities. The health insurance that we have will help if we are not ambulatory. If I am ambulatory I am supposed to go to the nearest healthcare facility, which is in Portland, Oregon, a good five hour drive from our location on Vancouver Island, B.C. That's why I think it's important to have SOS—a medical and evacuation insurance for travel in foreign countries. SOS is critical if you are concerned about the medical care when you are abroad.*
>
> *Rita A*

Since this interview, Rita was successfully driven from Vancouver Island down to the Portland health facility when she experienced a serious health problem. You just don't know when illness can strike and when you will need medical care.

Quality Healthcare

Benefits	Drawbacks	Compromises
In an emergency quick, available medical support can save your life.	If you are not close to appropriate, early response medical care it can jeopardize your life.	People living on islands or in other rural areas gamble they will be able to reach trauma or urgent medical care in time.
Living near doctors, specialists, and dentists gives you easier access to top-notch care.	The inability to access reliable medical care can make life difficult, especially in your later years.	People believe serious illness needing specialist care is not going to occur early in retirement and move to pastoral environments.
Maintaining your health with diet, exercise, and yearly medical check-ups can identify problems early on.	Living in another country or rural area may require you to travel great distances to obtain proper medical care.	

People often want to live in an exotic place or move abroad for their retirement; they may not see the importance of having accessible topnotch healthcare facilities. As you'll read later in this book, illness, sometimes serious, can befall us at any age, even early in our retirement.

CHANGE IS PART OF RETIREMENT LIFE

It takes a lot of energy to establish one retirement life, let alone two or more. After you spend all the time on research and make a decision, you may not want to spend more energy doing it over again. That's why it is so important to know what you want in your retirement life and investigate, visit, and spend time in the places you're considering. But, keep in mind that places change, requirements change, you and your spouse change. If you have to do it again, it won't be the end of the world.

> *We bought a small house in a desert retirement community that we thought we could afford and have been here for one year. However, our son-in-law was transferred back east. We are now considering buying a second home near family and old friends back in New Jersey. We would be on the east coast during the summer months and in that way see our children and grandchildren. My husband can't handle the east coast winters, so we plan to keep this house and return to the desert for the winter months.*
>
> *Barbara W*

Retirees told me they were surprised at the number of people moving in and out of their retirement community. The residents may have built their dream house with all the bells and whistles, and after a couple of years move away.

> *When my husband retired, we decided to start a new life and built a house in Steamboat Springs, Colorado, because our one son lived there. It was a big change from Pittsburgh, Pennsylvania. We took up skiing and lived there for six years. We knew living there would come to an end when I stopped*

skiing and the winters seemed too long. We started to look at retirement communities in Arizona, Nevada, and California. We received an unsolicited offer to buy our Colorado house and ended up selling it at a profit and buying a home in California. We have adapted to our new retirement community and we both have gotten involved in activities here.

Joan T

Change can come even if you continue living in your present home. Often people retire and continue living in their family home or select a retirement area that either doesn't agree with them or isn't what they expected. People move for all kinds of reasons—to move closer to family, friends, relatives, more space, less space or more conducive environment than the one they live in. Change is part of life.

SUMMARY

As you get older and settled in your retirement life, you may be more reluctant to change. Moving can even appear as taking a step backwards in retirement. You may think by moving you have to restart your retirement life all over again and question if you have the energy to do so. Don't be afraid to change if your life or situation changes. Which is worse—staying in an unhealthy area, suffering because you are miserable or changing for the possibility of something better? If you successfully changed once, the second time may just be easier because you already have the knowledge, skill, and experience to make a successful change.

QUALITY OF LIFE TOOL KIT

Questions:

Each person should answer these questions separately and then meet with your spouse/partner to discuss your answers. It will be important to talk about not only ideas, but feelings as well. Determine your priorities and what you each can compromise on.

1. What is your dream retirement?

2. What kind of climate and scenery do you want?

3. What would make a good place to retire?

4. What do you see yourself doing in retirement?

5. How important is it to us to be part of a community with friendly and compatible people? Why?

6. How important are support systems such as: family, friends, and professional systems?

7. How will our financial situation impact what we can buy and what we can do?

8. How important is it to us that quality healthcare is easily accessible?

9. If things don't work out or something happens, how willing will I be to change?

10. Do we need two locations to meet our retirement needs? Do we want to own or rent?

11. Are we interested in staying in our present home, moving into a retirement community, condominium environment, or vacation/resort location?

12. Are we interested in living abroad? Traveling abroad? If so, where?

CHAPTER 4 –
TAKING THE WHEEL
Physical, Mental, Emotional, and Spiritual Health

You have to have emotional balance. You have to have
physical balance. You have to have mental balance. . .
Balance means keeping things in proper perspective. . ..

— *John Wooden*

CHALLENGE:

To maintain your physical, mental, emotional and spiritual
health

PHYSICAL HEALTH

It's easy to get overwhelmed by the extensive amount of time
and energy it takes to maintain your health especially during
your retirement years. But, if you break staying fit into smaller
steps and incorporate it into your daily routine, it becomes
more achievable. You might walk to your various activities or
take a long walk and have a long talk with a friend. Try taking
the stairs rather than the elevator when possible. I know of one

retired couple who is specifically building a three-story house with stairs to climb up to a workout room on the second floor. You may not be that ambitious, but you can pay attention to exercising. Instead of driving around to find that close-in parking space, try parking somewhere in the lot and walk to a store or the movie theater. You can give yourself small doses of fitness, but remember to do it consistently and not sporadically.

During your working years you most likely didn't have a need to "check under the hood" to see how your health faired. You may not have paid much attention to your health at all unless you became ill or injured. But as you grow older, and health issues inevitably begin to arise, you develop a greater recognition of the importance of taking better physical care of yourself and exercising regularly in order to feel and look better.

> *I think one of the big changes for me in retirement is paying more attention to my health. I'm thinking about things in a different way. I didn't when I was young. I didn't have any health issues and I just didn't think about health. I just took it for granted that it would always be with me.*
>
> *Ralph S*

Do you ever notice that when you don't exercise for a couple of weeks, your body goes back to square one and you lose some mobility? If you go out and run, jog, toss a ball, or swing a golf club, you find yourself aching for the next few days. You get the message loud and clear from your body that you need to keep exercising to maintain flexibility and freedom from those aches and pains. In our working years, my husband and I were so busy in our individual careers we had to make a concerted effort to go and work out two or three nights a week. On many occasions

I dragged myself there after working all day. But, I always felt physically more in tune with my body afterwards. Now I have had to build in exercising daily into my retirement schedule. If I don't do it, I lose some flexibility.

Some people are naturally more mobile and physically active. Others tend to be more sedentary and idle. Those who include regular exercise in their daily lifestyle generally stay healthier and live longer than people who engage in more sedentary activities. If you're mentally engaged in and stimulated by sedentary work, you may have an even harder time pulling yourself away from those activities to move your body. Paradoxically, your mental life will be even more enhanced by taking a regular, physical time-out. Here is another opportunity for you to shape the kind of life you want for yourself in retirement by introducing some physical activity into your schedule.

By being active, you can:
- Increase your chance of fulfilling your dreams and plans for retirement.
- Travel to the places you dreamed of seeing and experience them first hand through walking, hiking, and being active.
- Delay or eliminate some of the illnesses you might contract such as obesity, high blood pressure, heart attack, etc.
- Add to your own functional longevity.

If you do fall to a genetic illness, even a relatively short-lived habit of regular exercise can help you through the surgery and recovery.

I think I was able to bounce back from heart surgery so quickly and get back to playing golf, volunteering, and my other activities because I was in good shape, ate well, and exercised. In fact, when I left the hospital, they gave me a menu of foods I could eat. My wife thought it was a wider menu than we normally ate before!

Steve B

Failing to maintain your physical health makes it more likely that you:

- Won't be able to do all the things that you worked for and hoped to do in retirement.
- Curtail your life span by engaging in poor health habits.
- Increase the likelihood of contracting a chronic or life-threatening illness.

Penny has such bad knee problems that she can't go up and down the basement stairs in her home to do her laundry. She knows it's a problem, but when she's been encouraged by her friends and family to see an orthopedic specialist, she says it just isn't the right time. Now she has twin grandchildren under four and a new grandchild, whom she enjoys, but may have some difficulty caring for.

Penny's Friend

For a number of years Penny has put off going to a specialist to get an assessment of her knees. Perhaps she is afraid of discovering that her condition is worse than she thought. Taking care of her grandchildren requires her to go up and down stairs in her daughter's two-story house, something her bad knees make difficult. If her knees had been operated on years ago, she most likely would be better off today. Underlying fear prevents some people from obtaining the care they need. Although it is generally better to deal with a health problem early, people may delay obtaining treatment because it means having to face their hidden fears. However, when you make the decision to obtain early treatment and face the fears, the chances of having a positive outcome are generally better. The key to a longer and healthier retirement is being self-disciplined about maintaining positive health habits and dealing with health issues early on. A positive change to take better care of your health can benefit you.

Here are some ways men and women on the road to a healthy future are working to maintain their physical health:

> *My husband and I go over to the fitness center, walk the track, and use the fitness equipment. He does his thing and I do mine. We meet to walk home together. We feel that it's important to exercise for an hour at least three times per week.*
>
> *Jan M*

> *In the years between 20 and 50, I was eating all kinds of stuff—steaks, potatoes, etc. because I was traveling and eating out a lot. When you get closer to retirement you realize that it isn't too wise to continue to eat the wrong things, drink, and smoke. You need to stop and radically change in order to have a better life. I'm not talking about just longevity, but a better life condition and life style.*
>
> *John B*

> *When I was working, two running friends and I used to run 20 miles together on a Saturday morning. Now I run*

to stay healthy and not to be competitive. I've accepted the fact that I am getting older and feel I have done all of the competitive running I needed to do.

Rick J

Sports such as jogging, timed running, tennis matches, or competitive golf do provide a work out, but are considered to be more "intensive" forms of exercise, which can put additional pressure or stress on some people. "Non-intensive" forms of body movement are walking, gardening, bike riding and swimming. Avid walking and exercising has been shown to help health maintenance as you age.

What I try to do now to lose a little weight and get a little more activity in the day is to get up an hour earlier in the morning and walk before I go to my part-time work. It's amazing how many people I meet doing the exact same thing, so I'm not alone!

Lorraine M

I do yoga and take a one-hour walk three times a week. Staying healthy does take a lot of time, but it's worth it. I started yoga about two years ago because my chiropractor and my physical therapist recommended specific exercises I could do for a sports injury. I find that the regimen of exercises helps me to be limber and to have greater range of movement.

Ann B

I never liked exercising for the sake of exercise. I like to involve myself in productive activities like pruning trees and gardening. I love the outdoors and do a lot of hiking in the mountains.

Bob G

I ride a stationary bike and watch TV while biking for 30 minutes when the weather is bad. In the summer I enjoy riding my bike on the quiet roads in the early evening.

Susan S

These people have found a variety of ways to maintain their health—exercising in the gym, walking, jogging, sports, yoga, tai chi, hiking, biking, etc. Building good exercise habits and healthy eating habits need to be part of your roadmap to a positive retirement, especially if you aren't doing it now. One of the biggest challenges in retirement is maintaining good health and taking the time out of each day to do it.

As cars reach the upper limits of their typical mileage, they need regular tune-ups. Your body needs them, too! You need to get regular yearly check-ups, a colonoscopy every five years after 60, and a review of the medications you are taking with your physician.

PHYSICAL HEALTH TOOL KIT

Questions:

As you prepare for retirement (and even if you're retired already) ask yourself these questions.

I. Are you satisfied with the way you are presently maintaining your physical health? If not, can you think about what keeps you from creating more satisfaction in the way you take care of your body? What would make exercising more pleasurable for you?

2. What physical exercises are you doing to keep in shape and in good condition? Do you enjoy them? How will you continue this regimen in retirement?

3. How can you keep abreast of the advances in medicine related to illnesses that run in your family?

4. How often do you get a complete physical check-up? What does the check up cover?

5. Do you have health insurance to cover catastrophic illness? If no, why not?

6. If you live part of the year in two different locations, do you have an appropriate doctor, dentist or chiropractor in both places? Does the doctor's office have a copy of your medical records? How often do you update the records? (This is especially important if you have had serious illness such as a heart problem or are in remission from cancer.)

MENTAL HEALTH

Maintaining balance in your physical, mental, emotional and spiritual areas of life can help you to lead a more effective retirement. You can't focus on one, at the expense of the others. By paying attention to all four areas of your life, you can maintain and live a more balanced existence. When I speak of the concept of mental health I'm referring to your psychological and emotional well-being—how well you are able to use your cognitive and emotional capabilities. In the context of this book, mental health is measured by how effectively you can function in your retirement life and recover from difficult situations that you encounter.

Intellectual Mental Health

As important as it is to exercise your body, it's just as important to exercise and stimulate your brain. Doctors have said that by the time we reach 85 years old, one-half of us will have some kind dementia. Fortunately, they've also reported that there are things we can do to delay the onset of mental deterioration. According to Dr. John Morley, Director of geriatric medicine and a professor at the St. Louis University School of Medicine, we need to challenge our brains so they will age healthfully.

> *What was interesting to me is that after three or four years of retirement, I felt that I was not expressing myself as well I used to when I was working full-time. In meetings I noticed that I couldn't put all the words together when I was trying to make a point. I felt that I was losing some of my verbal skills and that shocked me. So, I decided to go to*

*work part-time. It's amazing! I'm thinking faster and my
verbal skills are back.*

Rick J

Social interaction tends to enhance verbal skills and mental acuity. People report that they can think faster and respond more quickly if they are out interacting with other people on a consistent basis.

*In retirement, I was a tram driver and commentator at
the Living Desert Park for four years. I had to memorize
a talk and be able to speak and answer questions about all
the animals and plants. I never had a job that was so much
public speaking. I always tried to make it fun and educational. It really kept me on my toes.*

Marge G

*I found that presenting music programs to children in the
elementary schools has helped me to exercise my brain as
well as well as my creative side. You have to be sharp when
you are presenting a program to the youngsters.*

Steve B

As you get older, staying sharp may take a conscious effort. Intellectual mental health is the maintenance of active brain cells, which can enable you to retain brain function into your later years with the hope of stemming off dementia and/or Alzheimer's disease. Regardless of age, it's important to exercise your brain throughout your life.

*Mental health is important to me as dementia and
Alzheimer's disease run in my family. I do the word jumble*

*and word puzzle in the daily paper. I read one or two books
per month and belong to a book discussion group. We talk
about the subject matter; writing style, focus of the book and
how it might relate to our lives.*

Barbara C

*I use my computer as a tool to research all kinds of in-
formation. When I have a question about something, I go
online and do research—whether it relates to a new book,
or travel, or medical information.*

Barbara B

Being computer literate is a great advantage for anyone
working or retiring today. It provides you with information to
make an informed choice. The computer actually opens up a new
world to explore if you take advantage of it. Recently I wanted to
inquire about an acquaintance who was being treated for cancer
and was told that I could go to a specific website and check on
her progress and leave her a note. There's no end as to how the
computer can be used as a supportive tool in our lives.

There are many ways that you can keep your brain nimble.
You can expand your knowledge in the various ways the
interviewees above have done. It seems that learning about new
subjects, whatever your interest, can help you keep your brain
active and build its reserves of cells and connections. Another
way is to practice "neurobics." This technique uses your senses
to develop new connections in the sensory output area of your
brain. The idea is to use your senses in a new and different way.
Try to have a new experience by going a new way to a regular
destination; shower with closing your eyes; shop at an ethnic
market or do an everyday routine differently. It can be as simple

as using a different hand to comb your hair or brush your teeth. Or, it can be a more intensive experience such as traveling to a foreign country and immersing yourself completely in unfamiliar surroundings. The idea is to do something novel which totally engages you. You are never too old to search out ways you can maintain and increase your own brain vitality. Here's what Dorothy, who is 81, does:

> *I get up at 6:30 each weekday morning to take a two-mile walk to the latte stand on our island. There I meet young people having coffee and I enjoy listening to their points of view. We discuss the events of the day and what's in the newspaper. These talks help me to stay in touch and keep up.*
>
> *Dorothy N*

Given the choice, few of us would choose intellectual stagnation and mental atrophy. As we retire we want to continue leading positive and productive lives. The retirees I spoke with have found their own personal ways of maintaining their mental acuity and finding stimulation. Whether you decide to retire or are one of the 5.3 million people 65 or older who will continue in the workforce, maintaining your mental abilities will continue to be a paramount goal.

Despite all the mental and physical exercises, eating right and taking care of your body, breakdown and mortality are ultimately inescapable. Maintenance merely delays the inevitable. The gift of effective maintenance is that it can give you a longer delay than you might otherwise have!

MENTAL HEALTH TOOL KIT

Questions:

Take a few minutes to answer these questions:

1. How are you maintaining your intellectual mental health? Are you satisfied with this? If not, what activities might increase your satisfaction?

2. What are you doing that provides stimulation and exercise to your brain? Is it through reading, discussions, social or business interactions, volunteering, working, word puzzles, Sudoku? What else interests you?

3. What ways do you think you will maintain your cognitive skills as you age?

4. What stresses are you under currently experiencing? What can you do to dissipate that stress so that is doesn't escalate into a heart attack or stroke?

EMOTIONAL HEALTH

Emotional health is the ability to express your emotions appropriately and not get stuck in depression, anger, stress, or obsessive fears. When you are emotionally affected by an event that occurs, you tend to experience a physiological change.

When you become angry, your body responds by tensing your muscles or increasing your heart rate and blood pressure. You then unknowingly respond to this feeling. How you think as you experience anger can make a difference in how you act. You can have a positive thought, which acknowledges that you are frustrated and angry. This positive thought is a little like a mother holding a child who is having a tantrum. You have your emotion, and you have enough clarity or calm to simply witness the emotion without feeling forced to react to it. Or, as we've likely all had practice doing, you can get hijacked to think negatively and defensively. The cognitive response to your emotions then influences your behavior. A technique like Rational Emotive Therapy, defined at the end of this chapter, can help you slow down, sort out and untangle the emotions that arise in high intensity moments.

Emotions are hard to sort out because they often blend together. For instance, you may be jealous, fearful, and angry at the same time about a specific event that deeply affected you, but you may appear not to show it. Someone else in the same situation may stomp around ranting, raving and causing a commotion. The way we each express emotion and respond to events varies from person to person. Can you imagine what Gail felt in the following situation?

I received a shock a few years ago when I came home from visiting my kids I found that my husband had cleared out and left me for another woman. He had called both children and told them to give me the news. We had been married 36 years and the terrible way he left was the trauma. I thought I would be retired with my spouse and do all these wonderful things we had planned and saved to do together.

I never thought I would be growing old alone with partial financial resources. Immediately after this I had a car accident. The accident exacerbated my emotions and helped me to realize just how much turmoil I was in. I sought a professional therapist. It took me one solid year to get over grieving. But, I look back at this time as taking care of my self and dealing with all my old business. This way I wouldn't bring unfinished business into any new relationships I might have in the future.

Gail K

Gail survived this trauma because she was aware of her needs and wasn't ashamed to reach out to her friends and family. She credits their support as vital to her recovery. She sought out professional counseling help. She made up funny stories about the situation because she needed to rekindle her sense of humor to survive. All of this helped her to begin a new life. She now has a new relationship and is doing very well.

In addition to our various emotions, we also experience moods, which are longer lasting than an emotion. Perhaps you had an argument with your spouse in the morning, and you find that you are in a grumpy or irritable mood the rest of the day. Some of you may have temperaments that tend to cause a given emotion or mood. You might be prone to be melancholy, lonely, and dejected when something negative happens to you. Depression frequently affects older adults in retirement.

I saw my husband going into a rut about eighteen months into our retirement. If we didn't go hiking or on a day trip, he would have breakfast, go for a short walk and then come home and turn on the TV to check on the stock market and fall asleep in his chair right after breakfast. He was in his 50s and acting as though he was in his 70s. I recognized it as a sign of depression and I was concerned that he didn't recognize it in himself. He finally listened to a male friend who involved him in one of his business activities and I can see that my husband is now happier and is engaged in work he enjoys doing.

Lorraine M

A variety of events can trigger depression. Being aware of the symptoms and how they manifest themselves is important in seeking help.

The first months after my husband's death I was grieving and depressed. I let the house go. I would pick up the mail, look at it and drop it on the floor. It got so bad that I had piles of mail lying all over the floor. It's a wonder I didn't slip on the mail, fall, and break a hip. I finally got to the point when I said to myself, "you can't let it take over. You have to deal with it—even if you go to a movie alone or something. You have to take the bull by the horns. This is the way it is and the way it is going to be. Am I going to sit down and shrivel up like a prune and the let the rest of the world go by from now on? How do I want to handle it?"

Nancy E

I think my depression started when I had a knee problem and I couldn't play golf the summer of 2006. In the fall I decided to have a knee replacement operation. Despite the success of the knee operation, I felt lousy afterward. I was experiencing digestive problems that were making my life unbearable. I thought it was my heart because I felt pressure in my chest. I lost interest in everything and moped around the house all day. Then I read an article in the AARP Magazine that said if you had three of four symptoms, you should see a doctor to check you for depression. I had all four symptoms! I first went to my doctor and he sent me to a psychiatrist, who said I had a classic case of depression. He gave me some antidepressant pills at first, which were too strong for me. They made me wacky. I felt I was walking on two feet of air. He then changed my prescription to an antidepressant-antianxiety pill and that worked for me. I'm much better now but still not up to par. I feel that I'm on the road to recovery.

Robert D

Robert was experiencing pressure in his chest similar to the symptoms Jack Nicholson's character had in the movie "Something's Got to Give." Believing it was his heart made him more anxious, worried, and depressed. Some signs and symptoms of depression are: sadness, fatigue, losing interest in pleasurable pastimes or hobbies, social withdrawal, loss of appetite, sleep problems, diminished self-worth, increase in the use of alcohol or drugs, and thoughts of suicide. At times older adults can display a variety of symptoms or be hit with several types of illness, which complicates forming a diagnosis and providing remedies for recovery.

Some people I spoke with were able to work out of the situation on their own; others required the help of a spouse, friend, doctor, or counselor; some did not seek or listen to advice.

Although my husband has never really been a happy person, he is now so miserable and I think he made up his mind that he is going to make everyone else miserable. He makes derogatory remarks about some of our neighbors. I think he is angry because he sees that our neighbors are financially well off and can do a lot of things that we can't do. On several occasions he just jumped right down my throat for no reason. For a long time I just took it because I could see he was unhappy. Finally I just screamed back at him and asked him whom he thought he was talking to? I told him he couldn't talk to me that way because I reached the point I couldn't take it. He then was nice for a while. I think that he wishes he could have worked longer so we would be better off now.

Pat E

As a mature adult navigating the emotional problems and roadblocks of retirement, you may have to change from a faster lane into a slower lane when experiencing such illnesses as depression, ongoing anger, grief, and loss. There may be times that you just can't handle these problems on your own. It is then you need to pull off the road and obtain professional assistance before you can continue on your retirement journey. And do you know what? That is okay because slowing down and getting help can lead you to a more satisfying and meaningful life.

None of us is born with emotional intelligence. We learn it as we experience life and mature. The more you practice handling your emotions and impulses, the more skilled you will become. Just as you fine-tune a car, you can give yourself a tune-up by learning and practicing new approaches for dealing with the events and situations that continue to bring change to your life. One such technique is called Rational Emotive Therapy.

Rational Emotive Therapy (RET)

There are a variety of theories on how to manage emotion. Here's one that has helped many through emotional crises. It is a basic, direct self-help approach for dealing with negative self-talk and emotional discord. Rational Emotive Therapy (RET)—developed by Albert Ellis, Ph.D. and Robert A. Harper, Ph.D.—is an approach that helps a person to think and act more rationally in times of emotional stress or upheaval. It transforms thought patterns and helps shift the focus away from difficult emotion to objective fact.

Often referred to as the A, B, C method, Rational Emotive Therapy (RET) begins with (A) an activating event or experience. At point (B), your belief system, you might think that what happened is awful, terrible, and horrible. This leads to (C) an emotional consequence of feeling sad, sorrowful, dejected, and defeated. The resulting consequence derives from your belief system and thinking at point (B). If you tell yourself that what happened is terrible and horrible, you will be powerless to do anything about it. When an event occurs (A), the premise of RET is to change your belief system thinking based on objective facts (point B), to achieve a more positive consequence (C).

Using Gail's shocking experience as an example, let's say that your spouse leaves you for another person and you are facing a life alone after many years of marriage (A). You might feel furious, rejected, despondent, and depressed. You may say to yourself at point (B) that this is a horrible and outrageous thing to have happened to you. How could he or she do this to you? You might even feel guilty and blame yourself for not being able to keep your marriage together. You might mull endlessly about the awfulness of what happened to you and convince yourself that you are too upset to do anything about it. If you continue in this belief pattern, you won't be able to help yourself. It is at point (B) that you need to catch yourself in this irrational thinking and begin to look at the facts of what happened, which will help you think rationally. You begin by acknowledging that what happened as unfortunate, disadvantageous, undesirable, and frustrating. Then, tell yourself that no matter how earthshaking this event appears, you have the capability to cope with it. This can lead to a more positive consequence (C) where you will begin to have some control over your feelings and begin to pull out of this experience.

Like most self-analysis/self-help processes, the RET process requires a subjective personal assessment and motivation. It may not work for everyone. Some of you may wish to look for help and assistance from a professional psychologist, psychotherapist, family counselor or a grief therapy group. If you tend toward negative thinking, professional assistance can be extremely helpful.

EMOTIONAL HEALTH TOOL KIT

Questions:

Take a sheet of paper and answer these questions and give an example for each. Then you can discuss your answers with your spouse or partner.

1. Do you know and understand your own emotions? Can you recognize a feeling as it happens? How do you recognize when you are becoming angry, joyful, bored, or sad?

2. Are you able to manage your emotions so that they are appropriate to the situation? What helps you or hinders you in doing so? When your spouse does something that begins to make you angry, what do you say and when do you say something?

3. What do you do to calm or soothe yourself in order to shake off negative feelings such as anxiety, gloom and irritability? Do you use meditation? Take a hot bath? Walk around the block?

4. Do you think you have a flexible approach to life? Why do you think so?

5. When was the last time you had a good laugh or laughed at yourself?

6. Can you define a specific situation that is challenging you right now, something where you can begin to practice the RET – ABC's in your daily life?

7. In the midst of an emotional situation, what do you do to motivate yourself to collect your emotions and focus on a selected goal?

8. How can you recognize emotions in other people? How do you make yourself aware of what others might need or want?

SPIRITUAL HEALTH

In the United States, we live in a "fast lane" culture. We often have many responsibilities and tasks, and so little time to do them. Even television commercials picture us multi-tasking while driving our cars. During our working years, we don't allow ourselves much time for recreation, let alone solitude, and meditation. So, our spiritual health may not get the attention it needs during these hectic years unless we specifically make time to nurture it.

In retirement, some of you may look forward to obtaining some inner peace and harmony in your lives. You might elect to move to a quieter rural area of the country, the mountains, the beach, or the desert. In retirement you can take time to "smell the roses" by creating some quiet time for spirituality and reflection. The benefit of these practices is two-fold: they provide clarity in your daily practice and they give you something to draw on in a time of difficulty or illness in the future. Attending to your spirit is another way of keeping yourself "tuned-up." When you nurture the spiritual dimension of your life, you have something to draw on in time of need. When I talked with Lois K. Rubin, Ph.D. about spirituality she said:

> *I believe that spirituality can feed us, nurture us, and reduce our anxiety about aging. Spirituality is the universal need that we humans have to reconnect with source, with spirit, with the great Divine, the Divine Essence or whatever you wish to call it—God, Krishna, Buddha, and Jesus. It touches us deeply to have that connection and we need it for our nurturance, sense of life's purpose and for our well-being.*

Spirituality can be summed up as connecting with our higher selves and with God/the Universal Spirit or Divine Essence through meditation, prayer, or experiencing nature. Sometimes when I am walking along the shore of Puget Sound in the fall of the year, I see the sunbeams glistening on the water and I hear the lapping of the waves on the beach. At these times I feel very close to a higher spirit. Have you ever experienced a quiet time in the mountains, by the water, or in the countryside when you took time to listen to nature, listen to the birds' song or a hear a babbling brook? These can be special spiritual moments in your life, moments when you can slow down and connect with the greater forces at play in all our lives, the forces that bind us together with the rest of creation.

> *At times in my life when I experienced a lot of stress or anxiety, I turned to meditation, reflection, and prayer to give me the wisdom and guidance to see me through. I believe*

> *that God helps those who help themselves, so I wasn't look-*
> *ing for a miracle, just some sign that could steer me to what*
> *I could do for myself.*
>
> > Ann B

Depending on your spiritual beliefs, there are a variety of ways available to help you maintain your spiritual nature in good condition. You can pray for help or guidance. You can praise your God or creator and express your gratitude for what has been accomplished in your life. You can attend religious services on a weekly or daily basis. You can go on a weekend retreat and experience quiet reflection or do sitting meditation or walking meditation.

> *I've been meditating for over 30 years and I can't imagine*
> *my life without it. Meditation for me is the daily awak-*
> *ening to all of life's and love's possibilities. Meditation is*
> *about listening. It's about getting quiet and listening for*
> *answers and our answers will come when we are in a quiet*
> *place—when we aren't flitting around and filling our lives*
> *with activity.*
>
> > Lois R

> *I found that doing tai chi and daily meditation helped me to*
> *stay centered during a difficult time in my life. The stress*
> *and tension I was feeling raised my blood pressure. By do-*
> *ing the meditation and tai chi I felt grounded and calm so*
> *I could more easily deal with what was happening in my*
> *life. I was gratified to see that a side affect was lowering*
> *my blood pressure.*
>
> > Barbara B

Some people do tai chi daily and view it as moving meditation. Some people find quiet contemplation and renewal by writing in a journal. You can find methods that work for you, and you don't have to make it a formal thing. As you open to the possibility of meditating, you'll find that the world offers you many opportunities—walking along a beach, a forest, or a field of flowers. My neighbor Dan, who has been through a lot in his life, told me he loves to just walk slowly through the community, listening to the birds, watching the ducks in the pond, and contemplating life. He lets the fast walkers zoom past him and wonders why they are in such a hurry. Each of you has to find your own spiritual path and consciously walk it consistently throughout your life. Here's how some others are developing and maintaining their spiritual health.

> *When I was seriously ill, my whole life was threatened—all my plans and dreams changed. I found that this was not just a physical thing, but I was affected emotionally and spiritually as well. I began to think about the more serious aspects of my life—my family relationships and what is really important and meaningful in my life.*
>
> *Robert D*

> *I love one thing about being Catholic because it is one religion that helps you to take care of things. If you commit a sin, you go to confession and get redemption. If you pray, you get grace. We always have a way of resolving things. So whenever I have a problem or issue, I pray about it and then I resolve it. I don't look elsewhere for a resolution; I find it in myself through prayer and reflection.*
>
> *Marge B*

Spirituality doesn't necessarily mean religiosity, but religion can be a means you use to access your spirituality. Many people derive a special connection with their creator when praying in a church, synagogue, or mosque. Others find guidance and inspiration by reading the scriptures in the bible.

> *We have scripture verses that we base our life on. That doesn't mean that we are without conflict or problems. When problems do arise we have a source to go to, which gives us a clarity of thought, give us wisdom, give us direction, and helps us determine what way to go. I believe that spirit is part of every single person.*
>
> *Bob D*

> *When you are talking about spirit, that spirit has to connect to God personally. You don't just go to church and come out of church like you go into the grocery store and come out of it. You need to be transformed and love God body, soul, mind, and spirit.*
>
> *Lynne D*

Dr. Rubin suggests that retirement is a wonderful time to really get to know who we really are inside and to nurture that part of ourselves that we may have "glossed over" earlier in our lives. By paying attention to our inner self we each discover who we really are, what are our unique gifts and purpose on this earth.

Making time in your life for spiritual reflection doesn't have to be a big deal. You can take time when you get up in the morning or before you go to bed at night. Taking ten to fifteen minutes to meditate at night can help you to relax and possibly sleep better because you are able to release the tensions of the day and focus on your spiritual self.

Here is a way to begin preliminary meditation practice focusing on the breath.

* * *

MEDITATION EXERCISE

To practice a breathing meditation, choose a quiet place to meditate and sit in a comfortable position—on a chair, a mat, or a meditation pillow. You can sit in the traditional cross-legged posture or any other way that is comfortable for you. Try to keep your back straight to prevent your mind from getting sleepy or sluggish. Some people sit on a mat or pillow against a wall so that they have support to their back. If you elect to sit in a chair try to keep your feet on the floor rather than crossing them.

Your hands can be lying quietly in your lap, or you can have the right hand under the left with your thumbs meeting in the middle. Another way is to hold your hands open resting on your thighs and putting the thumbs and forefingers together to form a circuit of energy.

1. The first stage of meditation is to eliminate distractions and clear your mind of fleeting thoughts. You accomplish this by practicing a simple breathing meditation.

2. You sit with your eyes partially closed and focus your attention on your breathing. Allow yourself to breathe naturally, through your nostrils, but don't try to control your

breathing. Become aware of the sensation of your breath as it enters and leaves your nostrils. Concentrate on the sensation of your breath going in and going out to the exclusion of everything else.

3. As you sit quietly, you may find your mind getting very busy with thoughts and you will be tempted to follow these thoughts as they arise. Let the thoughts pass and continue to focus on the sensation of the breath. If your mind does wander, return your thoughts to the breath. Getting caught up in your thoughts is not a failure. Every time you notice that your attention has wandered from your breath, you have an opportunity to practice kindness toward yourself by gently returning attention to your breath. These moments are the heart of the practice. Refocus on the breath as many times as necessary until your mind stays with the breath.

4. If you are able to practice these steps, your distracting thoughts will gradually subside and you will be able to meditate and achieve a sense of inner peace, calm, and relaxation.

Note: You can look for meditation classes and trainings within your own community, on the Internet or in books on meditation.

SPIRITUAL HEALTH TOOL KIT

Questions:

Answer these questions for yourself on a sheet of paper and then discuss with your spouse or partner.

1. What do you do now to develop your own spirituality? How often?

2. Are you interested in practicing meditation? If not, why? If so, in what part of your day might you be able to set aside ten to fifteen minutes a day to practice breathing meditation?

3. What are some other ways that you can develop your spirituality? How can you develop spirituality as a couple?

4. How do you see spirituality assisting you in a time of illness, loss or care giving?

5. Do you ever discuss your spirituality with your spouse or partner? Why or why not? What do you know about his or her spiritual beliefs?

CHAPTER SUMMARY

Our physical health, intellectual mental health, emotional health and spiritual health are like the four tires of a car. When all four tires are inflated and in good condition, you can drive anywhere and do anything. They support and balance one another; when one tire begins to go flat, the other three tires may help to bring you to a safe stop. And, you still need a spare tire in reserve to move on again. Attaining an ideal balance of health may be a matter of developing and maintaining a critical reserve in the four areas of health so you have a spare tire to turn to when you need assistance and support in time of illness or an accident. The more you can maintain yourself in these areas, the better you can fulfill your dreams and plans for an active and productive retirement.

CHAPTER 5 –
BUMPS IN THE ROAD
Illness and Giving Care

We never planned on our health not being good. We had always enjoyed good health and thought that we would never have many problems.

—*Liela S*

CHALLENGE:

How to effectively deal with health changes when they occur, in order to have meaningful and rewarding retirement years.

ILLNESS

Generally today, most of us can anticipate greater longevity than our parents. While long life has many blessings, it also comes with great challenges: we now have to contend with a greater number of various physical and/or mental illnesses as we age. Such illnesses can be sporadic, chronic, or life threatening. The stories I collected about this aspect of retirement are informative, moving, and inspiring. Many of the people I talked with were surprised to experience their illness much earlier in retirement than they anticipated. Gail is in her late 50s, has only been retired for four years, and has been blindsided by fibromyalgia.

> *My friends and I were surprised at how much time it requires to take care of your body and the preponderance of medical problems we are experiencing. What surprised us is that we didn't expect it at our early age. We thought it would be when we were older.*
>
> Gail K

Men and women will experience illness sooner or later in their retirement years. It can be a short duration problem such as the seasonal flu, allergies, or cataracts. It also can be more serious and traumatic, such as a heart attack, cancer or stroke. As you drive the highway of retirement life, you will encounter some of these illnesses. When we're young, we tend to think we're invincible. Later in life, we discover we're actually quite vulnerable.

How you face illnesses that come during your later years will make a difference in your recovery and resumption of a positive retirement. If you see illness as a mere bump in the road or temporary setback from which you can recover, you'll likely accommodate the experience with relative ease. If you see the illness as driving on a very rough, bumpy road, while desperately hanging onto the wheel, you may feel like a helpless victim. In the victim mentality you are powerless and unable to make a change.

> *We designed our retirement so that we would be in an active community to enjoy ourselves and participate in activities.*

Then the illnesses started to hit. I found that I couldn't do a lot of things I had planned. Instead of enjoying my life I feel like I'm between a rock and hard place. All my dreams have gone by the wayside.

Jim B

There are times that our situation may appear impossible and we may feel powerless. However, it's up to each of us to make the decision to either take some control or be powerless. You might wonder, "How can I prepare for illness?" You can begin by reading about others' experiences and widen your perception by what they have done when faced with serious illness. You can apprise yourself of what resources are available to you. In other words you can drive defensively. Not long ago I was driving on a multilane highway. While preparing to pass a large truck, I checked the lane on my left to make sure it was empty. Having looked around, I was able to change lanes quickly and avoid an accident when the truck driver pulled out to pass another truck. Thinking about your options when life is smooth and relatively calm can provide you a modicum of control to make good decisions, if illness does strike.

Illness is never planned and serious illnesses are often a surprise. No one expects their body to betray them, which is part of why sudden illness can be so shocking. You may know that Grandpa Gus had a stroke, or Aunt Helen died from a heart attack. But until we've faced serious illness more directly, we're able to maintain an illusion of invulnerability. We comfort ourselves with the idea that our good habits will keep us safe no matter how many friends or relatives get ill or die. Our good health allows us to shield our eyes from the inevitable. But averting our eyes keeps us from learning that we actually may have more internal resources to face these challenges than we might have known. Some of the following stories illustrate how a positive attitude helped minimize the emotional impact of an unexpected illness.

Bumps in the Road

Some people who have a positive view of life compare their illness experience to a sudden jolt or bump in the road. You experience illness and then go on with your life. Depending upon your view of change, bumps can be anything from serious illness to a generally mild disorder.

> *One morning I was home eating breakfast with what I thought was the flu. I passed out and my wife called the paramedics and they found out I had an irregular heart-beat—an arterial flutter. I spent the night in the hospital and it apparently cured itself. I am now religiously taking a specific medication and the cardiologist says I will live to be one hundred.*
>
> *Patrick S*

> *Because my wife is a good deal younger than I am, I thought she would be taking care of me, as we got older. However, two years ago she went in for a routine test and they found a tumor on one of her kidneys. She went through the operation, the tumor was encapsulated and they got it out. She is now left with one kidney, but she's doing well and doesn't see it as a problem.*
>
> *Richard H*

I had a heart bypass twelve years ago and have recovered to full-speed activities. Last year I had a small stroke and was sure glad my wife knew the three symptoms to look for in someone having a stroke. I could raise my hands over my head. I was able to repeat a sentence back to her, but when she asked me to smile, I couldn't do it. She immediately called 911.

John L

The doctors determined that John had a light stroke and changed his medications. Stroke symptoms are sometimes difficult to identify and the stroke victim may suffer severe brain damage if he or she doesn't receive help within three hours of the attack. The three steps to recognize if someone is having a stroke are: ask the person to **Smile**; ask them to **Talk or Speak a Simple Sentence**, and ask him or her to **Raise Both Arms** above their head. If they can't do all three, call 911 immediately and describe the symptoms to the dispatcher. The couples, who shared their stories hit a bump in the road and were able to continue on with their lives. They don't know what lies ahead, but realize that more serious illness is possible and are mentally attempting to prepare for it.

Speed Limit

Aging is often synonymous with slowing down. After years of pushing the edge of the posted speed limits, we're accustomed to driving at the maximum speed the law allows. But as we age, we sometimes experience a disconnect between what we think we should be able to accomplish and what we can actually accomplish. Over the years, you gradually lose some energy, slow down and you may not even notice it, because fatigue sneaks up on you.

> *Some days I get up and I have tons of things I need to get done that day. I may only complete a third of what I hoped to do. I now have a lot of osteoarthritis and that slows me down. It's frustrating but it's nothing I can't live with. I just take one day at a time and do what I can.*
>
> *June L*

> *There is no getting away from it, as you age your energy does decrease. When I was 30 I could climb the moon. When I was 40, I still could climb the moon, but a little slower. When I got to 50, I looked at the moon and said things are changing here. When I hit 60, I said well, they are really changing. We used to go on month long vacation trips, and now we plan our trips carefully to compensate for the lifestyle changes we are experiencing.*
>
> *John A*

> *In my younger life I was a middle distance runner. I knew what kind of condition I was in because I measured it by a stopwatch. The last few years I am running slower than I did five years ago. Although I don't feel different, I see a fatigue problem creeping in. I plan on continuing to run, but will run in older groups as I age.*
>
> *Patrick S*

When you realize you tire more quickly, you gradually adjust or limit some of what you've been doing in order to protect your self. However, even if you do have to slow down, you can find ways of compensating for the limits you encounter.

Accident

When you drive safely and stay within the legal speed limits, you certainly don't foresee having an accident. It's the same thing in life; you might think if you do all the right things and eat all the right things, you can retain your health and mobility. But you can't keep changes from happening. What you can do is react proactively and do what you can to compensate for the loss.

> When I retired, I joined the bowling league in my retirement community and was still bowling fairly well until my knee went. After my knee replacement, I went back to try bowling several times. The first time I couldn't get down to the floor with my left knee, as I am a right-handed bowler. I then tried bowling again, this time standing up, but I ended up at the chiropractor because I was pulling my back out. So I had to give up bowling and turn to other more appropriate sports, which was hard to do.
>
> *Ralph S*

> When I retired, I was able to play tennis three times a week and loved it. Two years ago my shoe caught on the court and I took a bad fall backwards, but I still got the shot back! It turned out that I injured my left hip. After consultations with two sports clinic doctors and doing physical therapy exercises daily, I have gained some flexibility of movement. I have taken a detour from playing tennis and have turned to yoga, aerobics, tai chi, walking and golf. There is life after tennis!
>
> *Bev A*

Detour

Detours require us to deviate from our course or usual routine. As with road detours, illness in retirement may require you to go in a different direction for an undefined distance, but often you're able to recover and pick up your life again.

> *I was 55 when we moved here. I jumped right in and got involved in all kinds of activities. About 18 months into retirement I found out that I had thyroid cancer. Between the surgery and radiation therapy, I lost nine months out of my life. I had the added side effect of voice loss for three months from the surgery and radiation therapy. Although I lost a chunk of that year, I saw it through and am as involved as ever.*
>
> *April P*

> *One month after I started a part-time retirement position, I was working on the computer and noticed I was having vision problems. I thought it might be eyestrain, as I had not been working on a computer for several years. After a lunchtime doctor's appointment, I found out it was a spontaneous retinal detachment and I had to have it operated on immediately. So I never returned from lunch and I had to quit my new position. After the operation, I was not allowed to work for over a year. I was surprised that when I informed the organization I was well again, they wanted me to return to work.*
>
> *Lorraine M*

Both April and Lorraine experienced reasonably serious illness, were sidelined from various activities for a period of their life, but were able to recover and resume a positive retirement life.

Closed Road

When driving, you may come to a barricade blocking your route, a closed road. You may not just be detoured from your route; you may have to find a new way to go on in your life. Searching out another way to deal with serious health issues that blocked their road is one way people have dealt with the changes in their health.

> *My hobbies were racecar driving and photography. I am now blind in one eye and this is hard for me, as my wife now has to do most of the driving. It's also difficult when shooting pictures. Although I can't do some sports, I can fence because you turn your head when you are fencing and I can have a good panorama. You learn to compensate for a disability. You might have been able to jump over mountains, now you can jump over hills. So what? You are still happy—you have food and friends. You still have a modicum of health. That is all that is important.*
>
> *John A*

> *Shortly before retirement, I went into surgery to correct a collapse of vertebrae. The operation was successful, but after the operation I fell in the hospital and broke my tailbone. After a month in the hospital I was transferred to rehab, where I got E. coli in my back. I had to have four more operations and spend three months flat on my back in the hospital. I asked myself, "Why is this happening to me?" I told myself that I would come out of this a whole lot stronger and happier. During this long, arduous ordeal in the hospital, the thing that saved me was music. Listening to spiritual tapes and my husband's support buoyed me up. A volunteer*

> *harpist taught me to play a small harp suspended above my
> bed because I was flat on my back. Today I can walk, but
> I can't bend over and I have had to learn to use special tong
> utensils to help me dress and do things in the home.*
>
> Betty D

Betty never planned on beginning her retirement in this way. At one point, she thought she might never walk again and feels she is fortunate to have recovered to enjoy her retirement years with her husband, even with her limitations.

Rough Roads

The stories up to this point have been about situations that allowed people to pick up their lives again. But people whose lives take them on rough roads may not necessarily pick up their lives in quite the same way, even when the road smoothes out again. It is difficult to drive over rough roads. You get jerked from side to side and don't know where it's going to end. The following stories show how strong and resilient men and women can be when faced with life-threatening illnesses.

> *I was 53 when we first moved to this retirement com-
> munity. I helped to initiate the "baby boomer" club and
> was the first president. The Monday after our first boomer
> dance, I was told by my doctor that I had stage two cancer.
> When I heard the diagnosis, all I could think was, "I don't
> want to die!" Apparently, spots had been noted for a num-
> ber of years and my previous doctor was never informed.
> This made me really angry. After surgery, I ended up on
> chemotherapy and because my immune system was so low,
> I couldn't go anywhere for months. I was getting stir crazy*

in the house. I've discovered that your attitude is important in getting well. You have to fight and say, "I'm going to get through this."

Diane D

After being very ill, it took Diane two years to build up her stamina. Although friends have told her she is a role model, she thinks that anyone would fight the same fight if they were in her position. She said, "Why wouldn't anyone want to live?"

Both my heart and back illnesses were unexpected and have impacted my life. I now have six stents in my coronaries and a pacemaker. My heart actually stopped during one operation. When this happens your planning horizon shifts from years to months, to days, and then to minutes. As time went on I could be pretty sure that I could last another day. I began to plan two to three weeks out and then found it reasonable to plan six months out. My view of my future is vastly different than it was before I experienced these physical challenges.

Rick S

Rick is in his early 60s and feels his body has betrayed his hopes for having a healthy life where he can ride on his motorcycle with his wife, travel, and enjoy the things that he always wanted to do.

Before the cancer, my life was moving along a superhighway like the Autobahn. When I was unexpectedly hospitalized with an allergic reaction to the chemo drugs I was taking, I felt like all of a sudden I had dropped down through a manhole. I was bumping along a dirt road full of rocks and holes.

Heidi S

Life-threatening illness can often come unexpectedly and really cause people to stop cold in their tracks. When such serious illnesses occur, people have had to go within themselves and draw on what courage, stamina, and energy they have to survive and live life the best they can.

> *I think there is something inside each of us that makes this little protective thing that keeps us going. I don't know what it is but I believe we all have it.*
>
> Marilyn T

When I asked people just what that special essence was that kept them going, they found it hard to put into words. It appears to me to be a long-standing positive attitude nurtured during a lifetime. That does not mean that the people I talked with did not have dark days; but they were able to get past them to survive and even thrive.

> *I had a strange reaction when I first found out that I had cancer. It was almost as if I was up above looking down on this person who suddenly had cancer. It wasn't me. Breast cancer doesn't run in my family. I had breast tissue removal and implants put in years ago, so I figured that I wasn't a candidate for breast cancer. It took me three days to really take it in. Waiting for the results of the biopsy was an anxious time. After we had the results, I was able to accept what I've got and go on from there.*
>
> Shirley L

Shirley had radiation treatments and remained in remission for a year, at which time she had reconstructive surgery and is happily recuperating.

In the last five years I've had a heart attack, rectal cancer and a stroke. I was first diagnosed with cancer and it was quite a shock. Someone asked me how I coped with that news and was I afraid. I said no. I look at it like a Marine, you put your pack on, sling a rifle over your shoulder and start through the rain and snow and you keep going until you get to the other side. It's the same way in life; you just start going and keep moving. I've had a wonderful life. I've got great kids and lots of great experiences. If I have to go tomorrow, I'll go.

John A

John has been a real trooper as he fought off his series of illnesses. Having successfully battled them, he deserves the Health Medal of Honor for valor and heroism.

Caution Curve Ahead

While driving, we've seen those signs warning us that there is a curve ahead. Perhaps in life a warning sign can help us to deflect future possible illnesses. Often it is only later in life that you become interested in the illnesses that run in your families. Among the people I interviewed, illness was not something that just affected a person late in life. People in their 50s and early 60s contracted cancer and experienced heart problems. You and your spouse need to be aware of what signs to watch for and try to protect yourselves from the disease, if possible. You may want to know more about family illnesses and get tested for a specific gene. You could then be proactive by talking to a doctor and putting together a healthy management plan. Others may not want to know about your genetic future and just want to live your lives the best you can while you can. This is a very personal decision and each person's situation is unique. However, developing an awareness about your own heredity and the illnesses you might be predisposed to gives you the benefit of being able to make appropriate decisions about treatment if and when you are affected.

> *People with cancer tell me that they are overwhelmed with the choices they are expected to make. Even Sandra Day O'Connor, when she had breast cancer, said that she was given a myriad of choices and was asked what she wanted to do. Physicians tend to leave it up to you to decide from various treatments.*
>
> *April P*

I've learned through my research and interviews for this book that no matter how hard you try, you can't totally control what happens to you. But you do have some control over how you respond to challenges or threats to your health. And how you respond to physical challenges will have significant impact on the quality of the rest of your life.

When illness affects the quality of one spouse's life, it also affects the quality of a couple's life. My husband and I, like many people in the boomer generation, felt that if we exercised and ate healthy, we wouldn't experience a serious illness until we were well into our 70s or 80s. We were both surprised to find out that he had a heart problem in his mid-60s and I had to become a caregiver earlier than I ever expected to.

ILLNESS TOOL KIT

Questions:

Answer the questions and discuss them with your partner. These questions may lead to more personal questions that you both want to talk about with each other.

1. What genetic illnesses run in your family?

2. Is it important to you to keep up with the progress of research in this area? Are you aware of available medications or testing?

3. Can you do anything now that can help you stay healthy and delay the illness?

4. Have you considered donating to medical research for illness that runs in your family? (This can be a concrete way of giving your self a sense of control and positive impact.)

5. Do you know the signs of a heart attack, stroke, and cerebral hemorrhage?

6. Do you have sufficient medical insurance coverage to cover catastrophic illness?

7. Do you have an Advance Directive that states your wishes in case of serious illness?

8. What do you think you can do to help your spouse or partner in time of illness? What help might you expect from your spouse if you become seriously ill?

GIVING CARE

A caregiver is simply someone who provides support to a person who needs help. Giving care could be one of the most important things that you do in your retirement life. Caregiver may not be a role that you willingly choose. It may be thrust upon you because of your love and devotion to the person needing care.

Care giving takes different forms, depending on the skills of the giver and the needs of the receiver. It can be giving a few hours a week to help him or her by doing such things as: buying groceries, driving them to the doctor's office, checking on them, or maintaining their house or yard. It can also require a greater investment of time and energy when you provide hands-on care, help make medical decisions and handle their personal business, such as bill paying, filling out medical forms, etc.

For six years I was the sole caregiver for my stepfather, who had emphysema. I bought his groceries, organized his pills and medications, and took him to and from doctors, hospital or nursing home. I arranged for Meals on Wheels, Medic Alert, and a 24-hour per day oxygen supply, but as time went on he gradually became worse. At one point he was in intensive care and I consented to putting him on a ventilator over his objections, because it was supposed to be a temporary treatment. It was a round robin of hospital, nursing home, his condo, and back again—requiring a great deal of time as my husband and I were still working. My stepdad and I investigated assisted living residences, but before he could move in he had another attack. I adhered to his wishes and did not allow extensive life support systems. He passed away within a day. That spring, we were selling a business, selling our home, building a retirement home, and dealing with my dad's illness, death, and sale of his property. When it was all over I felt like a huge boulder had been lifted off of me. If I had taken a stress test, I most likely would have been off the chart.

Although we try to plan, and perhaps stretch out changes in our lives, we can't control them to come in nice, easy segments. My husband and I were put under a lot of stress given all the changes that piled up at one time in our lives. In retirement, you may have to care for parents, as well as your spouse, and perhaps even have to provide care to children or grandchildren as well. Illness is not exclusively the domain of the elderly. You may find that you will have to provide care much sooner than you expected. The following sections look at various care giving experiences in the retirement journey.

TAKING THE WHEEL – CARING FOR YOUR PARTNER

In retirement, the person closest to you, your spouse or partner, may likely be the one needing your help in time of illness. If you're both healthy and active now, this may be hard to imagine, but there may come a time when one or the other of you may need to become a caregiver.

When my wife became ill, they diagnosed the disease and said she would have about ten years to live. She had a lot of ancillary problems associated with the cancer. I felt like the little Dutch boy with the finger in the dike. You plug up one hole and another would spring open. You name it and she had it. She was just breaking down. Her positive attitude toward life helped me get through it all. I had to think and project that everything was going to be okay. That helped me to put one foot in front of the other and just keep going. A few months after my wife died, I was giving a friend a ride to the airport and unintentionally ended in the hospital parking lot. I was so used to driving to the hospital, the car just went there by itself. This brought tears to my eyes.

Dan M

Sometimes when we're under extreme stress due to illness, all we may be able to think about is "putting one foot in front of the other" in order to go on.

I lost six months of my life. I was still working when my retired husband had a heart blockage problem. At first they knew that he had one blockage but couldn't deal with it until they got to the bottom of his kidney problem. The longer it went on it felt like a time bomb waiting to go off. Waiting for tests and referrals, my husband's blood pressure was going out of sight, partly because of the stress of having to wait. Twice the hospital could not take the kidney biopsy because his blood pressure was too high. It was a six-month nightmare before they dealt with the blockages. I was over the top with worry.

Sharon S

It was a difficult time for Sharon as she was trying to find a way to support her husband. Often you may not only need to be the caregiver, but also the steady, strong support for your life partner at a time when you too are stressed and worried.

> *Two years ago, on our first trip to Europe, my husband suffered a stroke on our return trip home. He has lost a quarter of his vision and can't drive. He will drive locally around town, but he stays in one lane because he can't see well to the left. So I have learned to do things that I never had to do before. I do all of the driving. I used to be the passenger and the navigator and now do both. I have had to learn to be more independent, even learning to do things around the house.*
>
> *Judith A*

If you and your spouse have traveled by car, taking on the role of driver and alternate driver/navigator will be familiar ones. You may have "taken the wheel" when the driver gets tired or wants a break. This analogy extends to an illness and caregiver situation. There are times when the alternate driver has to take charge in an emergency or serious illness of the driver. You may then become the caregiver who has to make all the decisions and choices with regard to your loved one. We may not have even thought of being in such a situation and we most likely are not prepared for handling it. As you think about it now, does it make sense that you should know something about the other person's wishes and choices? You need to prepare yourself for the eventuality of taking the lead, rather than waiting and being thrown into an emergency situation. In an emergency, you'll most likely be anxious and under pressure to make appropriate decisions and perhaps racked with self-doubt about your capability to make the right decision. Care giving may require swift action and quick decisions.

> *Although my husband sailed through his heart bypass operation, he had several problems afterward. One morning after he was home, as soon as I woke up, he told me that he had a sharp pain on his left side. What to do? Call 911? I immediately called the doctor. I breathed a sigh of relief when the doctor called back a short while later to discuss the situation with us. Based on the symptoms, he said that my husband was experiencing a fluid build up in his lungs from the operation and it was nothing to worry about. He would have to go into the hospital the next day to get it drained off. We were both relieved that the situation wasn't serious, but that didn't erase the anxious moments I had just experienced.*
>
> *Babs B*

With this experience Babs has realized that she might be put into a similar situation in the future and may again need to make the right life-saving decision for her husband.

Do you know when to call 911? Not wanting to consider these frightening situations can mean that we don't know when we need to make that call. Sharon in our next story wasn't adequately prepared, in part because medical authorities failed to give her important information about her husband's situation.

> *Two days after beginning to take morphine tablets for back problems, my husband woke up during the night and was breathing heavily and couldn't get his breath. After staggering to the bathroom, he flopped back down on the bed. I lay*

there wide awake until he slept again. The next morning I got up, had my coffee and got dressed. I woke him around nine o'clock and had to pull him to a sitting position. I gave him coffee to counteract the drugs he had taken, but the coffee just ran outside of his mouth. He appeared dazed and I kept screaming at him to breathe. He began to turn gray and I tried CPR on him, but I couldn't get any air into him. I called 911. Later they told me that as he slept on his back, his lungs had filled up with fluid and he had drowned in his own fluid. His brain had been deprived of oxygen during the night and that was why he was dazed. It all had to do with the drugs my husband was taking. If I had been warned by the pain clinic that there was a possibility of this with morphine, I would have called sooner and he would have known not to sleep in his back.

Sharon J

After Sharon's husband died, a specialist told her that it was a huge tragedy, like a perfect storm of several issues coming together. Whatever the level of caregiver role you take on, you probably haven't been trained for it. Instead you learn "on the job" as you face new responsibilities and unfamiliar tasks. Still, you can educate yourself about the things you need to do and the questions you need to ask, as well as the resources that are available to you. Check the Tool Kit at the end of this chapter for ideas and information on when to call 911.

Not only is the caregiver changed by this relationship. The care recipient is cast into a new and unfamiliar role too. If a spouse is independent and likes to be in control of what he or she does, it can be difficult on his or her partner when he or she is incapacitated in some way. The vulnerability that comes from compromised health and being suddenly dependent can be very uncomfortable. Couples may find that this new relationship requires them to communicate about how it is for both of them to navigate this new territory. Although they are going through the new territory together, they each have a very different orientation and perspective.

> *My husband had a heart bypass operation and was in the hospital for a week. When he came home, we had an experience that was quite different in our marriage. He needed help and had to be waited on more than he ever had before. He was used to fending for himself and became short-tempered with me because of his situation.*
>
> *Ann B*

After many years of marriage, both Ann and her husband had to search out a way through this experience in order to find the right balance of care giving, reliance and independence.

> *At one time I said to my wife, "Cancer is the loneliest trip I have ever taken." She looked at me and was insulted. She said, "I've been here every inch of the way with you." She just didn't understand. I told her, cancer is a lonely trip because even though she was at my bedside, was worried and wanted to make things comfortable for me, it still is a lonely trip because I am the one in the hospital with a gown on backwards so my body is hanging out. I'm the one lying on the operating table going under. The next day I wake up with tubes hanging out of me. I'm being stuck with needles, given radiation and chemo. I walk around with a little tree with my tubes, IV's, and what not.*
>
> *John A*

John believed that although his wife tried to support him and was with him in spirit, he had to face his illness alone. He felt that he had to forge ahead on what he perceived was a lonely trip, because, as John said, if he didn't he wouldn't be on the "right side of the grass."

Proactive Care Giving

Sometimes a caregiver has to act in a proactive way to find medical assistance and resources for the person being cared for. It is important to talk with people who have had a similar disease or circumstance in order to locate doctors or facilities that can help. Go online and do research about the illness or disease and try to locate resources and information. You may be surprised at what you'll find.

My husband's cancer situation took a year to resolve. Everything in our life stopped for the six weeks of radiation and chemo. I changed from working part time and traveling to being at home. We changed all of our dietary habits and went totally organic. After one surgery my husband was scheduled for a permanent colostomy. After some research, we found an oncologist who shrunk his tumor. When looking for a surgeon who could reconnect his colon, I obtained the name of one from a friend. I read the doctor's bio and I said this is the right guy. I called and he just happened to have an opening. All the stepping-stones led to that one person we needed. So my husband was reconnected and went through a second round of chemo.

Judith A

Judith and her husband used all their contacts and resources to find an approach to his health problem that would be successful. In this day and age, the caregiver and the patient, when possible, need to explore all medical possibilities and appropriate medical personnel. A friend of ours recently found out that she has pancreatic cancer and is presently going through chemotherapy. She has a specific complication, which required her to find a specialist who's an expert in dealing with this particular type of situation.

Generational Care Giving

If you are nearing retirement or are in the early years of retirement, you may have parents who experience serious illness and need care. You may be caught in the "sandwich generation" having to provide support to not only parents, but children or grandchildren as well. This can be a challenging time in your life. It will take a lot of energy and the ability to research your options, alternatives, and resources to deal with it. Perhaps you can learn from some of these stories.

> *My husband's mother is 92 and is living in a nursing home on the east coast. Her insurance ran out a long time ago. I think you need to plan, not only to take care of yourself, but your parents as well. If you end up not needing the money, that will be an unplanned bonus. Not only should you plan to care for parents, but also you'd better plan on some funding for your children in case they may need your help. We have seven kids between us, and one or more are bound to need some help at some time.*
>
> *Jo S*

A friend of ours lost his first wife to cancer. He married a long time friend and widow from the same couples' social group some years later. They enjoyed their life together and traveled to various parts of the world. However, recently his second wife has become seriously ill and needed round-the-clock care. Because he is a take-charge type of person, he proceeded to make the healthcare arrangements for his second wife. Then, her children from her first marriage stepped in and wanted a say in how their mother was cared for.

Ann B

Differing ideas about care giving can be a real life problem in today's modern world of second marriages. The husband and her children will have to negotiate an agreement about the best decision for her care. If both sides are adamant and unmovable, this can prove to be a very difficult and dangerous situation at a crucial and anxious time for the family.

You may expect to have to take care of parents, but you may not expect to be taking care of children or grandchildren in your retirement years. But this can also happen.

I have three daughters who have Myotonic Dystrophy. I lost my wife about fifteen years ago. I have been the sole caregiver for my daughters since that time. They are now in their late 40s and early 50s and live with my second wife and I in our retirement home. In the last eight years my daughters' health has regressed to the point that I can no longer care for them in our home. My doctor says that my nervous system is just ruined from my previous stressful job and years of responsibility. So, we have been searching for about a year for affordable care facilities for my daughters. It will take all I have, but the girls will be in a three-room suite in a nice assisted living facility. This was a hard decision for me but I think it will work out for all of us.

Jack H

A decision to place a loved one in a care facility can be a traumatic experience. In Jack's case, he did all he could do before resorting to placement. Nine years ago he re-met and married a high school classmate and they have "been there" for the daughters. Now the couple will finally have the opportunity to have more time to be "there" for each other.

Long-Distance Care Giving

Being a long-distance caregiver can be difficult. With today's mobile society, parents, children, and grandchildren live around the country and around the world. Distance makes it more challenging, but not impossible, to care for a family member. If you live at a distance from a loved one who needs care, research what resources are available in the ill person's vicinity. Caring for someone at a distance will likely require you to stay at his or her location for some period of time, depending upon the person's illness. Providing this care may very well interfere with your retirement life as it did for Margaret and her husband.

I was the caregiver for an aunt who had no children or family. She lived in Oregon and contracted colon cancer. I went up to try to help her and asked if she would like to come down to California and live with us. She agreed. Once established at our house, we had hospice come to assist her. My aunt got upset because she felt she wasn't ready for hospice. We tried to care for her here and found it difficult as we always had to have someone with her. She didn't want to stay and said she wanted to go back home. We drove her back to her own home in Oregon and arranged for a lady to come in to care for her. I visited her at Christmas and arranged for hospice service. She passed away in January.

Margaret C

My mother, who had Alzheimer's disease, lived with us for six months. Because we were still working, we had to place her in a home so she would have appropriate full-time care. She had a number of strokes and then passed away. Now my wife's mother is having health issues. Because we are now retired and live so far away, this presents a problem. I think that is going to be a stressful scenario and we don't know how it's going to play out. Her mother is now in a nursing home and may not be able to go back home. There isn't really anybody we are able to call to help. We just have to have some plan on how to maintain contact with her and see that she is all right and cared for.

Larry M

Distance can really cause a dilemma for children. When you can't be there in person, you need to rely on immediate or extended family to help. Often the care and support falls to the family member or members (such as siblings) who live closest to the parent and the question of fairness comes into play. The person or persons who carry the brunt of the care may feel taken advantage of by those family members who live a distance away.

> *My mother is living on the east coast, as are my brothers and sisters. My husband and I live in a retirement community in California. It's been difficult lately because my mother is ill and I live so far away, I can't really help. The burden tends to fall on my brothers and sisters. When I flew back recently, I was left to rent a car and do what I could for my mom. I think my brothers and sisters may feel a little resentful that I can't do my part to help Mom on an ongoing basis*
>
> *Michelle P*

> *When my mother became seriously ill, I had to fly to Chicago and handle all the aspects of care giving. Because I lived so far away and had responsibilities at home, I set up all the arrangements for my mom to be taken care of. I was lucky in that I was working part-time for hospice, and knew what to do to help her and make her comfortable. After she passed away, we made all the funeral arrangements and my daughter and I took care of all her possessions and sold her house.*
>
> *Lorraine W*

Because parents are living longer, many retirees find that they have a greater responsibility in providing care and support. Distance inhibits giving hands-on care, so children have to resort to researching and finding ways to care for their parent. There are a number of options you may consider. Might you move your parent closer to where you live? Or travel to where your parent lives so you can do "hands on" research and establish support systems? This can require relying on family to assist in his or her care. Or is the best option a professional assisted living facility?

Professional Care Giving

Over the last 20 years or so, more and more people have been turning to assisted living facilities and nursing homes for help. These facilities provide a way for today's families to care for an ill relative while limiting their own stress. However, the costs of these facilities are increasing as more and more people continue to need this service. Getting into a highly rated facility, where your loved one will get excellent care, is becoming more difficult and more expensive.

> *My mother, now 93, lives in an assisted care facility in Toronto, Canada, while we live in Southern California. She likes where she lives and has her own bedroom and bath and goes down to the dining room for three meals a day, plus she gets help with her medications. I'm lucky to have cousins who live in the area and can visit her. One cousin has her power of attorney. The assisted care facility costs $2,500 a month. She has a monthly pension of $2,000 so she only has to take $500 out of her savings. With the medical plan in Canada, when Mom has to go to the next level of care where she is bedridden, it will cost $1,300 for care and she will receive government assistance. My Mom would never be able to afford the health care here in the states. It is really a sad situation to have her so far away.*
>
> *Maggie C*

Maggie and her husband would really like to have her mother closer to them, but can't afford it. In addition, they feel they may need their savings for their own care as they age.

> *My husband, who is sixteen years older than me, retired early and we had a wonderful life. I can now look back*

and really feel good about all those memories. Now he has Alzheimer's disease. I've learned what Alzheimer's is all about and I can now trace it back to when he was around 65. We were on vacation at a Club Med, he was getting the award for the most active person there and he acted somewhat strangely. That's when I said, "Oh God, something is wrong here," but I didn't know what. Over time I ended up having to do everything for him—shower him, brush his teeth, change diapers, change clothes, change bedding three times a day. It got so that I couldn't take my eyes off of him for a minute. One time I glanced away and he was beginning to comb his hair with a razor. My Alzheimer's support group told me I would not be able to continue to care for him, but I just couldn't put him in a home. Finally, I found I could no longer physically care for him because I contracted blood poisoning from changing the diapers and sheets. I found a care facility where I was able to place him. They've taken marvelous care of him for six years.

Marilyn F

After much searching, Marilyn found a cottage setting where she placed her husband. She visits him there and feels confident in the care he's receiving. When placing a loved one, it's important to find a facility that you will be able to visit, relax, and make the best of a difficult situation. Depending upon the illness, some care recipients may do better with professional care. Much depends upon the ability of the family to care for the person, the kind of illness involved, and financial ability to pay for a facility. If you do need to use an assisted living facility or nursing home, be sure to check it out thoroughly. Research and find out the facility's rating. Ask to talk with other families who have relatives living there. Ask about activities available for residents and try to view them if possible. Drop in unannounced and visit often to be sure your loved one is getting the proper care.

In order to limit expensive professional care and to provide a more personal family caring environment, some families opt to take care of family at home. If you're considering, this option, be aware of the personal sacrifice necessary to provide personal, hands-on care to someone who is ill and try to get the professional support needed to make the job easier. Care giving doesn't necessarily have to be for long extended periods of time. There may be times that you may have the responsibility to provide short-term care giving. That's why it is so important that you at least begin to prepare yourself for this role.

> *When I found out that my mother needed heart surgery, I researched the best heart doctor and heart surgeon in my area. My mom and stepfather lived two hours drive away in a small town. She had the surgery at our local hospital and after the operation and hospital stay, we had her and my dad stay at our house for five weeks during her recovery. Visiting nurses helped her bathe and checked on her progress. She was also close to the doctor for follow-up visits. We were able to connect her to an excellent surgeon and alleviate my stepfather from having to take on the burden of care when she came out of the hospital.*
>
> Barbara B

Caring for a family member or friend is not easy. It is not necessarily something we are prepared to do, but it can be one of our most rewarding and gratifying roles in later life if we are able to balance our selfish and our selfless tendencies. This balance is especially important if you become a caregiver.

Care for the Caregiver

Depending upon the situation and persons involved, care giving can be stressful, physically demanding and emotionally draining. Hands-on care giving takes courage, stamina, energy, and a devotion to the purpose of aiding someone else. It can become a selfless task. It is easy to become so involved in giving care that you forget about your own physical and emotional needs. As a caregiver, you may intellectually know that you should be trying to meet your own needs, but have difficulty finding the time for personally taking care of yourself.

> *I didn't take care of myself last year. My whole year was devoted to Tom. Now that he has passed away, I am beginning to make doctor's appointments and get things straightened out. I made a vow. I told all my kids that they better be good to me because I have every intention of living to be one hundred. I want a birthday card from the president, whoever it might be.*
>
> *Nancy E*

Caregivers who don't obtain help run the risk of negatively affecting their own health. They may end up in the hospital or worse because they get run down and are susceptible to diseases. It can happen when they don't exercise, eat properly, get enough rest, or deal with their emotional stress and tension.

> *My mother was the one to care for my father who was passing out and had a heart problem. He was in the hospital to have a pacemaker put in and my mother was very upset and cried on my shoulder at the hospital. My father was to be operated on the next morning. I went home and during*

the night got a call from the hospital informing me that my mother had died after I left. I had to tell my father after he came out of surgery the next morning.

Fred S

Because it is so easy for an at-home caregiver to become isolated, most specialists advocate the need for a break or time away from the loved one being cared for. This is often easier said than done. Perhaps if the caregiver thinks of time away in a matter of minutes rather than a span of hours, he or she might be able to find fifteen minutes for a quiet cup of coffee or a telephone conversation with a friend.

My husband is on medication for his heart, for his demen-
tia, and for his Parkinson's disease. These medications have
to be taken three or four times a day, so I have developed
a chart to help remind us. I've always had the freedom to
control my life and I'm not used to always having to be
there to help him all the time. Last year I finally have gotten
somebody to come and stay with my husband so that I could
have a little time away—for part of the day.

Dorothy N

Taking a few minutes or a few hours to step back from giving care can make a big difference in the energy and attitude you can bring to caring for someone. One option might be to ask for help from family and friends. If you are family or a friend, it might be a nice idea to offer to sit with the ill person and allow the caregiver a short time away. This not only provides the caregiver an opportunity to go out for the afternoon or to socialize with friends but also allows them to gain a sense of connectedness and a balanced perspective of their situation.

SUMMARY

If you are in the situation of being a caregiver, it is often helpful to join a caregivers' support group where you can gain information, ideas, and emotional support. It is a group where you can discuss self-doubts about decisions you are making and feelings of guilt and anger about having to care for your loved one. You will find that the others in the group very often share your feelings and that you are not alone. Care giving help can be found in a variety of sources—family, friends, online through your local community agencies or local paper. Check the list of ideas and resources that can assist you to locate care giving help in the Tool Kit at the end of this chapter.

CAREGIVER TOOL KIT

Questions:

Answer the questions and discuss them with your partner. These questions may lead to more personal questions that you want to talk about with each other.

I. What experience do you already have as a caregiver? What wisdom has that experience given you about being a caregiver in the later part of your life?

2. What can you do to prepare yourself to be a caregiver?

3. Do you have the necessary paperwork and power of attorney to make decisions for your loved one?

4. Do you have a support group of family or friends to turn to if you ever need the help in care giving?

5. Do you understand the rules for reimbursement in your insurance plan for care giving?

6. Do you know the guidelines to obtain hospice care for your loved one?

CAPABLE CARE GIVING

To Become a Capable Caregiver:

- Take a CPR course and update your skills periodically.

- Check out what paperwork you need to have as a caregiver:

  - A power of attorney

  - Medical power of attorney

  - Care recipient's healthcare proxy

  - An advanced directive indicating care recipient's wishes regarding life-and- death situations.

- Check for caregiver centers in your community that can provide assistance and access to a database of resources for caregivers. They often have a library of information and can offer referrals and family consultations.

- Depending upon what illness your loved one has, check out the appropriate support group where you can learn more about the disease and share experiences with others going through a similar situation.

- When friends and family offer to help, have a written list of things ready that they can do for you such as:

  - Preparing meals or casseroles (specify food allergies, etc.).

  - Providing a couple of hours coverage time so you can have a break.

  - Reading to the care recipient.

  - Running an errand for you.

  - Shopping for you.

- Find ways that will help you to relax and alleviate your stress:

  -Meditation

  -Yoga

  -Tai Chi

  -Keep a daily journal

-Read books

-Walk, exercise.

CARE GIVING RESOURCES

- The National Association of Professional Geriatric Care Managers. The purpose of this organization is to provide assistance to the family and the primary client, whether the family members live close by or out of town. The Geriatric Care Manager can provide a variety of services, which will help the primary client, be it a spouse, parent, other relative, or friend. These services relieve the primary caregiver of many responsibilities and give the caregiver the support that is so often needed.

- Community day centers, which provide the care-receiver with opportunities for socialization and stimulation.

- In-home help two or three days a week to give the caregiver down time.

- Orange County, California, puts out a booklet called "Senior Care" which lists advisory services, retirement communities, home care and companion care agencies, social services, residential care facilities, nursing homes and hospitals, etc. Referral sources should be available in your own county or community.

- Caring Connections online provide a wealth of information about care giving, providing physical care, home modifications, community resources, end of life care, etc.

- Online support groups for cancer, stroke, and Parkinson's. Support groups are set up to provide a place in which patients with the specific illness can talk about living with the disease with others who may be having similar experiences.

- Source for checking assisted living facilities and nursing homes.

Information about Calling 911 for Help

Here are some guidelines as to when to call 911: what to do and not do. As a general rule don't wait for symptoms to go away by themselves. Call without delay.

For a suspected heart attack - Symptoms include chest pain or pressure, severe palpitations, sudden serious weakness, extensive perspiration and a sudden shortness of breath. Women experiencing heart attack may not feel chest pain but may experience heartburn, nausea and sudden fatigue. What to do while waiting: Take aspirin yourself or give any dose of aspirin immediately.

For a stroke - Sudden symptoms include overall weakness or dizziness, trouble speaking or understanding, weakness in an arm or leg, seizure. Some strokes are characterized by an especially strong headache. Most strokes are caused by blockage(s) to cerebral arteries. If the arteries can be opened in time, permanent damage to the brain can be prevented. What to do while waiting: Make a note of when the first stroke sign appeared and give the information to the emergency medical team. Clot buster drugs must be administered with three hours of first symptoms.

Severe pain or bleeding - Call for help if the person is in severe pain or if bleeding is severe and person experiences weakness or drowsiness. What to do while waiting: With severe bleeding elevate the affected area if possible. Apply pressure to the site.

Choking - If you see someone choking, coughing, holding his/her throat and unable to speak, call 911, especially if the person is unconscious. What to do while waiting: You can give five sharp blows to the back between the shoulder blades with the heel of your hand. If this doesn't encourage breathing, provide five abdominal thrusts. If the victim is unconscious, perform CPR. (If the patient is one year old, do abdominal thrusts. If patient is under one year old do back blows and chest thrusts.)

Severe allergic reaction or asthma attack - If a person is experiencing a serious allergic reaction to an insect bite, food or if an asthma suffered doesn't respond to inhalers or oral medications, call 911. What to do while waiting: Ask if the person has specific medication on hand they can take, where to find it and give it to them. Assure him or her that help is coming.

Information derived from Article "When to Call 911" by Dr. Isadore Rosenfeld, Seattle Times Parade Magazine, Sept. 30, 2007

CHAPTER 6 –
DRIVING IN THE CARPOOL LANE
Couples' Relationships

*The relationship after retirement changes from two
people being together but independent to two people
sharing one life together.*

Quote from Healing Journey

CHALLENGE:

To obtain positive outcomes for each person in a relationship through knowing the "Rules of the Road" on communication, activities, time together, space, conflict, and relationship.

If you have been a two-career couple, each with your own
field of endeavor and control in your work world, most likely
you've been leading separate daytime lives. Now, deciding on the
kind of retirement you want you'll need to discuss, negotiate,
and compromise as never before about what the rest of your life
will be like. Have you been able to coalesce your visions for what
you want to do with your future together? If you haven't, how are
you planning to resolve the discrepancy? You may need to ask
yourself: "How far am I willing to compromise on something so

important as the rest of my life so that my mate and I will both enjoy our retirement years?" In this chapter we look at various communication and collaboration issues that face all couples embarking on retirement.

Couple Identity

If you decide to move into a retirement community, you will be sharing one life, one home, one space, and one social environment. Most likely you'll be perceived and related to as a couple by the other couples you meet. In this atmosphere, your words and actions not only reflect on you, but your spouse as well. This can be positive or negative depending upon the kind of personae each of you portrays to your circle of acquaintances.

She said: While working, my husband and I had our own businesses. He had his world and I had mine. We now live in a retirement community where are worlds are more closely aligned. When my husband resigned from a club board in our retirement community because of conflicts with some of the board members, it put me, as a fellow board member, in a very uncomfortable position, wondering what to do. Do I resign or do I see my responsibility through to the end of my term? I was torn between my obligation to support my husband and my commitment to the board. I actually thought things could have been resolved, had he not been so rash in resigning. Because I was conflicted about this, I talked with my spouse about my concerns. He seemed to have no problem with me continuing, but I felt uneasy the rest of the term.

Barb B

He said: I believed that some of the board members were actually working against what I wanted to do as the president of the board and decided the best thing for me to do was resign and get out. I didn't need this kind of headache in retirement. I had enough of dealing with problems in business. If my wife wanted to complete her responsibilities, I didn't really care, but I didn't wish to be involved in the group.

Stan B

Barb became profoundly aware that she and her husband were now a couple in a couple's community. It was hard for her to say, "I'm not responsible for his actions." It was hard for him to say to her at the time, "You should be supporting me no matter what." Situations like this can easily happen and can cause friction in a marriage. Whether you wish to or not, you tend to be viewed as a couple. Because your actions can affect each other; you may want to assess how much individuality you want to maintain in retirement, and how you'll both function as a pair in a couple's environment. For some of you, this can be another challenging change in your married life.

Influence of Age

Often, there's an age difference between partners. One spouse may be ready for retirement and the other continues to work full-time or part-time. These differences in timing can create a predicament. You need to discuss and decide how you will work this out, as it will affect many of your other retirement decisions. Your "work or retire" decision doesn't only influence whether you move from your present home or not. It can also affect what you plan to do together, when you do it, and the time you have together. It can further affect the amount of money you will have to spend in retirement.

> *My husband took early retirement at 62 but I continued working part-time as a respiratory therapist for six years because I was only 50 at the time. However, in 1999 my mother died unexpectedly and my husband had to have six-way bypass heart surgery. We had been talking about moving to a retirement community in California. I looked at our life together and said let's go and do this as long as we can, given our age difference.*
>
> *Sharon J*

The unexpected death of her mother and the seriousness of her husband's illness made Sharon realize how vulnerable we humans are. She decided to retire in order to spend time with him.

> *I am retired and my wife is continuing to work in her profession and is working under some stressful circumstances. I told her I would get Medicare in December and that we didn't need her to work for my healthcare anymore. We also really don't need her income, even though it's been nice that we have it. She feels unsupported as she carries the burden of work and I feel that I am carrying the burden of the relationship.*
>
> *Rick S*

Rick is retired from his formal work and wants to share this time in his life with his wife. This is most likely a big shift in their married life. When partners are working, they may provide each other a safe place from work stress, a place to decompress and relax. In retirement the need for companionship, especially during the retirement transition, may outweigh the need for a safe haven. Rick needs companionship as he experiences the retirement process and his wife may still need to have him provide her with a haven from stress. These are the kind of issues that can arise when one person is ready to fully retire and their mate is not. If you have a wide age difference between you, you may very well encounter issues about working and retiring. If you retire and want to move to a milder climate in retirement, what choices does your spouse have if he or she wants to continue working? How do both of you reconcile your differences?

> *She said: When I met my husband I was 37 and he was a young 57. I didn't even think that he was going to retire or wonder if he did, what that would mean. I was still working full time when he retired. When I would come home, he would say he wanted me to spend more time with him. I came home drained from being with people all day long and I just didn't understand that he needed companionship because he was home alone all day.*
>
> Miriam L

> *He said: I retired at 65 and feel that I paid my dues and I don't have to do it anymore. I can live my life. Rather than servicing others in business, I can now spend time and service my wife, my family and myself. I was able to transition from work with that kind of thinking.*
>
> John B

Generational differences in age can and do affect retirement and work decisions. Age differences may not be an issue early in the relationship. Their similar interests, activities, and beliefs may overcome possible generational differences in values and perspective. However, when the older spouse reaches retirement age, or wishes to change his or her life stage, issues of age may come to the forefront and affect their relationship. Age differences often can occur in second marriages and need to be considered and discussed.

> *She said: When my husband and I met, he had lost his wife after 40 years of marriage and I had been divorced after being married 20-something years. Meeting him was like a miracle because I didn't think I'd ever marry again. My husband thought we needed to talk about our age difference and what it would mean. We went ahead and started a new life together. He is in wonderful health and I'm usually the one being taken care of. I understand that death is a possibility and life does not give us a guarantee on anything. We have been blessed with the years we've had so far.*
>
> *Jane L*

> *He said: After we had been dating for a while and were beginning to get serious, I suggested we talk about our 20-year age difference. We discussed the various things that could happen because I was older. I wasn't sure how much time we would have together. That's why my wife decided to retire at 50 so that we could spend time together. As it's turned out we have been married eleven years so far.*
>
> *Joe L*

Jane made a decision to sacrifice her job and retire early in order to make the years she had with her second husband meaningful to both of them. Other couples have discovered other ways of solving the issue of a working spouse.

When I met my wife I didn't know she was 20 years younger than I was or I probably would never have gone out with her. We have now been married 19 years. Twenty years was a big difference in my mind and my concern had to do with the generational difference in outlook on life. However our backgrounds were very similar. Recently I retired and we moved to a retirement community. I found myself home alone with not much to do while she continued working in real estate. So, I went for a real estate license and we are now a real estate team.

Rick J

Since this interview, Rick and his wife moved to a newer retirement community where younger retirees are purchasing homes and beginning retirement. What they and others have found is that as a couple you have to deal with your own issues, be they in personality style, communication, age differences, or roles. You both will need to find a way to function together.

Understanding Roles

Whatever your situation is, whether one of you is working and the other retired, or you're both retired, most marriages have a tendency to change somewhat in retirement. Prior to retiring you and your spouse may have already defined roles, such as the way you both contribute to running your household. You may pay the household bills, while he or she may be responsible for investments. You may do most of the cooking while your husband or wife likes to do most of the outside yard maintenance. These functional roles are often carried into retirement. But, since both of you will be in the home more of the time, your roles within the household may need to be redefined. Some wives, whether they worked outside or inside the home, may expect that the husband will take on more of the household chores.

> *She said: Since we retired, I have continued to do some of the house chores I did before, such as washing clothes, paying household bills, and cooking, while my husband is still involved in investments, fixing things, and yard work. However, we've sat down and redefined how we handle some of the other chores. We decided to have a cleaning person come bi-weekly so I don't have to clean. We made an agreement that whoever gets out of bed last makes the bed. My husband does more cooking since he retired and is actually enjoying it.*
>
> *Ann B*

> *He said: I don't think my chores around the house have changed too much. I still like doing yard work and fixing things. However we now sort of split housekeeping chores. I take out the trash and my wife does the laundry. Since retirement we share cooking as much as possible and we share dish duty. We negotiated that who ever cooks, cleans up after him- or herself. I think you just make an agreement with your spouse about what you both are going to do and do it, whatever it is.*
>
> *Sal B*

Ann and Sal looked at the chores they have done in the home and figured out how duties could be split up. In some cases, they both agreed to share duties for maintaining their home. Many couples continue to struggle with sharing chores and responsibilities in their new retirement life. Couples generally focus on the big issues they face in their relationship, but in retirement it is often the small everyday actions, whether positive or negative, that add to or detract from the couple's quality of retirement life.

I've seen some wives experience serious issues when their husbands retired. Friends of mine were shocked when their husbands were telling them what to do all the time. One person's husband retired on Friday and on Monday he walked into the kitchen and said to his wife: "This kitchen has always driven me crazy. I'm going to reorganize it." She was a tiny lady, only five feet tall and the kitchen was set up where she could reach things she needed each day. He took everything out of the cupboards and reorganized them alphabetically. It made no sense for someone of her height. That lasted about a week and she said, "You put everything back and go work in the basement."

Carol T

Many of the women I know whose husbands have retired feel that house tasks have become more of a burden. Many husbands sit and wait to have their dinner served and resent the spouse's active life. One friend has to be home by five o'clock to serve dinner. I think retirement is a time when the men want to focus on the home and the women want to focus outside the home. So you have a dilemma. Here is the man saying, "I have time I want to spend with you." The woman's message may be, "You aren't meeting my needs. I have more fun outside the home."

Gail K

These differing needs create an interesting dichotomy. Although some couples are challenged by this change in needs and desires, many couples find ways to gain more independence so that they can achieve their personal dreams and goals.

> *She said: When I work part-time, I can leave a to-do list of things I'd like him to do when I am away and he gets everything done. Things are just fine. But if I am running around the community doing social things and leave him a list of things to do, it's not going to get done. He's going to say, "Why should I work while you are out having a good time." I'll ask him when he thinks the laundry gets done, the house gets cleaned, or the marketing gets done? He doesn't like to do those things.*
>
> *Helen S*

> *He said: I'll help if my wife and I can work together on house projects. I like projects where our roles are defined and clear. Some of the best times we have had are when we sit down and plan a whole project or plan a trip together.*
>
> *Paul S*

Both partners need to be comfortable with the new division of labor. You may want to talk about the issues related to tasks such as time spent, difficulty of the project, or your reluctance to do certain tasks.

Each married relationship is different and there is no set pattern that works for each couple. Some couples want to do most everything together because they see their marriage relationship as the central point around which their life revolves.

Others see that a strong relationship with their significant other is important in their lives, but don't feel they need to do everything together. You might want to discuss how you each see your role in the marriage now and in retirement. Defining your roles and reviewing them yearly, or as needed, might be a good idea to see if you both are fulfilling each other's needs in the relationship.

Activities — Separate or Together?

Couples who have adjusted well to retirement can comfortably maintain their connection, but allow themselves the freedom to pursue new activities and interests.

> *He said: Someone once pointed out to me that married life is not a three-legged race. You are not tied together as in a sack race. If you really like the other person, life together is more important than anything else, but you don't have to spend every minute of every day together. So you go to different places and come back to share your knowledge and experience with the other person. Recently my wife and my daughter-in-law did a six-day hike together and came back to tell me all about it.*
>
> *Patrick S*

> *She said: My husband and I both have our routine activities. He often says that life's not a three-legged race and the husband and wife don't have to always be together. He's learned over time that a happy man is a man with a happy wife. I love to go places and do things more than he does. He has no problem with me going on a hiking trip with other women and even said he would be happy for me to go.*

I think that when you are both involved in other activities
you bring something new to each other when you share your
experiences.

Susan S

You are a much more interesting person to your spouse and also to your friends if you go out and do things. If you are active, you have a lot to talk about and share with him or her over the dinner table or when you are together. Wouldn't it be sad to go out with your spouse to a lovely restaurant and eat in silence because you have nothing to say to each other?

She said: When one of you or both of you are working you
kind of go out of your way to be nice to each other. You
don't get on each other's nerves. When you see each other
24/7 it's different. He might be spending time out golfing.
I may prefer to spend time reading a book. Sometimes I
have felt guilty because I thought I should be taking time to
play golf with my husband. I bought golf clubs and I tried
golfing. But I don't like golf and it hurts my back. So he
spends time on the golf course and I prefer working on the
community newsletter and other activities. This schedule
works for us.

Pat D

He said: My wife spends time on her interests and I'm oc-
cupied with mine. If you enjoy doing different things, you
don't always have to do everything together. I can work on
the computer or go down to hit golf balls without feeling
guilty about it. We don't always need to be together during

*the day. But we do plan time together whether it's during
the day or evening.*

Bob D

Each couple will need to determine how much time they want to have with each other and when they want to spend time doing their "own thing."

Retirement provides some people with a sense of freedom, which they use to focus on themselves. Some spouses feel that this is a time for them to do everything they have ever wanted to do, regardless of how it affects their spouse or others around them.

Before we were divorced my husband said that it was his turn and he was going to do what he wanted. I looked at him and said, "When have you ever done what you didn't want?" It was ironic. I hear a lot of men and women saying something similar. So many of my friends survive by leading separate lives from their husbands. It isn't what they want and they don't like it, but they do. They stay in their marriage because they think it is too late to change or leave.

Gail K

This type of philosophy can cause serious friction and conflict in marriage. Although you may feel a sudden rush or urgency to do the things you've waited years to do, you're still in a partnership. You need to balance your newfound freedom with the need to continue collaborating and negotiating with your partner.

Extensive time focused on separate pursuits leads some couples to live what is called "parallel lives" in retirement. He's on his track, she's on hers, and their tracks never cross. Unless you both prefer doing all your activities separately, you might want to guard against "leading parallel lives" in retirement, because it can separate the two of you even more.

Sometimes you may have the best of intentions, but you miss the mark. You may try to do what you think is the right thing, but it doesn't resonate with your partner. When this happens, it's often because you actually never asked what he or she really wants.

> *He said: Since I retired I am focusing attention on building a lasting and worthwhile relationship with my wife. I want the relationship to contribute something to her life as well as mine. It's somewhat difficult because we both have had failed marriages. I've had to learn, change, and compromise a lot and be more accepting of somebody else's foibles and ways. Although there is a difference in our ages, there isn't a lot of difference in the way we think. We have the same orientation around the value of the individual and the psychology of life and so I think this similarity carries us through our generational gap.*
>
> *John B*

> *She said: We were talking the other day about how much of our marriage is his agenda and how much is mine. I said I think it is 75 percent yours and 25 percent mine and that was exactly his take on it. He didn't seem concerned that it's not 50-50. Getting concerned might be a good idea, but we don't always have that kind of conversation. A lot of*

the problem is that I don't know myself what to ask for or what I want. These are big life questions that have come as a result of this retirement.

Miriam L

A generational age gap between a husband and wife can lead to differences in perspective, ideology, and perception of self and of others. These differences tend to become more prominent at retirement age and need to be seriously considered and discussed. In John and Miriam's case, he is so intent on making a success of their married life, he doesn't seem aware of her need to participate in the process. As more and more boomers (the very people once defined as the "Me Generation") retire, the individual versus couple orientation is likely to continue to cause friction in retiree marriages. It might be wise to remember that if you are a part of a couple, retirement isn't all about "you," it's all about "us."

Time Spent Together and Apart

The amount of time you spend together in retirement depends a lot on your past experience, independent nature, personal interests, and need for companionship. The time you spend together or apart is heavily determined by the routine you established prior to retirement. If you tended to spend most of your free time doing things together, you most likely will continue that after retirement. However, if you both devoted time to interests outside the marriage, you may very well continue spending some time separately. Each couple has their own history and experience. Couples who are in a second marriage may feel differently than couples that have been married 30, 40, or 50 years.

She said: When I was working, I would be gone from seven a.m. to seven p.m. and my husband was retired doing part-time consulting. We'd just get three or four hours together for dinner and the TV news. We used to joke about this and say, "Do we have time to put a log on the fireplace or do we have to use the Duraflame?" That's why I think we changed our life in retirement because we hadn't been married very long and didn't have a lot of time together. I enjoy his company and I think he feels the same about me, but we aren't together all the time.

Jane L

He said: I have my interests and my wife has hers, but we manage time together every day. We add to our relationship when we share different interests. We balance time with family and friends with our time together.

Joe L

Many of the people I talked with had established a pattern of "together" time that resembled the pattern they had while working.

She said: Approaching retirement you may think that you will be with your husband 24/7. But if you are busy, you may see him at breakfast and again at dinner. My husband and I plan some time together every day. It is usually in the evening. This is just "together time" and doesn't include other couples. I think that you still have to plan individual time that doesn't involve others something exciting and different from your daily life. We even plan going away time for just the two of us.

Jo S

He said: The time we spend together is basically the same as when we both worked. Now that we are retired I do my thing during the day and my wife does her thing and we spend evenings or parts of an evening together. I need time for myself. She has never said so, but I believe she does, too. I grew up as an only child and I think I am basically a loner. I'm just as happy being alone as I am with a group. I have the time to do what I want and so does my wife, but we spend a tremendous amount of time together.

Frank S

If one person retires at an earlier time than the other, he or she tends to develop his or her own retirement routine and may find that when the other person retires, things change quite a bit. The time to discuss this change is before it happens, or as you begin to notice it.

She said: I think that if you have been married to the same person for 40 or 50 years it may be easier to be home with that person all the time rather than a person like me who has only been married 16 years. We came into the marriage older and we had things we enjoyed doing and were set in our ways. We may grow old together, but we didn't grow up together. Although I believe in the old adage that the husband is boss, being home all day with a boss may be difficult. So I think that will be a challenge for me.

Marge S

He said: Prior to moving to the west coast we were both retired for two years and were together all the time and there was never a problem. Since then my wife went back to work full-time and I'm still retired and plan my own day. I am never bored and have so many things to do. We basically have our own patterns in the house and it works out pretty well. If she were home we might be spend more time together, but we both would be doing things separately too. I don't envision any problems when my wife will be home a hundred percent of the time. We'll probably have to make some adjustments. If I'm going out I'll need to communicate a time I'll be back and where I'm going, where now I have the freedom to just go.

Ralph S

When you become aware of a problem, it's best to sit down and discuss it with your partner. What do you want and what does he or she want? By each talking about your feelings and wants, you can begin to compromise and find a reasonable and acceptable solution for you both, which can make both of your lives a lot smoother and easier.

I retired earlier than my husband and began to make a life for myself. My friends had told me that my husband was going to expect a lot of my time after he retired. His retirement has been a big change for me, as I was used to having the whole day to myself and we only spent evenings together. Now I find that I have feelings of guilt when I leave him during the day to do whatever I have always done before. I don't go shopping or out to lunch with friends like I used to because I feel I am leaving him alone. It is a difficult transition, but we are working on it.

Liela S

Consciously planning time together is an important aspect of a retirement marriage, according to many of the couples

I talked with. Although they may spend much of their time involved in various activities, they seem to save time for each other. Some couples put aside time in the morning to spend a leisurely hour together, others put aside time in the evening. Couples who found a balance in the amount of time they share and the amount of time they spend on their own pursuits believe they are both richer for the experiences they bring back to the marriage.

Couples' Communication

A successful relationship needs the three C's: caring, commitment, and communication. If you communicated, cared enough to treat each other with respect, and had a commitment to negotiating difficult issues prior to retiring, these attributes will stand you in good stead during your retirement years. Being able to talk quietly, sensibly, and diplomatically about the issues that arise in your marriage is an important ingredient in a positive relationship.

> *She said: We don't have any hesitation in telling each other what we are thinking good or bad. One day we were riding down in the elevator and I said to my husband, "Don't you ever get tired of being with me?" He said, "No" and he meant it. He wasn't saying it to make me happy. To which I said, "You know what, I get tired of being with you all the time. If you don't mind." In retirement, I would like to have a little more of "me" and not always "us." Perhaps it is because women have fought so hard to be independent that they don't want to give up that part of their psyche.*
>
> *Jane S*

He said: A few months ago going down in the elevator, she looked at me and said, "Do you get tired of being with me all the time? I said, "No." She said, "Well I do with you!" I said that's fine. We've been married 34 years. We generally don't say it in those words, but we realize that each of us needs some time alone. We each have to respect the other person. I will have to admit that living in the condo is harder because we are in closer quarters, while when we are at the summer cottage, I can spend time outside and she can be inside reading.

Fred S

Fred and Jane felt free enough to discuss their concerns openly. Sometimes you may be afraid to speak to your partner about something that is bothering you. However, stewing about it alone won't solve your problem. You need to get your concerns out in the open and resolve them before they grow in magnitude. Your ability to share your needs, express yourself and listen to your mate can be vitally important for a successful retirement life.

She said: Although I am pretty easy to get along with, there are a couple of things that will strike my flame and I will go up like a volcano. Lots of time I will just say, "What are you doing?" Bringing the issue to my husband's attention, gives him the opportunity to step back and think. He may not realize what he's doing. I don't think that you can just sit there and take whatever is dealt to you. Each of us should be able to speak up. I like to know if something I do irritates him and also be told when I do something positive.

Marge S

He said: Sometimes we may have a lack of communication as to schedules. My wife may have to go back to teach at night and I may not know about it until later that day. She may have mentioned it earlier in passing, but I may have not heard her. That is frustrating sometimes because I may have planned something for us to do. That's when we need to talk it over. We have such a busy calendar that if we don't write appointments down and remind each other that something is coming up, we can get our wires crossed and miscommunicate.

Ralph S

A continuous effort to communicate is important to a positive relationship. Real communication hasn't occurred until the receiver of the communication hears the intention of the message in the way it was sent. You may send what you believe to be a clear message, but your spouse may not hear it that way. He or she may miss hearing the intention of your message because it's being blocked by old hurts, prejudices, hopes or assumptions. Sometimes couples are so used to listening to one another talk, that they may not truly be "hearing the message." Taking the time to pay attention to what is said and verify the meaning, by responding with what you think was said, will demonstrate acknowledgement and caring.

She said: Sometimes I try to talk with my husband about something and he shushes me up because he is watching CSPAN or some other TV program. I realize it perhaps wasn't the right time, but it happens so much that I some-times feel like the television has become more important to my husband than I am. We don't seem to take the time to really talk with each other as much as I thought we would in retirement.

Barbara B

He said: Sometimes when I am interested in something else or watching a special program on television my wife will just start talking to me. I don't want to miss what's being said and tell her " not now" or "shush." I guess that is one of her traits—she just begins talking even though I'm not interested. I guess I tend to hurt her feelings when I'm so abrupt about telling her to be quiet. We have talked about this and are trying to find a compromise about when is a good time to talk.

Stan B

Television and computers tend to replace conversation with each other. Often the television news comes on first thing in the morning and is the last thing people watch at night. During the day one or the other spouse is most likely to be on his or her computer utilizing it for a variety of activities—finances, paying bills, sending e-mails or instant messages, obtaining information, or playing games. This is why it is critically important for couples to set aside time to actually communicate with each other. No television, radio, or computers. Some couples use the dinner hour to talk with each other. Others have told me that they set aside time at five o'clock each day as their "attitude adjustment hour" and they sit down, have a drink, and talk about their day. Setting aside actual time for conversation is important, whether you take a walk together, sit on your patio, or curl up by the fire. Giving your full attention to your partner goes a long way in saying, "you are important to me and I want to be with you."

Knowing the Rules of the Road

Just as there are unwritten rules of the road, there are unspoken and unwritten rules in marriage. Because rules are unwritten, people make assumptions and confusion can result. A couple needs to discuss what their expectations of each other are in retirement, because expectations lead to assumed rules of the road in a relationship. When one or the other breaks these assumed rules, conflict results. He or she may not even know they are breaking an unwritten rule until the partner gets angry or upset. Sitting down and listening to your mate, discussing your perceptions, and coming to an agreement of how to get along can alleviate a lot of conflict and provide both of you with a smoother, less frustrating retirement life. Make clear your "rules of the road."

> *She said: Listening to your spouse tell stories for the thousandth time you just have to smile because the other person hasn't heard it yet. You might be thinking "Oh my God, here he goes again" but you shouldn't say anything or criticize your spouse. I think you need to have agreements when you go out in public as a couple that you will not criticize or bring up old issues. You need to portray a couple personae that other people look to and respect. You can discuss things that come up later at home.*
>
> *Jo S*

> *He said: We've seen couples have some conflict when they play cards. The woman will say something and the husband will look at her or say something and she will say to him, "Why are you looking at me that way?" I believe you should air your dirty laundry at home.*
>
> *Frank S*

Both Jo and Frank understand the importance of their couple rules of behavior and are aware of others who don't. You might think about couples you're acquainted with who have a great public relationship, and you believe that they also have a positive private relationship and are comfortable with each. They may make it look easy, but it's not. They have to work at it.

> *When I was working in my career, I was always trying to find a win-win situation for those concerned. You have to be a master of compromise. So in a marriage relationship you see something where there is a disagreement, you need to look for a way to make a compromise. My wife feels the same way, as we both absolutely hate conflict. That is what caused both of our first marriages to dissolve.*
>
> *Rick J*

Maintaining a good relationship with your spouse in retirement takes just as much, if not more effort, than when you were working. It takes a lot of behind the scenes work and like the tide it will ebb and flow. There will be better times when the relationship may not need fine tuning, and then there are times it falls back to snipping and shortness of temper when you live through it.

> *I can see why people who have been married 45 or 50 years get divorces. I think you have to continually work on that relationship and on being really aware of where things are going. When you start to feel angry and pushed about something, instead of lashing out, excuse yourself and go to the bathroom and try to figure out what triggered your instant anger. This will give you four or five minutes to get yourself under control, so that you don't make the situation worse.*
>
> *Harriet S*
> *(See Resolving Disagreements at the end of this chapter.)*

The secret of dealing with conflict situations is to nip problems in the bud. Don't wait for issues to build to the point where you're about to explode. Deal with the small, irritating ones as they crop up. Also, don't be surprised if you have to discuss the same issue several times until some behavioral change does occur. The ideal is for each person to adjust or adapt a little to the other. But, sometimes you may just need to "go with the flow" and function around a problem behavior. As they say in poker, "know when to hold them and know when to fold them." Joan in our following story has learned this lesson well.

> *My husband gets his own breakfast and lunch and I usually cook dinner. I then excuse myself and he cleans up the dinner dishes. My husband has told me that I don't know how to load the dishwasher. I used to speak up about this, but I figure that if he does it better, then he can be my guest.*
>
> *Joan T*

Personality Characteristics

In marriage, spouses learn to adjust to the difficult aspects of each other's personality. In pre-retirement both of you may be working and are not together all day. Thus, you may have found ways of working around the challenging personality traits of your mate. However, characteristics that you have, and that your spouse has, often tend to become more prominent in retirement. These personality traits seem to multiply or expand to the point of irritation. Perhaps it has to do with more time spent with your mate. Behaviors that were acceptable in short-term increments appear to loom much larger when you are faced with them day in and day out.

She said: I am totally a micromanager and am incredibly organized. I was organized in my job and I am organized in planning meals and doing the laundry, etc. My husband is totally unorganized which tends to irk me. I can't stand going into his closet because he throws things in, doesn't hang them up, or put them in any order. This was something I had to adjust to and I've solved it by just letting him be responsible for his own areas of the house. I've let him deal with his own trait.

Joann A

He said: My wife is a "get it done, take charge person" and I am more of a laid back procrastinator. My procrastination doesn't seem to bother her until it gets to a point that she can stand it anymore and then I get things done. However, in ten years of marriage we really haven't had an argument that I can say was of any consequence whatsoever.

Frank A

Certain aspects of your spouse's personality may become an irritant in retirement because it may be more pronounced as he or she ages. I've observed several things can occur to men and women in the retirement stage of life. Some people become more self-oriented and feel this is the time to do what they want, when they want. Others may become more aware and tend to become less tolerant of their mate's actions or faults.

I do think some personality traits do get stronger with age. I see my husband becoming more short-tempered. I don't know if he is just angry because he is getting older. I can't figure it out. My friends have told me that my husband sounds abrupt on the phone when they call. I don't feel that I can say anything because it doesn't seem to help. It's difficult to change a person. How many young brides think they can go and change their husbands. But the bottom line at this stage of life is just adjusting.

Joan T

I've seen and heard of similar scenarios as Joan's. One woman was embarrassed by and often had to apologize for her husband's abrupt and gruff behavior. When angry or upset he could be verbally abusive of others. It seems that some older adults develop rigid behaviors, which can be really frustrating to his or her spouse. For some people, changing in later life can be very difficult, but that doesn't mean they shouldn't try. Each of us can modify our behavior if we really want to. We may need to be convinced of its importance and relevance, but it is possible. It's best when negative behavior traits are addressed early on.

She said: My husband has a controlling aspect of his person-ality and most of the time it doesn't bother me but it can be irritating. Every once in a while it will get to the point that I say, "wait a minute, I am not going to do this." When I feel it becomes intolerable I speak up and he says okay and tries to change. I think we communicate quite well and we understand what the other is thinking.

Jane S

He said: I guess we have discussions about the idiosyncrasies that irritate us now and then, especially when we are tired. My wife isn't very mechanical where as I am. She'll ask me how to do something. I explain it all, but she still won't get it and I tell her to read the instructions. I think friction is something that is just there it doesn't happen any more than before retirement. Jane and I tend to accept it and try to compromise. If you do this, I'll do that.

Fred S

Irritating personality traits are often part of life and cause frustration and friction in a relationship. Some individuals will even shy away from spending time around their spouse because they feel perturbed and angry. Maintaining distance is just a temporary solution and can contribute to a further breakdown of the relationship if continued for a length of time. You need to sit down together and discuss it calmly and respectfully. (See Dialogue Approach at the end of this chapter.) However, when a situation becomes intolerable, you may have to seek help from a relationship counselor. Many times guidance from an outside source is helpful because with advice, you can obtain objective observations and conciliatory ideas. With regard to personal characteristics, it's important to focus on the positive aspects and reinforce those, rather than to harass your mate about the negative issues.

Personal Space

Another issue that couples have to negotiate when suddenly spending a lot of time together is that of "space." A couple celebrating 60 years of marriage was quoted as saying that their long marriage was due to commitment, communication, and two TV rooms. This humorous comment underscores the need for having both together and alone time. Because a positive marriage relationship takes work, sometimes you need time alone to recoup and restore.

I probably irritate my wife with watching too many sports on television. I am very sports minded and if there is a sporting event on television I will turn it on without even thinking. Although my wife's adjusted to watching sports, if there is something she wants on, we have enough TVs in the house that one of us can go into some other room to watch. But if we want to watch together, one of us has to adjust to the other's program.

Ralph S

Sharing space in retirement can become an issue if you or your mate feels that you need some place to do what you want to do in peace and quiet. In my talks with interviewees, space was one of the priority areas of concern when discussing people's activities and time. Couples have found various ways of dealing with this issue. Some couples try to share space and have found ways to make it work for them.

She said: I think patience is important in retirement. We only have one computer and we both like to use it. We do share the computer pretty much. I use it in the morning because he is always out golfing or at a meeting, so that's my time. Otherwise I have a nice area in the bedroom where I read. We always have dinner together and afterward we literally part unless we have company. I go to the bedroom and he goes to the den to work on the computer.

Joan T

He said: My wife and I generally have a system where I use our den in the afternoons to play poker or do business

at the desk such as paying bills, etc. She uses the computer in
the morning as I am usually out of the house at a meeting
or playing golf. After dinner we each have our interests and
I work in the den on the computer.

Ralph T

Initially you may not feel that you need your own space,
but as you are thrown together with your spouse more than you
have been in years, you may find that an additional room can
be a haven to which you can retreat. It can provide you with
privacy and a place of your own to work, exercise, meditate,
or watch a TV show. It can be a welcome change from being
together 24/7.

She said: When my husband and I retired, I was tentative
about sharing an office with him as we have two different
working styles. He assured me that he wouldn't be in the
office much as he would be playing golf. But, as we adjusted
to retirement, I found that he was spending a lot of time in
the office. It took me several years to figure out a way to
easily expand our home so that we both can have a place of
our own when we want. We now each have the freedom to
work on the computer, read, talk on the phone, or listen to
our favorite music.

Ann B

He said: My wife thought we might need separate offices
in the house we were building for our retirement. But the
standard model we chose had only three bedrooms a master
bedroom, guest room, and den that we could use as an office.
I really didn't think I would be spending much time in the
office and thought we could share it. After several years, Ann

*felt she needed an office of her own. At first I really couldn't
see it, but since we now have our own separate offices, I
appreciate that I can listen to my favorite radio or TV sta-
tion or work on my computer. It was the right move.*

Sal B

Although Sal didn't initially feel that they needed rooms
of their own, by developing separate spaces it added a new
satisfaction to their retirement. They both now have the freedom
to do what they want in the time they aren't together. Some
retirees knew in advance that they would need their own space
and planned accordingly. They incorporated this need in their
criteria when buying or renting retirement homes or condos. Ken
and Lorraine even gave up a guest room in their new house to
have separate offices.

*The biggest question we had when we retired was whether to
have one den and office with our desks and computers in one
room or shall we not. We worked it out by having separate
offices. We spent a lot of time discussing that issue because
neither of us wanted to intrude on the other. It's a significant
point when you realize that my wife is an extrovert and
talks on the phone all the time and I am not.*

Ken W

Use of the telephone brings up another point. Some couples
felt it was worth the expense to have either two house phones or
a house phone and one or two cell phones so that they have the
freedom to make calls when they wanted. Maintaining your own
space where you can work on the computer, read, paint, or do
other hobbies should be something you discuss as a couple when
planning your retirement. One couple built their retirement

home with enough space that they wouldn't be bumping into each other all the time. They love each other, but they didn't necessarily want to spend every waking moment together. Often people didn't consciously define a specific space for themselves, but after retirement, they realized that it was very important and contributed to a more tranquil environment and more meaningful relationship.

Romance and Intimacy

The secret of a happy marriage is to keep the romance alive—yes, even, perhaps especially once you've retired. Falling into the trap of just living each day without looking forward to new experiences with each other can make both Jack and Jill very dull. Earlier in your life, you were involved with work and family responsibilities. In retirement, you now have the time to devise ways of showing your love for each other. It doesn't have to be some expensive piece of jewelry or a lavish trip. Often it is the little things that we do for each other that are remembered and appreciated.

> *She said: When we were working, one of my employees told me about having a date with her husband. It sounded like a good idea and I invited my husband on a Friday Night Date. So we started it about 20 years ago and we still plan dates for each other at least twice a month. Sometimes we go to a movie and have dessert and coffee later. One of our favorite inexpensive dates is to go to a local restaurant's happy hour and have appetizers, then browse through an old secondhand bookstore, get an ice cream cone, and walk*

along together. We just hold hands, talk, and enjoy each other's company.

Betty B

He said: Every Sunday when we get up one of us makes the coffee or gets the Sunday newspaper. We sit in bed, listen to music or the news, and read about what's happening in the world. These are one of the times I enjoy just snuggling in bed together without having to rush somewhere or do something. We have romance in the morning. We also try to experience what we call "discovering Washington" outings. We plan two-three day trips to explore the area since we aren't natives of the region. This is when we really talk about our life together. These are fun and we can get away during the week now that we are retired.

Steve B

Close married relationships experience different levels of intimacy. Intimacy can mean different things to different couples and its meaning can change over the time of a marriage. If you have been married 40 years, intimacy now may have a different meaning than it did when you were young marrieds. When you are intimate with someone, you let him or her into your private space. In a sense you extend your personal and emotional boundaries to include each other. In intimacy you experience shared moments and closeness, which may include sexual relations, but it also may not.

An online article on intimacy and aging by the Mayo Clinic suggests that the need for intimacy is ageless. You don't outgrow your need for affection, emotional closeness, and intimate love just because you have retired. Retirees aren't different from other adults in their need for a fulfilling relationship and intimacy with their loved one. What does happen is that both men and women experience physical and psychological changes that can make some aspects of sex more difficult as they age. You can go online to MayoClinic.com for helpful information or discuss these changes with your doctor. After obtaining additional information, sit down with your spouse and discuss the role of intimacy and sex in your marriage. What does intimacy mean to the two of you? Do you both share the same understanding and feeling about sex at this time in your life? If so, what do you plan to do about it? If not, how can you deal with the difference in views?

The Two of You Can Make It Work

In addition to what's been covered in this chapter, three more ingredients will help you to provide the framework for a positive relationship: *consideration, respect,* and *honesty.* You're *considerate* when you think about how what you do will affect your partner. You show *respect* when you're thoughtful about how he or she may feel about what you do or don't do. Attempting to view things from the other person's perspective goes a long way in creating a more congenial environment. *Honesty* is being candid, truthful and sincere, but doing so in a kind way, rather than being brutally honest and unkind to your loved one.

> *I can't tell you how many times I have promised to be more sensitive and considerate. I think you have to do more than get along with your mate; you have to honor her needs. My wife is a very insightful person and in the process of her own insight, she has educated me. I have learned a lot about*

vulnerability and sensitivity. You learn over your married life about each other's personality traits and needs. We sort of "sand each other's rough edges."

Ken W

Your spouse's behavior won't magically change in retirement. What often happens is that because you're around him or her more, you become more aware of both positive and negative aspects of behavior. It is a time of adjustment and adaptation until you find a level ground or plateau where you both can settle into comfortably respecting and showing consideration for each other.

She said: To have a positive couple's retirement experience I think you need to be flexible and look at things from different points of view. You should be willing to compromise rather than just doing what you want to do. I don't just compromise. I compromise and know why I do it. When one of the pair has had health problems you might tend to compensate more towards their needs than you would otherwise because you don't know how long you are going to have that person.

June S

He said: We usually take walks together. I took a bad fall going up some steps when we were traveling in Italy. So I am very careful now and don't walk as quickly. My wife is somewhat protective and tries to warn me about steps coming up when we are walking. I've told her that I hate it when she does that, but I understand why she is doing it. She has my welfare at heart.

Frank S

Understanding why your partner is acting in a certain way helps to accept their behavior. Frank realizes that his wife's concern is her way of showing her love for him. You can express appreciation in words by saying thank you for something your spouse may have done for you or some consideration that he or she shows you. It can be something as small as emptying the dishwasher when it wasn't your turn, or buying a special treat at the bakery on your way home. These small acts help to show you care and you are thinking of the person you love most.

> *She said: Pat and I are different in similar ways. I am just one of the high-energy people and he, on the other hand, is a very calm, quiet person. What in fact happens is that his calmness will at times, especially difficult times, pull me out of an anxiety situation. I, in turn, have gotten him to do more in retirement by getting him to walk with me. In a sense I think we balance each other.*
>
> *Susan S*

> *He said: My wife and I have been married for 15 years. This is our second marriage. She is a high-energy person and is involved in a variety of activities in the community. I gain from what my wife does and I'm able to share my knowledge and experience with her. We support each other.*
>
> *Patrick S*

Recognizing and appreciating each other's contributions to the marriage is key to a positive relationship. Sometimes, if you've been married for a long time, you may not express your appreciation or may not even recognize that your spouse has done something for you. You just assume he or she will. You would be wise not to take these things for granted.

SUMMARY

The emotional nature of most marriages changes like the ocean ebbing and flowing, rising and receding. You experience frustrating times where you may think you can't stand him or her a minute longer. And then there are placid times where you truly enjoy each other's company and wouldn't want to be with anyone else. If you have been through generations of marriage and are still together, I'm certainly not telling you anything new.

However, as you age, you change and may no longer have the same relationship with your spouse as you had in your earlier years. Because you both can experience a change, you may find your relationship is not living up to your expectations or is in trouble. Couples in similar situations have sought counseling. Depending upon the individual situation, agenda, and mindset, counseling often helped.

A constructive and satisfying relationship with your life partner can make retirement the best years of your life. That's why it is essential to dialogue about how you both feel about your marriage in your retirement years.

COUPLES TOOL KIT

Questions:

You and your spouse, partner, or significant other can answer these questions separately and then sit down to discuss your answers.

1. Do you need to think about your "couple personae and reputation" in a retirement community? How might you establish your reputation as a couple? How do you think you will be seen as an individual?

2. Have you had any issues or problems arise because of age differences or time of retirement issues? How have you handled meeting your partner's needs during these times? How does each of you feel about it?

3. How do you each see your role in your marriage? Do you see these roles continuing or changing?

4. Do you do a lot of activities together now? Do you plan to continue doing them as you move through retirement, or do you anticipate a change?

5. What does effective communication with your spouse mean to you? Do you think you both communicate effectively and if so, how? Do you truly listen, make eye contact, not interrupt, and give your spouse your full attention?

6. How often do you say, "I love you" to your mate? How often do you write him or her a note or e-mail message? Do you try to surprise your spouse with a small gift, flowers, or a special treat for dinner?

7. Can you speak honestly about your relationship to each other?

8. Do you each have a fair or equal chance to talk and share your feelings?

9. When you disagree, do you think you compromise more or does your spouse?

10. How have you handled conflict situations between you in the past? How can you improve your conflict resolution skills for the best outcome for each of you?

11. What does intimacy mean to each of you? Are you each satisfied with the level of intimacy in your marriage? If you haven't discussed it, is there a reason why?

CREATING A BETTER COUPLE RELATIONSHIP

There are many ways to create a better relationship with your spouse in retirement. The following two approaches have worked well for many couples who wanted to improve the quality of their marriage.

A Dialogue Approach

One way to increase communication and share feelings is to use a dialogue approach. This approach helps partners share their feelings without being judged or analyzed. By following basic guidelines and techniques you can begin a process to discuss some of the issues or problem areas you encounter in your marriage, whatever age you are.

Dialoguing employs various methods such as discussing, writing, and negotiating. One method that works well is to write down your feelings about a specific topic or question, read each other's written dialogue and then discuss what you have read. This process actually functioned well for my husband and I when we experienced the process 35 years ago on a Marriage Encounter retreat. This is my variation of that method, which we have used since that time.

Guidelines for dialoguing:

1. Take fifteen minutes to **write** a letter about your feelings on a specific topic or issue you both have decided to write about. Remember this is about feelings and not what you *think* about the topic. Focus on "how I feel" and not what the other person has done. Stay away from absolutes such as "you always" or "you never."

2. Then **exchange** your letter with your spouse or significant other. Take time to read it over several times, at least twice. Pay attention to the feelings of the other person. Identify and select a feeling or topic in the written message you believe is important or needs clarification that you want to dialogue about.

3. **Dialogue** for fifteen minutes on the strongest feeling or most important topic in each of the letters. You might need to allow an extra five minutes for the dialogue session to actively listen to each other and discuss both of your feelings. Don't be accusatory or sarcastic. It doesn't help to say, "You shouldn't feel that way." His or her feelings are real to him or her. Also don't jump to problem solving at this point. Just discuss feelings.

4. **Select** a topic and time for your next dialogue session. Often the topic or question for the next session will derive from your fifteen-minute dialogue as you may need more time to evolve a better understanding of an issue.

5. When you are both ready, select a specified time after the dialogue session to discuss possible ways of meeting each other's needs and begin to focus on actions each of you can take.

This dialogue approach uses "active listening" that is, being really present when your partner is talking and verifying in your own words what you think you heard. Envision the conversation being like rowing a boat. You both have an oar in the water and participate. If only one-person rows, you will just go in a circle and get nowhere.

Another important point about dialoguing is that just because you have shared your feelings, your spouse may not change behavior immediately. He or she may need a gentle reminder again in the future. However, you can positively re-enforce the appropriate changes in behavior by acknowledging positive behavior changes.

(This dialogue approach is based on our experience at a Worldwide Marriage Encounter Weekend for couples.)

* * *

RESOLVING DISAGREEMENTS

Most couples argue at some time or another. What's important is how you settle the argument. Do it in a way that shows respect for your partner and maintains your relationship or makes it stronger. When you find yourself stuck in an argument with your spouse, try to follow these guidelines:

1. Attempt to remain calm. By staying calm, you help to keep the disagreement from escalating. When you take a minute to calm yourself, you can think more rationally and reflect on what's happening. This helps to focus the argument on the controversy at hand.

2. Use words that express how you feel rather than how you think. "I feel disappointed and less important when you pay more attention to the television program than you do to what I am saying."

3. Be sure to keep the discussion focused on the current problem and don't deviate into past discussions or old arguments. Don't attack your partner with personal comments; attack the problem. Negative personal comments are hurtful and inconsiderate.

4. Actively listen to what your partner is saying. When you truly listen, you hear and understand what the person is saying to you. To be sure you understand, repeat back in your own words what you hear the person saying.

5. Remember that the person you are disagreeing with lives with you and sleeps with you. By realizing this, you can more easily get past the disagreement and begin the healing process.

(Based on resolution ideas from Peter Post's book, *Etiquette Behind Closed Doors*)

CHAPTER 7 –
TRAVELING TOGETHER IN AN RV
FAMILY RELATIONSHIPS

*Other things may change us, but we start and end
with family.*

— *Anthony Brandt*

CHALLENGE:

To maintain and expand positive relationships with family members in order to better understand and fulfill each other's needs.

Not long ago I watched as a family matriarch talked with a television interviewer at the Iowa State Fair. As they toured the recreational vehicles park, she pointed out all the RVs belonging to members of her family. Several generations of family were represented—children, grandchildren, parents, aunts, uncles and cousins. Every year they all converge on the state fair from all parts of Iowa to celebrate this traditional event together. I was struck by the importance they placed on family, connection, and togetherness.

When retired, you and your spouse may feel challenged as you try to both pursue personal dreams and attend to your family responsibilities. Retirement from work can mean the freedom to do what you want, when you want to do it. At the same time, family involvements and responsibilities may lessen, but they don't go away. Many variables will determine how much time, effort, and focus you will have to expend on family. Because there is no typical family, there are no typical experiences. Your family may be nuclear, consisting of you, your children, and grandchildren or extended to include parents, sisters, brothers, aunts, uncles and great-grandchildren. Many couples who don't have children include best friends as family. In fact, some retirees are closer to their best friends than they are to family. Whatever your particular family configuration, retirement may trigger you to rethink these relationships and how you want to nurture them. How do you want to relate with your parents, children, grandchildren, siblings and in-laws? What kind of relationship do you want to have with your family relations? This will have a bearing on how much time and energy you spend on this area of your life.

In retirement you have the opportunity to better know your children as adults and to develop special relationships with grandchildren. You might see it as an opportunity to establish, reinvigorate, and focus on these relationships. However, there are a variety of issues that may impact your plans. Consideration of these issues will better prepare you to successfully handle them when and if they arise.

Timing and Distance

One challenge to spending time with family might be differences in timing. You now have the time to spend with your children, but they may not have the time to spend with you. In the prime of their lives, they are likely preoccupied with work and family, as you once were. You're available, but they aren't.

> *We specifically decided to live reasonably close to each of our children for part of the year. We thought we would be more accessible for them to visit us more often. Our plan was to have the grandchildren visit us for several days or a week so we could do things with them. However, what we have found is that our sons have limited vacation time, which they use to travel with their families. The grandchildren are busy and involved in summer school, sports, or scouting commitments. Thus, it's hard to set up a special time for them to come and see us. More often than not, we are the ones that have to travel to see them at their house.*
>
> *Barb B*

Barb and her husband have found that the right time for them isn't necessarily the right time for their family. You may have the vision of spending more time with family, but it may not work out that way. When your expectations are disappointed, it's easy to feel angry or resentful. You may take it personally when family members reject your overtures. If this happens, you need to remember what it was like when you were bringing up your family and dealing with all the responsibilities you had at the time. That shift in perspective may help you gain a better understanding of your children's situation. However, if after several rejected offers and invitations, you feel that you are being rebuffed, you need to sit down with your son or daughter and quietly discuss how you feel. (Use the dialogue approach from the Couples Tool Kit in chapter 6) Being thoughtful and having the ability to see the "big picture" (especially in the midst of difficult conversations) will be an asset in retirement.

Each family's happy medium of closeness and distance will be different. Some families live on the same street or in the same town and see each other all the time. Others in this age of transition are spread all over the country or all over the globe. When you retire you have a choice of locations. If you select a distant place to retire to, you may see family members occasionally. You can select a site that is reasonably close and easy to drive to, in which case you may see them quite often. Or, you can move close to your children and see them often.

> *We feel that if you have family, you should try to be near them. You don't have to be next door, but you should have easy access to family. We are approximately two-three hours from each of our children. We're close to family but not too close because we figured that they needed their space too. When family members live with in driving distance, it makes it easy to celebrate holidays and family events together.*
>
> *Steve B*

If you have more than one child, you may need to choose which one you'll live closest to. Generally, it isn't wise to live so close that you end up being involved in the every day lives of your kids. They need to live their own lives and you need to create your own life. But, don't be surprised if they don't come to visit you as much as you expect.

> *Before moving to our retirement house, we had a large house and my husband's kids would visit us all the time. They*

would fly in for a few days, see us and use our house for a jumping off point to see tourist attractions in L.A. Now we live in a retirement community and are surprised not to have them visit here as much. It seems to be more difficult with little children because there are too many restrictions on the use of facilities. We had assumed that things would continue the way they were before and it hasn't turned out to be that way. Even my mother and stepfather have gotten to the age where they can't drive out to see us. We have to do all the driving in order to see people.

Judee W

Judee's comments have been reiterated by a number of other retirees. Their children and grandchildren don't visit as much as they would like them to and they wonder why. My research indicates that there are a number of things that impact the frequency of visits from offspring. One is that when they come to visit you, they have to interrupt their lives and perhaps take your grandchildren out of committed sports events, music lessons, scouting commitments, etc. A second problem may be weekend traffic, which can extend the time of their trip, as they are only free to travel on the weekends. Third, if you choose to live in an adult retirement community, where there are often rules and regulations about the use of facilities, these guidelines can hamper use by young families. In order to get our children to visit us, I found that we must make advance arrangements to accommodate all these limitations.

Family Celebrations

If you remain in your own home, and it has been the gathering place for the family, it may still continue to be. However, as you become older and your family grows, continuing to do all the work for such an event can become burdensome. In the future you may want to divvy up some of the cooking responsibilities among family members. However, when family members live in various parts of the country, their far-flung living arrangements may very well affect family celebrations. They have to travel or you do.

> *When we first retired, I felt a little let down at not having the family at our house for Christmas. What we do now is to spend Christmas with one son and his family one year and visit our other son the next Christmas. It isn't ideal, but it has worked out pretty well. In the past we had a traditional family tree with all our children's handmade ornaments on it. I have given all these decorations to them and now can have a decorator style tree if I wish to. The Thanksgiving holiday is rotated between our one son's house and ours. This way I don't always have to cook the entire dinner and to be honest that is a relief. This year we won't even be home for Thanksgiving, as we will be traveling.*
>
> *Betty B*

Giving up the family home, where your memories of family holidays were formed, can be very difficult. If you downsize and move to another area it may become more difficult to continue holding the celebrations at your home. In retirement you may no longer have a home large enough to have everyone over for the holiday. Where once your home was the gathering place for family, moving to a retirement community can make you less accessible. This can be a disheartening change if you have always enjoyed entertaining family.

We always had the big celebrations at our family house because we had the room for it and enjoyed doing it. In retrospect I see that people were able to come for the day or just a few hours and drive home again. They didn't have to spend the weekend, unless they wanted to. Now, no one can come even for the day because it's too far away. They say that they have to come for three days to make it worthwhile. We had thought that we had taken everything into account when choosing our retirement life in a desert resort community.

Judee W

In your planning you will try to think of your needs and what might work for your family, but you won't be able to think of everything nor be able to anticipate all future life changes.

During our marriage we lived all over the country. There were many times we couldn't travel to celebrate holidays with family. We would get together with close friends and celebrate. Now that we are retired, if for some reason we can't spend the holiday with family, we meet with friends. Being together on a holiday has actually solidified our friendship.

Bonnie B

Whatever holidays you do celebrate as a family will most likely change somewhat when you both retire. It may be a time to "pass the torch" to the new generation to carry on the family traditions. If you have expanded your family by a second marriage, you may be establishing a whole new approach to dealing with holidays. You now have two family groups, which may require more careful consideration and sensitivity about where you spend holidays and who visits whom.

> *You have to plan ahead how to cover all the birthdays and anniversaries—all the kids' stuff you didn't plan for before our marriage. We have seven kids between us and they are married or have girlfriends. We also have seven grandchildren and we give presents to everyone. Christmas is huge and becomes "undoable." I start planning for that in June and work the whole year round.*
>
> *Jo S*

> *This is our second marriage. We both had children before and so we have six children between us. Since our children were older when we married they don't have much in common. They don't have the same family history and thus, aren't close. We have gotten them together for holidays. They tolerate each other, but they don't like being together. Christmas is an important holiday for me and I want to be with people that really want to be with me. I want to celebrate it with my kids and grandkids. We take turns having the families over. I think when you have a combined family it's like vying for attention. Who do you care more about, this new family you have moved into or about us? It's hard for them to understand that I really love all of them.*
>
> *Judith A*

Judith's situation shows how couples sometimes have to rethink how they celebrate holidays and revise past traditions or incorporate new ones when several families are involved. Whatever holidays you celebrate, whether these are religious holidays or birthdays, you'll likely have to consider how to manage the gathering.

Family Connections

Ten years ago, Steve and his family began to have family reunions with his mother, sister and her husband, brother and his wife, plus the children and grandchildren.

> *Our family gets together for a weekend reunion in August of each year. Because we live in various western states, we select an acceptable place and date way in advance. We spend time eating, drinking, playing sports and family games. Each year we take a picture of all the grandchildren sitting on a giant log that is down by the water. We now have a series of pictures and see how all the children have changed over the years.*
>
> Steve B

"La familia" has traditionally been important to Steve and his relatives and they have begun to see connections established between cousins and even second cousins. Family memories are being developed for Steve and his family members for years to come, whether they are able to continue maintaining contact or not. They have established a family tradition that may be carried on by the younger members of the family. Have you thought of how you can maintain family connections? Can you get together with family members or perhaps visit them? How can you maintain a connection, if you feel it is an important element in your retirement?

Relationships with Adult Children

Generally by the time you get close to retirement your children are grown-up and are out on their own or at least in college. They may even be parents themselves. As they have grown up, your relationship with each child has probably evolved and changed. Each of you most likely developed a personalized relationship with each child because men and women tend to relate differently to their children. Retirement is a good time to enhance your relationship with your children. It takes time and opportunity. Perhaps you can take a walk together when they visit you. Mothers and daughters may plan a day at the spa, while the men of the family might plan a hike or fishing trip. Have you ever thought of traveling with members of your family? We found time to talk with various members of our family when we took them on a seven-day cruise of the Mexican coast. Interestingly, in planning another family trip my husband and I considered another cruise, but our children have suggested going to a dude ranch. At our age, this wouldn't have been our first choice, but we are willing to go along. However, these suggestions point out the differences in what younger families want to do on vacation and what retirees want to do.

> *Although our relationship with our daughter is fine, we have a problem because she wants us to participate in everything her family does, including vacations. Both she and her husband want to travel with us because they say they have fun with us. I think that it is a real compliment that they want to spend time with us, but our travel ideas are different now that we have retired. We feel that we have just so many years left to travel and we don't necessarily want to do the same things a younger family wants to do on vacation.*
>
> *Harriet S*

Finding the right balance of family time and time for you and your spouse to do what you desire in your retirement can be a challenge. It will vary from couple to couple and from family to family. Some families tend to have very close, daily relations. If you have been living close to children, you may want to continue this pattern or you may feel you need to break that pattern and establish a new retirement life for the both of you.

> *I knew retirement would be different because you are obviously changing your lifestyle. What keeps coming up for me is our children's perception of what our retirement is. They think because we are retired that we aren't doing anything; so we are free to baby-sit for them or come visit for a month. We have things to do. We want to live our life while we can. We saw what happened to my husband's parents. When they became ill, their independence was taken away from them. His dad died and his mom is now alone. We love our children but want a different life.*
>
> *Jeanne E*

Whether you have a positive relationship, or one that is broken and needs patching up, retirement can be a time for reassessment and renewal. You might be reassessing your relationship with each of your children as to where it is today, what you want it to be and what is possible. Part of that reassessment will be to determine how, when, and where you will spend time with them.

Relationships with Grandchildren

I've heard people say that grandparenting is a lot better than raising your own children because you can enjoy the fun experiences without the responsibility of being the disciplinarian.

Retirement is a time to enjoy your grandchildren especially if you accept them as they are and don't try to correct every behavioral flaw you notice. Instead of correcting them, be positive and look at what they do right rather than wrong. Nothing can light up your face and warm your heart as quickly as seeing a grandchild running up the walk to your house to give you a great big hug!

> *Just knowing my grandchild is very special to me. Having that one-on-one relationship is important. How would I have really known her if I only saw her a few days per year? Once, someone asked her, "what makes you happy?" She said, "Gommie makes me happy." That meant the world to me. We are purchasing a small retirement home back on the east coast because our children are moving back there.*
> *Barbara W*

Developing a special relationship with grandchildren adds to your life and theirs. Recently I got a birthday card from my young grandsons. It showed a mod grandmother with sunglasses rocking in a chair while snapping her fingers to the music coming from a boombox. The card read, "You rock!" What was even more touching to me was the scrawled personal note, which said, "You are the best Grandma in the universe!!! You are cool!!!" It's hard to beat that. I treasure the times I've crawled around the floor at their house playing "Traffic Jam" with matchbook cars.

You have a choice about the role you play and the time you spend with your grandchildren. If you live close by and have a good relationship with your children, you most likely will see your grandchildren often. But if you live in another area of the country or state, it might be more difficult for you and for them to travel back and forth as often as you would like.

I think of myself as a family man and have done babysitting for our son. I have a good connection with my two older grandchildren. With the younger ones the times I get to see them are few and far between because I haven't been invited over to their house in a while. My son is busy and the kids go to school and are involved in activities, but we communicate by telephone several times a week. They come down to see me on Father's day and Thanksgiving so that's about it. I don't get to see the kids, but I know they have their heads on straight and they aren't in trouble with the law. What more can I want?

Dan M

If you don't live close by, you can still make the time you are with them count. You can help them to explore new worlds and they can help you learn how to explore their world of video games, TV shows and "Game Boys."

Our grandchildren are lucky enough to get presents from their parents, other grandparents, and family. Early on we decided to provide experiences for our grandchildren rather than material presents. When they are six we begin with small events such as taking them to a special tourist site for their birthday. I still remember our grandson's surprised look when he got a giant sundae smoking like a volcano while having lunch at the top of the Seattle Space Needle. Experience gifts are different for each child and depend upon their interests. Sometimes we have combined birthday and Christmas presents for one larger event or we have combined having two children do the event with us. We have experienced such things as sleeping in a tent teepee in the middle of an animal park, visiting an Indian Village, seeing the Ice Capades, and driving out to a national park at night for a cookout and a telescopic look at the planets. Imagine how we felt when we heard our grandson proudly tell his friends about seeing the moons of Mars.

My husband and I try to select local, diverse experiences, which not only expand our grandchildren's horizons but ours as well. You might feel that this may be difficult for you if you don't live close to your grandchildren. We too don't live very close to grandchildren full-time. Sometimes we have had to delay the outing until we saw the children. However, we've found that when the children are young, it's best to have the outing reasonably close to their birthday or holiday, if possible.

Being with a grandchild away from the parents provides an opportunity to get to know them as a person. You have an opportunity to talk with them about their school life and to learn about their interests. It can be an enjoyable experience for both the child and grandparents when you establish an open relationship.

A number of the grandparents I talked with take a more active role in caring with their grandchildren. Several of the grandmothers took care of their grandchildren. They may see them off to school and are there for them after school because both parents work. This provides grandparents with time to stay in touch with their grandchildren's every day life.

> *Because I don't live far from my daughter, she drops her son off on the way to work each weekday morning. He watches the TV or plays games until I drive him to school. In the five years we have done this, there have been times that he needed to talk about a problem and I was able to help him*

think through the emotional situation at school or with other children. I'm gratified to have these occasions to help not only my grandson, but my daughter as well.

Judy D

Maintaining contact with grandchildren really can be a challenge because they are so busy with school, friends, and sports or perhaps don't live close to you. People tell me that the best ways to keep in touch are through phone calls and Internet.

I use the computer to send e-mails to keep in touch with our four children, nine grandchildren and one great-grandchild. We are fortunate to have such great kids, with no marital problems, no kid problems and no drug problems. With that many grandchildren in this day and age we could have those problems.

June L

If you do have a computer there is a lot you can do to maintain contact. Not only can you e-mail children and grandchildren, but you can also begin to learn the instant messaging programs youngsters use to communicate. If you don't own or know how to use a computer, you may very well want to learn as e-mails, instant messaging, text messaging, and cell phone calls are their communication channels. Using these channels doesn't provide the same kind of contact as face to face. But it is contact nevertheless, which can bridge gaps of time and distance between your family gatherings. In fact, these little technological contacts can make the larger family gatherings smoother because when you're together, you have some context and familiarity with what has been going on in each other's lives. You don't have to spend time doing a lot of catching up in person, because you've been tending the relationship via technology. By using these devices, you not only keep in touch with grandchildren, you keep up with the technology age.

Relationships with Parents

In retirement you may also be maintaining your relationship with one or both of your parents. If they are physically well and independent, that relationship might be relatively easy. However, as parents age, there is bound to be an increase in dependency. Some of you may have the responsibility for caring for them or having to make appropriate living arrangements that would be most helpful to them. If they have health issues, you may need to provide assistance for a short term or even for long-term care.

> *I had my hip replaced a few years ago, which caused a change in our lifestyle for a while. I didn't go through the rehab center, but arranged for a therapist to come into the home. Upon my son's insistence, we stayed with him and his family. The first night we were there, our son took off from work and he set up a card table in the guest room with two TV trays and the whole family ate together in my bedroom. It was a fun thing for them to do because I couldn't come to the dinner table. Initially I thought we'd stay a week, but we ended up at their house for six weeks. Staying there worked out well both ways, because they were busy working at the store and we could make dinner. I sat in a chair and did pricing for the store while I was on the mend.*
>
> *June L*

June told me that she and her husband were able to get closer to the grandchildren and this experience ended up being a pleasant one for all concerned.

If your parents are well and live independently, it is important to talk with them about their preferences and wishes for the future. Making appropriate arrangements for help whether you care for parents in your home or theirs. If you are forced to select assisted living, the Caregiver Tool Kit in chapter 5 can help. However, I encourage you to go online and see what resources are available in your vicinity, as each situation is different and each community provides differing resources.

Single with Family

Some divorced retirees maintain their relationships with children and grandchildren separately from their former spouse. They have an opportunity to individually establish the kind of relationship they want to have with their children and/or grandchildren. Some were able to establish a personal bond with their children.

> *I have three daughters, four grandchildren and am now divorced. Although they all don't live near me, I have a close relationship with all of them while my ex-husband doesn't. My daughters and I have a bond similar to the one I had with my father when I was growing up. He was kind of a mentor to me and I could easily discuss things with him. Our bond is like cement because they feel free to come to me with anything—for advice, money issues, or recipes. I also*

can discuss everything in my life with them. I didn't have that kind of bond with my mother.

Marcia W

Since my husband and I are divorced, I am the one who is close to our son and daughter. My husband is missing the important events in our children's lives because he alienated himself. These are the times when we had expected to be rejoicing together. That part is sad, but I'm glad to have a significant other who goes with me to family events. He accompanied me and gave me support when I recently met my son's future in-laws.

Gail K

A parents' divorce can be a difficult time for the children involved. It can put them in a precarious position as to how, when, and to whom they give their support and allegiance. Sometimes families are split up because of differing alliances to either of their parents.

I have a close relationship with our four children. When my husband and I divorced, they were all married and away from home. In retirement, he decided that he preferred to live his life with another woman in our neighborhood. The children didn't expect this, but they were not surprised at our separating. I see them quite often and I spend holidays with them. My husband maintains contact with them by telephone. They had no choice but to accept the other woman, but don't have much contact with her.

Jo G

A divorce in the retirement years can be difficult not only on the spouses involved, but the children as well. One or both of the spouses may need advice and support from their children. The amount of involvement and advice given by each of the children will vary, but it needs to be done with sensitivity for everyone's feelings. Jo went on to share:

> *I am presently selling the family house and have gotten a lot of advice from the children. They each have different opinions about what I should do and that can be a little wearing on me, but I appreciate their support. It's hard for me to sell my long time home and begin the next chapter of my life.*
>
> *Jo G*

Family Traffic Jams

When conflicts have occurred in the past between either of the parents and their children or any other family member, they often experience estrangement. Sometimes all contact is cut off. Retirement can provide a time of renewal. It can be a time for rectifying mistakes and healing hurts that have occurred in the past or occur in the present.

> *I took good care of my wife during her long illness over many years. She died a few years after we moved to our retirement home. A short time after her death, I off-handedly invited a woman friend from my paddle tennis group to try out a restaurant in our town. Since it was a short time after my wife's passing, my daughter became unglued. She was extremely upset when she heard I was going out with someone. Much to my surprise, I exhibited an enor-*

mous amount of patience, especially with my daughter. It took a good two and a half years of semi-estrangement, but I kept the lines of communication open in spite of things that were said and done. The nice thing is that we are now both on the same page and the relationship is a thousand percent.

Dan M

Dan was pleased that his daughter finally accepted the situation. But, that didn't end his difficulties because his going out so soon after his wife's death also upset his son, son-in-law, and granddaughter. It took a long time for the family to adjust to the fact that their father/grandfather had the right to have some happiness in his life after spending ten years caring for his wife. During the estrangement Dan stuck to being patient, even though he said it was out of character for him. Finally the rest of his family also came around to acceptance.

Difficult family issues can arise from an array of challenges: new relationships, ill health, and death.

A few years ago my family went through a fairly negative period. There were a lot of health problems and one of my brothers had cancer and was dying. I was stressed out try-ing to be a support to my mother who was falling apart. My other brother and I had a falling out about this time. I don't know what my brother's problem was, but he got angry with me about something that I had or hadn't done and proceeded to rip my life apart. I was saying, "Stop! What are you talking about?" He refused to talk to me. A week later our brother died and I couldn't even talk to him. I felt like I lost two brothers. It was an intensely difficult,

emotional and negative time for me. I ended up seeing a
grief counselor, which helped a lot.

Sally S

It's often during traumatic family times that everyone's dispositions are stressed and conflict occurs. Sally said that within her family she was a safe person with whom people could vent their anger. They could say things to her that they couldn't say to anyone else and she would support them. She and her brother finally reconciled. As you age and mature, you too may be faced with difficult family matters. That's when you will want to draw on such attributes as patience, understanding, endurance and acceptance.

One of the things that happen as we mature is that we discover that we want to pass on some of this learned knowledge and experience. When we retire we also now have the time to notice and address family situations and behaviors, which we were too busy to notice before. Thus, we may attempt to share wisdom and provide guidance, which we believe will help our children and grandchildren.

I read a book called The Care and Feeding of Husbands
and felt it was very informative. I bought three copies—one
for each of my daughters and one for my daughter-in-law.
I read the book and felt there was a lot of things I did do
and a lot of things I didn't do in our marriage. I told them
I was still learning and that it was not a condemnation of
how they do things. It had more to do with the fact that I
was still learning after 42 years of marriage! I didn't want
them to be offended, as I just wanted to share information
that was helpful. My one daughter said that it was funny

*that I was giving the book to her as she just went to a semi-
nar recently that was saying essentially the same thing. My
other daughter thought it was an anti-feminist approach to
marriage.*

Carol C

*I try to be very careful to not give advice to either of our
sons or daughters-in-law unless I am asked. I once sent an
excellent child-rearing article to my daughters-in-law. One
daughter-in-law became upset and misread my general intention to educate. Sometimes, it's hard not to say something,
especially when I see possible mistakes they are making in
rearing our grandchildren. But, when this happens, I say
to myself that we had our chance to influence the rearing
of our children and we did a good job. Trust them to learn
for themselves. It seems that when I do have some concerns
about the grandchildren, something positive happens that en-
courages my hope for their future.*

Barb A

There is a fine line between giving advice and meddling.
Much of it is in the perception of the receiver. If you do have
suggestions, you might try to check out the situation first to
see if advice or guidance is even wanted. What I have found
is that if either of our children are wrestling with a behavioral
problem with the grandchildren, they will at some point share it
in conversation. If they ask for my thoughts, I do share them. I
might show empathy with their situation, share my opinion, or
support the positive action they plan to take. If you are asked,
remember that you are just sharing your own opinion. They
don't have to follow your guidance even if it is based on many
years of experience. In turn you are not obligated to follow their

advice. You may just want someone to talk with about your situation.

> *Family is important to me. They are a vital part of my life and I care for them even if my family sometimes disappoints me. I don't stop loving them. I depend upon these relationships when I need to talk. My youngest son is my very best friend and always has been. I can talk with him about anything in the world. I could call him up and he might tell me what he thinks I should do, or he might just listen.*
>
> *Dee H*

Family Coming to the Rescue

There are times in our lives that we need the help and assistance of family. It can be in time of illness of a parent or it can also be an illness or accident to one of our children or grandchildren. You don't know when something is going to happen to a family member.

> *My second husband had three children and the fourth, the youngest child was mine, but we kind of threw them all in a pot and let it go at that. The oldest son was killed three years ago in a freak auto accident. That's when my husband's health started going down hill. He kept it all in, where I talked it out and cried. My husband died the next year. Family is especially important during times of crisis. My other son was wonderful through his dad's illness and kept asking if I was okay and he wanted to be sure I had enough money. He was concerned about my welfare.*
>
> *Nancy E*

As with Nancy's situation, often it is in times of crisis that family becomes even more important. For Susan in the following story, the time when she and her husband moved into their retirement house was her "Golden Period" of retirement. It was a time when things were going well and her family was all right. Then everything started happening.

> *First my brother became terminally ill. My mother, who lives on the east coast, needed my support and still needs some help. My grandson stuck himself with a needle while playing in a public park and we went through nine months of testing for Hepatitis or HIV. While on a rafting trip in Idaho with my husband, I got a satellite phone message from one of my daughters to call her. I thought perhaps my grandson had died because you don't get satellite phone calls in the wilderness. At first I couldn't reach anyone in the family. I didn't know what the problem was and felt physically ill. It turned out that my daughter-in-law, who was a little over five months pregnant, went into labor while visiting her parents in the north woods of Wisconsin. After a wild helicopter and ambulance ride, she prematurely gave birth to our granddaughter. We didn't know if the baby would live. At the time I felt this just isn't fair. However, my baby granddaughter overcame the odds and is alive today.*
>
> *Susan S*

Things seem to be going well again for Susan and her family, but she understands that you never know when it will change. Not all family situations are as serious as Nancy's and Susan's. However, there are times when you will be asked to help out or to be available if you are needed. The importance of having accessible parents can be meaningful in time of need. You might be asked to just help your children out by babysitting for an evening or for a period of time when a transition is going on in your children's lives.

> *Our oldest son has now experienced adversity in life. He and his wife have divorced and share custody of our grand-children. He has the kids one week and she has them the other week. They live close enough in the same area so that the children can go to either house and attend the same school. Although there is a housekeeper that goes between our son's house and his former wife's house weekdays for the children, we've been asked to help out at times. We drive in to take care of the grandchildren whenever we can help.*
>
> *Lorraine M*

> *With regard to children my favorite expression is that you are never off of the hook. I had some concerns about some of my children's financial matters, but by and large they take care of themselves.*
>
> *Dan M*

Many of the couples I talked with felt that their children could "take care of themselves." However, there is always that time when help is needed and it may be important to be there for your family. If you are leading a busy life in retirement, by traveling, participating in sports, hobbies and organizations, you may give the impression that you aren't available. You might assume that your children know you will always be there for them, but if you project a very busy life, they may get a different impression and not feel comfortable in bothering you to ask for assistance when they need it. You may have to specifically let them know you are available for them and they can call you.

The same can be said for you if you need help. If you tend to be a self-sufficient, independent couple, you may find that at some time you too will need to ask your children or even your parents for help. One friend who contracted cancer was fortunate to have her mother and father come from the east coast when she had to have surgery and was bedridden. She said her father, who was in his late 70s, even got up in the middle of the night to take her dog outside to pee. As discussed in the Destinations chapter, many times retirees move to be close to family so they will have support in time of age-related illness.

Second Marriages and Families

In today's world of divorce and remarriage, family relationships tend to be more complicated. This is also true in retirement, as spouses separate or pass away, their partner may remarry someone who brings their own children and grandchildren into the marriage. With the differences in family experience and background, there may be a greater possibility of misunderstandings, conflicts, and non-acceptance.

> *We've been married for ten years. Most people that I know who try to merge two families that are older like ours will tell you quite honestly that they don't merge. I've talked to a lot of people who have married again later in life like my husband and I have done. They get together for holidays and see each other a couple of times per year, but they don't bond as a family. My husband's four stay as his and my three stay as mine. They are compatible for vacations, but that is it. They don't bond because they are too old and set in their ways.*
>
> *Jo S*

The task of combining adult members of two different families can be a daunting one. Depending upon the personalities involved and the circumstances, it is worth a try. But, don't be surprised or disappointed if it doesn't work out the way you expected.

When my husband's sons come to our house, if they are married, their wives make it a lot easier for me as the stepmother. The wives don't have the same family history as the boys and I believe women are more socially conscious. The boys just show up and want to be entertained and fed. The daughter-in-laws come in and ask what can they do to help and they remember birthdays, etc. These young women have come into the family as outsiders just as I did into this second marriage. I think this creates a sense of comradery in the kitchen as we women work together.

Judith N

My second husband died after we were married for eighteen years. We had a combined family of nine children. After a number of years alone, I married for the third time to a man whose wife died of cancer and left three grown children. So, we have a large family totaling twelve children. I keep in touch with the children from my second marriage and my own three, but we don't see them very often. When we married I said that if his children accept me that's fine, but if they don't, that's fine too. I'll telephone his kids once in a while, but I keep telling him, "They're your kids. They don't want to hear from me. They want to hear from you." He just says, "They know my number." They are nice kids, but I only call after pushing him to do so. I've told him, "Everything you do reflects on me. You don't understand that it comes back to me and yet I'm the one encouraging you to call."

Darlene L

As you can see, retired couples face a variety of challenges when it comes to mixed families. Often where the children are adults when a couple remarry, the couple interacts separately with each of the families or children. In situations where the woman or man was responsible for the break up of the previous marriage, it can be more complicated. There most likely will be negative relations with the children.

> *In a second marriage where there is a prior divorce situation, it depends upon what caused the break up of the old union. If either of you were involved in that break-up, you just better prepare yourself for misery. Often the children don't want their father married to that woman. She was the other one or he the other man. It can happen where the wife or husband only died two months ago. The children might say, "How could she do that to dad, he isn't yet cold in the grave." It is tough to carry this emotional baggage into a new marriage. I was lucky because I met my husband five years after he separated from his wife.*

> *JoAnn S*

A variety of circumstances can affect your relationship with your children and your spouse's relationship with his or her children. If you did get divorced and it wasn't an amicable separation, it may help you to focus on your relationship with your children and not to concern yourself with what your former spouse does. What is important to remember is not to allow your prior conflicts to effect your present and future relations with your children. If conflicts do arise, try using conflict resolution remedies such as the dialogue method in chapter 5 to limit the situation. However, the best method to deal with it is to try to anticipate it and establish an environment where such a negative climate can't begin.

Relationships with Extended Family

Some people have a hard time breaking away from their family or home territory when they retire. They have family and friends there with whom they don't want to lose contact. So, they try to look for a solution that will meet their familial needs and their spouse's need for a new locale.

> *Although we moved permanently to the island, I sort of have my feet in both my old community and my new one. I see my family and old friends when I go back and I baby-sit the kids. We see the family a lot and I talk to them every day. I find it hard because I can't participate in some of the grandchildren's activities as much as I'd like. I never want to give up my old attachments and extended family—sisters and brother-in-law because they are like best friends. They are a support system for me.*
>
> *Linda R*

Linda is having difficulty in letting-go of the benefits of living near family. She's struggling to find an answer that will solve her situation. She thinks the answer may lie in buying a condo in their hometown for the winter months and spending summers on the island. They could then go back and forth.

There are couples who have decided to go back to their original home turf to retire. Perhaps they have fond memories of living in that area as they grew up or when they were young marrieds. Jean and her husband in our following story elected to move back to her hometown and found that this was to be the first time in her adult life where she would be surrounded by family.

We moved back to the island where my extended family lives. There is my mother, two brothers, wives, nieces, and nephews. It is a lot of family all of a sudden. But, it is surprising at how well I am getting along with everyone. I thought I would be seeing everybody all the time and found out this doesn't happen. Although we see my brothers quite often, we see the nieces and nephews about five or six times a year. The best surprise is that our daughter moved to the island from Vermont. That has been more fun than I imagined. We haven't lived together since she went off to college. We have a new adult relationship with our daughter that's good.

Jean M

Moving back to a familiar area sometimes works out well and sometimes not. Remember that your birthplace may have changed over the years and the people you used to know may very well have changed too. Going back for a high school reunion and enjoying all your old friends and family in the short term is one thing, but going back to live there may be something else. You will need to scout it out, just as you would any new retirement location.

SUMMARY

Although there may be roadblocks, traffic jams, and hazards as you reassess and redevelop relationships with family members, the benefits will generally outweigh the potential issues. This can be a wonderful opportunity for you to renew, reestablish or enhance your relationships with children, grandchildren, parents and siblings. What you both have to do is to be clear about how you view the importance of family in your retirement life and what you can do to pencil in time for family into your busy schedule. Allowing time and opportunities to establish or strengthen these relationships can add enjoyment and satisfaction to your retirement.

FAMILY TOOL KIT

Questions:

You and your mate can answer these questions for yourselves and then sit down together and discuss your answers. After you come up with possible actions you want to take, discuss some of these questions with your children or your parents to get their viewpoint and expectations about your future relationship.

1. What kind of relationship do you have with each of your children? Your parents?

2. Is it the kind of relationship you want it to be? If not, what can you do to improve it?

3. Have you shared your retirement plans with your children? With your parents?

4. How can you renegotiate your relationship with your parent(s) and what do you anticipate they may require from you?

5. Discuss ways that you believe you can help your children or grandchildren. What do they need from you? What do you need from them?

6. What kind of relationship do you wish to have with your grandchildren? Will that be possible? How can you make it happen?

7. What special talents and abilities do you bring to being a parent? A grandparent?

CHAPTER 8 –
VAN POOLING
Friendships and Informal Support Systems

The only way to have a friend is to be one.

— *Ralph Waldo Emerson*

CHALLENGE:

To maintain friendships and establish new friends and support systems in retirement.

The importance of friendship changes as you move through life's stages. When you were young, friends may have been important in determining what you did and how you saw yourself. In your mid-career years, the importance of friendship may have waned a little, as you were heavily involved with work and family. Usually when you're working and your friends are working, there's an unspoken understanding that you both are busy and you may only see each other occasionally. Often the weekends for working couples are filled with family commitments and personal responsibilities such as going to the cleaners, grocery shopping, etc. You may have a limited amount of time to squeeze in social engagements with friends.

However, in your mature adult years, friends can become more important again, especially if you live away from family. Friends may even become your second family. You might rely on friends to help you in times of trouble. You'll probably spend more time with friends than your family if you don't have family living close to you. Given the importance of friends in our later years, it's important to consider this aspect of life when planning for retirement. This chapter focuses on some of the "friendship" challenges that have faced retirees in this book and how they have met them.

FRIENDSHIPS

Whether retired or not, friends can be an asset in your life. You may not have thought about it, but not all friendships are the same. You've probably experience various levels of friendship in your life.

> *Best Friends — one or two people you can talk to about anything and they give you emotional support when you need it.*
> *Close Friends — who share your common interests and you see quite often.*
> *Social/Casual Friends — people you see occasionally; play golf or tennis with, go out to dinner with, see at interest group meetings.*
> *Neighbor Friends — could be any one of the above or just good neighbors.*

Work Friends — people with whom you work, have lunch,
ride to work with or know professionally.

Depending upon the level of friendship, being a friend does take time and effort. Being a best friend can require a lot of time and personal involvement. In fact, your spouse or partner may be your best friend. A best friend is one you see and talk with often, while close friends are seen somewhat less often but seen consistently. Social friends are generally seen occasionally or just at meetings, events, or social activities.

Establishing or maintaining your various friendships in retirement can take more time than you anticipate. Whether you partially retire or fully retire, friendships take on a new meaning. More may be expected of you. There may be a presumption that since you are retired, you can spend more time with friends.

Retaining Work and Professional Friendships in Retirement

If you continue to work into your mature adult years in the same vicinity where you now live and work, you most likely will keep your friends from the workplace, professional organizations, or social organizations. However, if you no longer work at the same company as your friends, nor go to the same professional meetings, you may find that you now have less in common with them than when you worked.

> *What I found is when you no longer work for your em-*
> *ployer; you begin to forget some of the people and the politics*
> *of the workplace. The politics change so rapidly in a large*

organization. The company evolves, new people come in and the dynamics change. The main focal point of their lives is still their jobs, while I've moved on in my life. It was hard to maintain my work friends because our interests drifted so far apart.

Judith A

I have two close friends who are continuing to work in the same field I was in before I retired. Because we no longer live in the same area and see each other rarely, we mostly communicate by e-mail or cell phone. When they write me about their work and their special projects, I still care about hearing from them, but am becoming less interested in their work projects as time passes. My head just isn't in that same work arena anymore. It feels like this is stepping back into the past, while I'm focusing on my future and the life I now lead.

Barbara B

When you meet your work friends for lunch or dinner, most likely they will talk about what's going on within your former organization. You might hang in there for a while, but gradually you tend to lose interest, because the people you know have changed and the gossip and "scuttlebutt" may no longer be of interest. You may even experience a sense of loss at not being involved with your former colleagues.

I used to drive 20 miles once a week to see my friends in my former town, just to have coffee with them. Over a five-year period I began to go less and less to the point now I rarely see my former friends. Things just changed and we no longer have as much in common.

Peter B

I found that because we moved to a new retirement community, I really didn't have the interest in participating in the professional organizations to which I belonged. While actively working, I took a leadership role in these organizations, but after I moved from the area, my interests changed and I found that it was time for me to move on with my life

Ann S

I still keep in contact with the people I worked with at Boeing. We have lunch every few weeks or so. There are six or eight men I keep in contact with and all but one of them are retired now.

Dave V

In order to keep work or professional friendships alive, you have to maintain contact and interest in their activities. If you are retired and they're not, this can become more difficult as the months and years pass because their lives continue on a different road than the one you're on.

Establishing and Maintaining Personal and Couple Friends in a New Environment

Prior to retirement you most likely had personal friends and your spouse had his or her friends, and you both may have had couple friends with whom you shared outings and activities. If you decide to move to a new location or retirement community, you will have to establish new friendships.

If you're a baby boomer, establishing friendships may be easier for you than it was for your parents because boomers generally had more time as single adults, before marriage to develop adult friendship networks. Also, if you've been involved in the workplace since the 1990s you may remember and use the concept of "networking." Through networking you most likely developed the skills to make connections, obtain information, and meet new people. Networking skills can come in handy in meeting and establishing friends in a new retirement community.

When my husband and I moved around the U.S., I learned that I had to get involved in the community, schools, social organizations and "sift through" numbers of people to find friends who had like interests. In an active retirement community, this process is made a lot easier because there are clubs and organizations established which you could join. By getting involved in stimulating activities, you connect with new friends of like interest and maintain your interpersonal skills in the process.

Barbara A

I learned that in order to make friends as an older adult, you have to get involved in something. If you stay home and aren't a joiner, you will be a very lonely person because no one is going to come knocking on your door to ask you to come out and play.

Bill G

When you relocate to a new retirement community, you're generally anxious to meet new people. Your first contacts may be with neighbors, the people who live around you. You may initially make neighbor friends. Sometimes these people become your best or close friends, but they may just remain neighbor-level friends as you expand your friendship circle through your interests and activities. Moving to a new location in retirement will require working to establish new friendships. As Barbara noted, you may have to "sift through" a variety of people to finally develop close or best friends.

> *I left all my friends in Florida when we moved west. I had a couple of girlfriends who were best friends. I think that women bond and have stronger friendships than men do. When I moved here I missed a couple of my women friends so badly that I had days that I was weepy because I have not made a close friend here. I have made friends here, but so far no one I feel comfortable enough to tell my troubles to.*
>
> *Pat E*

> *I don't think you necessarily have to have a best friend. As an active adult, I have friends I exercise with, friends I go to the movies with, and different friends I discuss books with in my book group. I am pretty versatile and enjoy having friends with various interests as this expands my knowledge and my social network.*
>
> *Mary B*

The secret to developing friends in retirement is what I call "forced contact." You need to participate in some activity, which provides you the opportunity to personally interact with people on a consistent basis, in order to develop close or best friends. By activity, I don't mean going to a musical performance or social dance where you may not have much time for personal conversation. It needs to be some activity or involvement where you participate and talk together. People who get involved either on committees, boards, or have some participatory role in a club or group, have "forced contact" because they attend meetings together, and have to be in contact with each other either by telephone, e-mail, or in person.

> *My wife and I learned from our past U. S. military experience abroad to believe in the old expression, "When in Rome, do as the Romans do." Treating people in other countries with respect is a two-way street because you get it back. While at our summer home on Vancouver Island, B.C. we've attempted to assimilate into the community as quickly as possible. We got involved with community organizations and recreation groups right away. My wife is very active in ceramics, painting, and the Red Hat society. I am active in some charitable groups in Canada and do volunteer work at non-profit organizations. We have used these as stepping-stones into the life of the community.*
>
> Bob A

In a large retirement community there are a proliferation of clubs and interest groups so you can search out friends with like interests. Wherever you live, you need to take the initiative to locate groups where you can meet people who share your avocations. Of the many people I have talked with, most join a number of groups, clubs, or organizations where they have been able to establish friendships.

> *Here in this retirement community I don't think men and women would have any problem making friends. Everybody here is from somewhere else. You join an activity group and make friends. I told my husband that I was going to put a moratorium on friends as I have too many now. I can't keep up with everything now. Somebody calls every*

day saying, "Do you want to do this, and do you want to that?"

Phyllis W

I think if you are an outgoing personality and you like people it helps you in making friends in a new retirement community. Years ago my mother gave me a wonderful piece of advice. She said, "don't go into a school and make friends too quickly. Go in for three weeks or so and kind of stay to yourself. Be friendly but don't get hooked up with any group. Kind of check things out and you will see where you would like to be. This way you don't make too many mistakes in beginning friendships with people you really don't know well." This philosophy works in starting a new retirement life. Finding the people that can be your friend and developing a friendship with them does take time and shouldn't be rushed.

Harriet S

Harriet brings up a good point—sometimes, lasting friendships need to evolve as you get to know someone's personality and identify your similar interests. It may not be in your best interest to act impulsively and become too involved with specific groups until you've had a chance to get a sense of the people and environment.

Your friends most likely will come from the various groups each of you joins. Because you and your wife or husband's hobbies in retirement may be very different, you may find that you make friends in different interest groups. If one of you is more outgoing than the other, that person will be out in the social environment more and thus meet more people on an ongoing basis.

Recently I dug out my old high school yearbook and read about all the clubs I belonged to. When I think about my life in retirement, I see that I belong to a large number of clubs and have made a lot of lady friends. I'm just a joiner. It is easy to be over-socialized when you live in an active community. I think it works for me because I am an extrovert. However, my husband is more of an introvert and doesn't get as involved.

Lorraine W

Because Lorraine is more socially active and her husband is more comfortable staying home working on the computer or doing projects, she tends to be the social coordinator for the couple. However, he is willing to go with her to the couple social events. Whether this is your situation or not, each of you may find that making friends is your responsibility, if you want personal connections.

In retirement some men think that the women will establish the social environment for them. Once they retire, they have to go out and develop their own friends. It takes a lot of time to make friends and to be a good friend. That is a big surprise to a lot of the men. All of a sudden they think now they are going to do all these things and they don't have the same type of connective group to do them with.

Carol T

As a couple in retirement, you may want to identify the amount of time each of you wish to spend with each other and with personal friends or couple friends. This generally just works itself out, but it can become an issue if one person is out all the time with his or her friends and the other person is sitting home thinking that they aren't spending enough time together. Judee and Barbara and their husbands have found a happy balance of time spent with individual and couple activities and friends.

My husband and I like diversity. He has the friends he's met at his activities and I have my friends from the groups I belong to. However, even though we have our separate interests we are also happy if it is just the two of us as well.

Judee W

Because we have such varied interests, my husband and I each have made different individual friends. He has his golf buddies and friends from his investment group. I have my book club friends, Red Hat friends, and tennis friends. But, we also have developed friendships with couples whose company we enjoy from some of the couple groups we belong to.

Barbara B

You'll need to find your own level of comfort or balance of friendships that will work for the two of you. Sometimes friends that one of you makes separately become friends of both of you. One thing to consider with regard to couple or personal friendships in retirement is how to remain a friend to a person who is left alone due to a divorce or death of the husband or wife. Sometimes these friendships dry up, just when the single person needs them most.

The best thing I did when I was married is to make my own friends as well as couples' friends. Now that I am single I still have my girl friends, as well as the couples friends that include me when they go out for dinner or to a movie. I pay my own way, but it is nice to be able to go with friends. I'm invited for dinner at their home and I have entertained my friends at my house. In order to be really happy in a retirement community, you have to create your own circle of friends. I know spouses that have done everything together and when one spouse dies, the other is at loose ends.

Gail K

When making couple friends, you and your spouse need to feel reasonably compatible with each of the people in the other couple. Many times women or men become friends and they want to do things as couples. They make arrangements for what we used to call a "double date" for dinner or some social event. If the husbands or wives find they have nothing in common to talk about, one or the other may be reluctant to go out with the other couple again. Generally if you just see the other couple sporadically, this might still work out for all concerned. But, neither you nor your spouse may want to drag the other out with people he or she isn't comfortable with, and then come home to hear about the awful time he or she had.

We bought a modular home in a senior park in a small California coastal town. An old friend of my husband lived there and he thought he'd pal around with him and the wives could be friends too. We moved and my husband began reestablishing his friendship. By the second summer my husband's friend got bored with retirement and obtained a fulltime sales job. So my husband lost his buddy. The friend's wife was also never available to be a friend to me, as she was always busy in the home doing laundry and watching Oprah. I saw that she and I had different interests and not much in common. We ended up selling the home and moving to a new retirement community where we've made a lot of friends of various ages.

Liela S

This experience helped Liela realize how difficult interaction is when dealing with people who might be the same age, but have dissimilar backgrounds and education. She and her husband weren't afraid to make a change to locate a more friendly and welcoming environment.

Age to some people can be a criterion for establishing friendships. They may think that people of similar age have more in common, than people of different generations. If you walked into a room where you didn't know anyone, would you tend to gravitate to those people who appear to be of similar age? This may be because you believe they have the same historical reference as you and have more in common with you. Although this may be true to some extent, you may be surprised at the differences of view and experience, once you get to talk with them.

I think having similar interests supersedes age differences when developing relationships. I try to connect to people through a common interest. So it is an entree to people of all ages. I like young people because they are full of human vigor and have lots of new ideas. They think outside the box. It keeps me young and active.

John N

There is an age range difference in our friends of almost 20 years. I know that some younger retirees prefer to be with people their own age, but I think they are missing something

special because some of our older friends are more active
and involved than some of our younger friends. We enjoy
people for who they are and how interesting they are, not for
how old or young they are.

Ann B

If you enjoy and appreciate the friendship of a person, age can be irrelevant. My husband and I tend to have friends older than we are as well as friends the same age and also younger than us. We have often gained knowledge and ideas from older friends that we have put into practice in our own lives. With people of similar age we have shared past and present experiences, while with younger friends, we may be the ones to share our experience and knowledge and can learn from them too. Friends are friends, no matter what their age.

When I was 55 I had a friend who was close to 90. He
was still working and he spoke often of the changes he'd seen
as his friends passed away. He tried to offset that by as-
sociating with younger people.

Patrick S

We have friends of various ages and we like to entertain
by having dinners and parties. We have friends who are
retired, friends who are still working and friends who have
young children. We even hosted a wedding reception for two
friends who didn't have family in the area. Since we moved
here, our friends have become our extended family since we
don't have family living close by.

Rick S

During your adult years you can have contacts with people of various ages, who can become friends of yours at some level. It depends upon your interests, personalities, needs, and connection points.

Developing and Sustaining Friendships in Two Locations

You may be one of the myriad of retirees who plan to live your retirement in more than one location. Some of you decide to maintain your present home and have a winter or summer place to go to so you can escape the cold winters or hot summers. Others will decide to have two homes or condos in two different localities. Even if you are renting or leasing a place for a short time, you most likely want to meet and make a few friends while you live there.

Although we live in an island community for only five months during the summertime, we wanted to have friends to do activities with and invite over to entertain. We knew only one couple and the real estate broker when we first bought on the island. We made it our mission to make friends. The first summer we had a dessert party at our house for the neighbors and anyone else we knew. We joined the golf and country club for golf, tennis, and pool. We also joined the church and volunteered to work at their fundraising events. The second summer we started a neighborhood golf and dinner event, which we sponsored for the next three years. We found that it takes several years to develop friendships, especially since we were the part-time "new kids on the block" in a more stable, long-term resident community. But with a concerted effort, we found ways to make friends through participating, volunteering, and getting involved in community organizations during the months we live there.

Living part of the year in two places can mean that you may have to do "double duty" in spending time to make and maintain friends in both communities.

> *If you live six months in one place and six months in another part of the country, you need to reestablish liaisons, friendships, and even acquaintances. So for my husband and I, our anchor in both places is tennis. We come back and play with the same tennis people. I also play bridge and pick up with my bridge friends. But you have to reconnect every six months. It takes some effort on our part to do that. When we are back in Cape Cod, we make ourselves very visible to say we are back. We stop to talk to neighbors and ask if they had a good winter or let's have a block party. You have to put yourself out. You have to make the effort, not them. They didn't go anywhere. While you're away their lives went on without you. When you return you have to get back into their lives.*
>
> *Jo S*

Jo says that it takes a lot of physical and emotional energy to renew friendships, keep up the friendships, and move them forward. It's a matter of reinserting yourself into the social life of the area.

> *What I have found living in two different communities is that the time it takes to maintain friends in both areas increases tremendously. When I am in one location, I try to at least sporadically keep in touch with my friends at the*

second location by e-mail, cards, letters, and/or cell phone. Thank goodness for the Internet, because if I do think of a friend or find out he or she is sick or celebrating a special event, I can at least send greetings or a note to them, whatever the time of day. I do find, however, that it is difficult to leave a best friend for six or seven months and then return back into her life again. So much happens that you can't convey it all long distance, even in today's high-tech information world.

Ann B

Having friends and acquaintances in both of the places where you live can increase your enjoyment at both retirement locations. It will take some effort and does have some drawbacks in the amount of time available to spend with specific friends.

To be a Good Friend or Good Neighbor in Retirement

Friendship is a give and take relationship. In order to have friends you have to be a friend. Giving might mean being available for friends in time of need. When your best friend or close friend needs someone to talk to, you can provide a listening ear and emotional support in time of illness or trouble. One of the advantages in having close friends is that with their help, you can bounce back quicker from crises and problems if you have people you can confide in and express your fears, grief, or concerns to.

Women generally seem to find it easier to talk with women friends about their personal issues and problems than men do. Often men maintain friends around some hobby or activity, such as golfing, bowling, watching football games, or playing poker. Although they may not usually discuss personal issues or problems with their golfing buddies or poker pals, men may discuss serious issues with a best friend or close friend they trust. Although some people become "fast friends" quickly, most people's friendship is something that grows and develops over time.

Since friendship is not only taking, but giving as well, being helpful to friends and neighbors is also important. It might be driving your friends to and from the airport when they travel or giving them a ride to the doctor. You might be asked to take in a neighbor's newspaper and mail if they plan to be away for a few days. It might be picking up some groceries for a friend if you know they are sick or housebound. In a retirement community a neighbor might ask you to keep an eye on their house while they are on vacation or at their second home. Just as there are levels of friendship, there are levels of reciprocity among friends and neighbors.

> *One of our summer neighbors offered to check our house when we are at our primary residence. It gives us a secure feeling knowing that our neighbor is looking out for any trouble or problems. After a small earthquake occurred near the area, we felt relieved when our neighbor reassured us that there was no damage to our property. We've found it difficult to pay him for his help because he won't take money. We try to repay his kindness by taking he and his wife out for dinner at a special restaurant when we are there for the summer.*
>
> *Steve B*

> *The day we moved here our neighbors living across the street and on both sides of our new house came over and introduced themselves. They asked if they could be of any help to us. It was a very warm welcome and we have become friends. Where we lived before we had a few neighbors, but not friends.*
>
> *Nancy E*

Sometimes friends show up at your doorstep, but often you have to go out and find them. If you are open to meeting people, you never know when people you do meet can become friends. Often you have to take a chance and talk to people.

> *My husband and I were at the gym one afternoon and my husband was using the treadmill. He's not normally an outgoing, gregarious person, but I saw that he was in deep conversation with the gal on the treadmill next to him. I finished walking the indoor track and he waved me over to introduce me. She, in turn, introduced her husband and now he and my husband are the best of friends. They just hit it off. I have met more people and made more friends in six months in this retirement community than at our last house where we lived for four years.*
>
> *Jeanne E*

To Establish and Maintain an Informal Support Network in a New Community

If you are newly retired or about to retire, you may question the need for an informal support network of friends. You perhaps plan to travel or live a vacation type of life in some resort area somewhere in the world. The two of you may be independent and see no real need for establishing new close friendships or for an informal support network of friends or non-professional community groups.

I learned early on in my husband's retirement how important support can be. Within a short time after moving to the desert retirement community, my husband underwent heart bypass surgery. Because we hadn't had the time to develop close friends that I could reach out to, I spent a long, lonely vigil in the waiting room while they operated on my husband. I feel fortunate that if this happened today, I would have friends I could rely on and a support group to lean on.

> *We had plans to live in other countries for periods of time and to travel the world. But what I have come to realize in retirement that what I need is a community of people that I'm a part of. If we spent all our time traveling and being vagabonds, we would meet people along the way, but we wouldn't have those friends and close ties, a support system that we all need. It really came home to me when our son, Michael died. We had just been living in Sun City a year. When we came back from his funeral in Santa Fe, the out-pouring of support and love we felt from people we knew here just overwhelmed me. It really showed me how much you need to be part of a community for the times in your life when there is a crisis. You just don't know how much that means until it happens to you.*
>
> *Lorraine W*

Sometimes tragedy can lead to positive outcomes. Lorraine found out that two of her friends had also lost children. Their support of her caused them to begin a parents' grief support group to help other people in the community. Group members offer empathetic listening, discuss coping skills, and offer mutual support in a small group atmosphere of confidentiality and understanding.

The advantage of living in a retirement community is that there are many informal support groups like this who meet on an ongoing basis. Most of these groups have been founded or initiated by people needing other people. They are coordinated by volunteers and provide information and support to people living in the community. The groups focus on helping people who are dealing with cancer, diabetes, visual challenges, Parkinson's disease, and stroke. Groups such as these provide a haven where you can learn about an illness and obtain reenforcement and help.

> *I have been involved with the Sunshine Club for eleven years. What we try to do is to cheer up residents who have been ill, hospitalized, or had an operation. We send get well cards and one of our members calls on the ill person to deliver "bundles from the heart" in the form of gift baskets, plants, or flowers. We obtain our funding by collecting aluminum cans and recycling them. Twelve men, who we call "Good Samaritans" collect the cans from the donation bins and take them to the recycle center two or three times a week. With the funds, we are able to provide our "bundles from the heart" and make donations to specified charities in the name of a resident who has passed away.*
>
> *Edie B*

In addition to these organized support groups, there are many informal social groups meeting in homes within the community where people have an opportunity to meet, share information and help one another.

> *I was invited by a friend to join a Red Hat ladies group in our community. I hadn't been a member of this kind of group before and hesitated joining. It seemed that the group did frivolous things and just went out to lunch and had a good time. I wasn't sure this would be a group for me. However, because several of my friends encouraged me, I joined. Shortly after, one of the members died of cancer. The group joined together and hosted the refreshments for a post-funeral brunch for the family and people who attended the funeral. I began to see how such a sisterhood was beneficial to members. Since then I've participated in providing dinners for ill members or for members whose husband was seriously ill. They pull together to help and this is way beyond the perception of a flighty ladies' group who are just interested in having fun.*
>
> *Betty B*

Whether you're in a retirement community or not, you'll need the support and comfort of friends at some time in your life. If you live in a town, city, or suburb, you need to locate what is available in the form of a support network. It can be through your church, synagogue, or mosque or through a community organization.

> *When I moved to a retirement community, I joined different clubs and groups within the community. It was really easy to meet people. Now that I just relocated to Sedona by myself and live in a mixed age neighborhood, I am finding new friends and support as I joined the local Synagogue.*

After looking through the newspapers to see what kinds of activities that are available, I will be attending workshops and classes with the expectation of meeting people with common interests. In addition, I'll join a book club and begin participating as soon as I finish unpacking.

Gail K

SUMMARY

Whether you live in a retirement community, spend time in two retirement locations, or move to a new area, friends can come from a variety of sources. It's a matter of going out, meeting them, and spending time and energy to know them. By taking some time to delineate how important friendships are to the both of you and the amount of time you want to spend with personal friendships and couple friendships can help to make for a smoother couple relationship and more rewarding personal life.

FRIENDSHIP TOOL KIT

Questions:

Each person should answer these questions separately. Then meet to discuss those questions that apply to both of you to determine what will work best for you.

1.   Think of your friends and acquaintances. Try to categorize them as best, close, casual, work or neighbor.

2.   How important are friend relationships in your life now? If you are not yet retired, do you see this changing in retirement? How might friends or a support system be important to you in later years?

3.   What is the maximum number of friends that you can comfortably give your time to? If you feel over socialized, how could you cut back? What are the signs that tell you that you are overextended? If you feel under socialized, do you want to expand your friendships? And if so, how?

4.   Is it important to you to have a best friend? Do you have a best friend? If you have best friends what does that do for you?

5.   When you feel discouraged and depressed whom do you turn to?

6. Do you and your spouse/partner have couple friends? Is this working out for both of you? Do you need to make any changes?

7. If you haven't yet, discuss how much time you each want to spend with personal friends? Couple friends? Do you mutually agree about the time you each spend on separate friends or couple friends?

CHAPTER 9 –
PAYING AT THE PUMP
Financial Issues and Changes

The earlier you start saving the more time your money has to grow.

— *U. S. Dept. of Labor*

CHALLENGE:

To develop and maintain the financial means to live out your dream retirement

If you don't pay at the pump you won't have the gasoline to run your car or drive where you want to go. The same holds true in retirement. If you don't have the financial means available, you won't be able to live out your planned retirement. If your present tendency is to live for today and spend your earnings accordingly, you may limit your options as to what you both can do in retirement.

You may have already assessed your retirement savings and if so, you're ahead of the game. Many organizations provide seminars that concentrate on the financial aspects of retiring. By attending one of these seminars, you propel the two of you much further along than people who have not done the research and learned about the financial issues in retirement. You are on the way to properly funding the kind of retirement you both dream of.

The intent and scope of this chapter is not to provide you with detailed financial advice. Instead it focuses on providing you with ideas about how retirees have planned ahead, how they are managing their finances, and how they are dealing with the financial changes they've encountered. You can observe what worked for them, what didn't work and how they are spending their money.

Planning and Saving Early On

Twenties: The ideal time to put a little money aside for retirement is when we're young. But most people in their 20s don't because they are often more focused on living their lives to the fullest. They are beginning their careers and are more interested in acquiring the accoutrements of the good life. In today's culture there is a tendency to live for today and let tomorrow take care of itself. Saving for retirement may be the furthest thing from young adults' minds.

> *When I first started teaching, I didn't care about what pensions were. I just didn't want them to take too much out of my check. Since then I have learned that you need to talk about saving early on and do some serious thinking about it. Don't leave it until last minute. We saw how important*

*it was to save by observing my parent's retirement. They
started saving early and were able to travel and enjoy their
retirement. A friend told me, "We want to do exactly what
your parents did. They are great models for us." I believe
it's important to save money early to take advantage of the
multiplier effect.*

Fred S

Thirties: Couples in their 30s are generally married or living together. They may be paying for a mortgage on a house or condominium, paying rent and/or raising a family, all of which take a large slice of their income. Saving money for retirement can also be difficult at this stage of life. However, saving even a little through a pension plan, a 401(K), or an Individual Retirement Account (IRA) will multiply over the years ahead.

*In 1978, I was 39, married and had two children. I began
working for a non-profit organization, which allowed me
to put money into an IRA as well as a pension fund. It
didn't seem like I contributed much into the program at the
time. I didn't even miss the money. Four years later when I
left, I had about $3,000 saved. In the years that followed
it just sat there and kept multiplying. In 2001 when I
took early retirement, the original small sum had grown to
approximately $20,000 and it is still growing. Today the
sum is closer to $30,000 and I should be able to draw on
it soon without penalty.*

Benita S

Forties: Couples this age tend to increase their combined income, but their expenses also multiply. A greater portion of their income is spent on family necessities. If you are a baby boomer who married later in life, you may have children in college and are paying a lot for tuition. You might have mortgage payments, furniture payments, and car payments. In addition, you may be responsible for caring for aging parents. These bills, along with rising living expenses, can gobble up a good portion of your net income, leaving little, if any, to save for retirement. If this is your situation, you are most likely operating in the "fast lane," trying to make ends meet and may not have the time to plan, nor the money to put towards retirement. That is why participating in company plans or starting your own (IRA) is so important.

Late Forties and Fifties: Depending on your forecasted retirement, at this point, you need to be saving for retirement in some appropriate pension plan. If a tax-sheltered savings plan like the 401(K) is available, sign up and save as much as you can. You can put up to $4,000 a year into an IRA and gain tax advantages. It isn't easy to save for retirement, but if you don't save anything, you will be left with little or nothing when you are in your 60s and 70s. You may find yourself working for an income and health insurance, versus working because you enjoy it or being retired.

> *When you plan well financially, you won't have a lot of surprises like we did with the loss of $40,000. By planning well you can handle a few bumps in the road. When you run up against a couple of big surprises in life and you don't have a good-sized nest egg, it causes problems for the rest of your retirement years. Believe me that's not a good thing!*
>
> *Pat E*

Pat and her husband feel locked into a retirement life that they didn't plan. They feel stuck because of their financial situation and don't see how they can make a change.

Saving may look difficult, but it's a matter of budgeting your money effectively. Budgeting money forces you to look at your income and expenses and make choices about your discretionary income. How you spend your discretionary income often relates to how you view and relate to money. Some people see money as a means to buy what they want or need, while others view the accumulation of money as representing security or filling an emotional need. You and your spouse may need to assess your emotional relationship with money in order to complete your financial plan for retirement. Question one in the Tool Box at the end of this chapter gives you an opportunity to reflect on your predisposition or reluctance to financially plan for your future.

You might be saying to yourself that saving for retirement is easier said than done. You are right. Financially, the early years of work and mid-life can be busy and difficult times. At times, it may seem impossible to save, but others have found a way and so can you.

> *I'm kind of glad that we are from the old school where we planned from the very start to be money conscious. We planned for our children's college and also saved to set aside money for retirement. That didn't give us an awful lot of money to live on when we were working. But you learn and you progress in your career, you get a little bit more money because life generally does get better. You need to just stay with it.*
>
> *Marge G*

When beginning retirement, the key thing is your financial picture. Are you in a condition to have a retirement? Can you accommodate yourself to your financial resources? I think that is the first thing that has to be answered. It should have been answered 20 years before. That is the key for what you are able to do.

John L

One way to think about saving for retirement might be to not think you are giving up something when you save, but to think of it as investing in your future. Six hundred dollars invested in your future can be worth far more in the years ahead than purchasing a nice-to-have $600 item that will most likely depreciate in value. Once you have made the commitment to put money aside, especially if you've had it taken out of your paycheck and directly deposited to your retirement account, you'll soon learn to live on the remaining amount. You'll forget that the money is "gone" and unavailable for spending. So it's really just a matter of making the initial decision to save, then letting the money go and forgetting about it.

As a couple the choice is yours to make. You can obtain financial advice, budget your money judiciously, and find a way to save something or not. Each couple has to find their own way of balancing "living for today" and "saving for tomorrow."

When you are working you have to live within your income and be able to set aside something for savings. I found it a challenge to see where we stood each year in relation to savings. We also found a way to invest in property, which we were able to sell to financially help us build our retirement house.

Bob G

One of the ways you can experience some benefit today while investing in the future is to build equity in your home. If you feel comfortable in investing in rental property, this too can provide you with additional ongoing income and future funds, especially if property values rise. Perhaps you or your spouse can become knowledgeable about real estate, which will provide you with greater insight into this kind of investment. If the real estate market is rising or already exceptionally high, you'll have to weigh the value of making a particular purchase. The best possible scenario is to buy as low as you can and sell when property rises.

The three guiding principles of real estate are "location, location, and location." If you see real estate investment as a viable way to save, become knowledgeable about property in areas beginning to grow and develop. While on a week's vacation stay in a rental near the water, my husband and I heard scuttlebutt about a marina being built in the area. So we checked it out. When we saw evidence of cranes on barges building the breakwater, we decided to grasp the opportunity to purchase a small house in the area. We were 30 years old, had two young children and house payments, but we scraped together $2,000 to put down on a small house in the vicinity of the proposed marina. We rented the house for ten years and then were able to sell the house for four times its original value. We put that profit into a four-plex apartment building in the same area. We saw this rental property investment as part of our retirement savings. Twenty years later we did a 1031 exchange on the apartment property and bought a small rental house on the water in the Northwest. After renting it out for a number of years we were able to renovate the house and now use it as a summer home. Our success could be attributed to timing and luck. But it also was due to acting on some basic knowledge of real estate values, taking advantage of a growing area and a willingness to take some risk.

Prepping for Retirement

The United States Department of Labor provides information on preparing for retirement (www.dol.gov/ebsa). Also, the American Association of Retired Persons (AARP) provides excellent material about financial planning for retirement (www.aarp.org). In addition, extensive articles and books written on financial planning for retirement are available to you. Get them. Read them. Discuss them together to get your thoughts and ideas on the table. With this information, you'll be able to determine where you are financially and what you may need to do.

If you aren't involved in a savings plan or 40I(K), I urge you to read the many excellent books on the market that give details about how to save and what you might need to do financially to have a comfortable retirement. Also, talk with a financial counselor about saving for your future.

As you approach the last ten to fifteen years before your forecasted retirement, consider taking these steps: First, sit down and discuss what you both want out of your joint retirement (Vision and Planning in Your Roadmap—chapter 12). Then, if you haven't already done so, estimate your future income from social security, pensions, real estate rents, and financial investments (Financial Planning in Your Roadmap—chapter 12). If one of you is retiring and the other is not, take that into consideration. Then proceed to develop your roadmap so you can determine when you can retire, where to retire to, and how much you will have to retire on. The sooner you seriously think through your planned retirement life style and assess both of your views of money, the more knowledgeable you will be to make better decisions.

> *It is an odd feeling when you worked your whole life to know that you won't be going out to make money again. While working, if the cost of living went up, you decided to work a little harder. I threaten to go out and get a job because there isn't that "free flowing money" coming in. The waterfall stopped but you get used to it over time.*
>
> *Judee W*

When you both are retired, the cruel fact is that you and your spouse are no longer earning money. Hopefully the money that you saved is earning dividends. You might need to experience a "change" in how you think about money. As Judee says, the waterfall has stopped and if you overspend this month, you can't make it up next month. It isn't replenished so easily. You can't afford to make choices that you can't financially live with.

> *Initially when you retire you're going to spend more because you'll want to do all the things that you didn't have time to do before. It's easy to run up those credit cards. I think that some people don't want to adjust their lifestyles when they retire. If you don't have solid investments that return a good capital and you haven't financially planned very well to begin with, your lifestyle will have to change. If you were buying a car every three years, you may not buy a car that*

often in retirement. Your attitude will also change towards buying that new car too. You will say, "Hey, why go out and buy another $30,000 car when I've got one here that's working fine." In addition, in retirement you have more free time so you probably will spend more because you start doing things to fill your time. You might go on a day trip up the coast or out to a tourist attraction and the next thing you know, you have spent $300.

Larry M

When you first retire you might continue to spend at the rate you did when you were working. If you buy a new home, move to a location, experience new endeavors, you may need furniture, a different wardrobe, or sports or hobby paraphernalia and that will cause you to spend as before. Eventually, however, you do come to the realization that you may have to change your thinking pattern from one of spending to one of conserving. Your attitude won't change with the snap of a finger. It may take some time for you to change your thought pattern to one of "tightening your belts."

Having inherited conservative values from our parents, my husband and I creatively utilized our furniture in our new retirement house rather than buying all new furniture. Since the house is smaller, we were able to consolidate furniture and put the extra furniture up for sale in a consignment store. We got enough money for it to help us partially pay for a new media center. Moving into a new home still required us to purchase appliances, window coverings, patio furniture, and landscaping. We didn't want to run through all our money in the early retirement years and decided to establish a general budget. The idea of going on a budget put

*me off at first because it reminded me of how constrained we
felt on a tight budget early in our marriage.*

Barbara B

Barbara overcame her initial repulsion to return to a budget and found that budgeting wasn't so limiting, but actually gave her sense of clarity, priorities, and values. Although budgeting may seem confining, it is really a tool for bringing more awareness and consciousness to one's spending.

As you determine the extent of your financial capability, the two of you may have to decide what is negotiable and what is not. What must you have in your lives? What can you live without?

*You really need to think about what your needs are in
retirement such as do you need as much clothing as you did
working? If you and your wife have two cars, you may
need to assess if you still need two cars in retirement. Each
couple has to look at what their needs are and assess if they
can really afford a lot of those things or not.*

Ralph S

Some people come to the realization that they need to conserve more quickly than others. They calculate what they can spend and chose accordingly. Others are smart enough to anticipate their new conservation status and begin to prepare for it.

*There are things you can do to help you as you begin retire-
ment if you think about your retirement needs in advance.
In my case, I sold my representative business to a younger
partner. As part of the buy out, I was given my company
car and my computer system. This helped us initially as we*

*didn't have to go right out and buy a second car or com-
puter. As a matter of fact, I am still driving the car eight
years later. It is a Volvo and I anticipate it can go another
120,000 miles if I want to keep it.*

Steve B

*Because both my wife and I had no company pensions, we
realized that we had to start saving small amounts 30 years
ago. Today we try to live off of our social security, plus taking funds out of our non-IRA savings. When I become 70
I can begin to draw on my IRA savings without penalty.
So far we have been doing pretty well. Like most everyone
we know, we lost some money in the 2002 stock market
decline, but we didn't get wiped out because we diversified
our investments.*

Stan B

One thing that is hard to absorb in retirement is risk. That's
why it is important to diversify your investments and invest
conservatively when you are retired. There are books and articles
that can educate you on a mix of investments and how to balance
stocks and bonds, etc. Be sure to check these out. Take the
positive step of looking at the AARP website for information if
you haven't already done so.

Managing Your Money in Retirement

Both you and your mate may have spent a lifetime earning,
budgeting, and saving for the time you can enjoy your retirement
lives. Unfortunately you aren't finished thinking about money
quite yet. When you retire you have to work together to manage
the money efficiently so that it lasts you during your lifetimes.

Especially now you need to practice financial skills and make use of financial guidance.

> *Financial skills are important to have in retirement and we don't always learn them in school. That is why I believe AARP is a key education tool. They use their magazine to teach people and help them understand what they need to do. Good financial management is contrary to one's emotional wants. We all wish we were unlimited resource kings. One rule in investment management is that you never spend capital because that generates future income. That means, of course, that you wind up leaving everything you have to your kids.*
>
> *Patrick S*

> *You have to have mathematical skills to know what you are living on. You need to be able to know how much is coming in and going out. Manage your cash flow. You've got to know thrift. You don't hear this word used much these days. Thrift to me is really a big thing—to live within your means and make it good. Don't expect the moon. Don't expect riches when you retire. Be satisfied with what you have.*
>
> *Ruth B*

Managing your cash flow is an important principle of business and it can be important in managing your finances in retirement. For example, you might have a cash flow issue if your charge account bill is due on the 13th of the month, but your social security check is deposited on the 14th of the month. Since paying on time is important, especially with 18 percent penalties or more each month, you'll need to know what amount of money to maintain in a non-interest earning checking account or a low interest money market account to cover these kinds of charges. It's amazing how quickly billing due dates roll around each month. Another way to conserve in retirement is to pay off your credit cards monthly. You'll be amazed how much you can save when you analyze your spending patterns.

In retirement we still have a budget and spread sheet and we enter all the checks on it. It isn't as tight as it was when we were younger. Unless you are really mega wealthy, all of us have to say to ourselves, that if we buy this new car this year, we won't be able to go on a vacation. There are always trade-offs. You can't just have everything you want all the time. That wouldn't be so great anyway. It probably wouldn't be as much fun as you thought it would be. In retirement, you still keep your values and your ideas about spending money. I see how some young people spend their money and I wonder how they are ever going to retire.

Marge G

One thing is I never felt comfortable with finances in the sense of investments. I came out okay financially, but a lot of it was luck. I was in a stable work environment and that was a big help because working for a long time with a good company gave me a retirement benefit. Now that I am retired, I am putting in more effort with regard to investments and am doing a decent job at it. Another awakening is that because I am on a fixed income, I am more concerned about the investments.

Bob G

The reward for paying attention to money matters is a greater sense of power and control over your own finances, even if you're not rolling in dough.

Spending Your Money

How you spend your savings in retirement is probably as important as saving it in the first place. Many retirees have said that when you first retire and move to a new home or community there are a lot of initial expenses. There appears to be a "financial honeymoon period" in retirement where the couple tends to spend as if they were still earning. After a period of time, about eighteen months to two years, a realization sets in that they are on a fixed income and may need to seriously budget their funds.

> *When we were first married, we were on a budget and now we feel we are sort of in the same situation. By budgeting, we at least are more careful with money and keep track of where we spend it.*
>
> *Bobbie C*

Understanding how much money you will have to spend in retirement to purchase a home and be able to live the lifestyle you plan for is critical to your satisfaction and happiness.

> *Some people move to a nice retirement community and use every bit of their resources to buy a house and then are strapped to do anything once they are retired. They worry about money and it takes a lot of the joy out of your life. I think some people make a big mistake to try to get as much*

as they can and then extend themselves so much that they can't enjoy the daily things in life. They can't afford to throw a party or to travel. They could move somewhere that is less expensive and less cushy and start a social life that they would enjoy.

Marge G

It is pretty easy to fall into the habit of initially overspending in retirement because you may not know what your cap is on spending. If you move to a new community you may want to attend all the events, concerts, dances, dinners, etc. Your goal might be to meet and make new friends. So, you might extend yourself and spend more than you planned to attend pricey events.

We found that we needed to pick and choose the social events we wanted to go to and could afford. It is easy to go to the wine tasting group dinner one week at $190 per couple, join the gourmet restaurant group for $210 on another week, and then go to dinner and attend a theatre perfor-mance, which may cost $350 on the fourth week. Before we knew it we blew over $750 in one month just on these events, let alone just going out for a night at the movies.

Len M

Len began to realize that doing all the things they've enjoyed in their work years loom as large expenditures for a month in retirement. There is nothing wrong with continuing activities that give you pleasure as long as you can afford it. When you watch your hard earned money "go out the door" faster than it came in, you may come to the same realization Len did, that it might be wise to monitor your expenses.

Another point made in some of my interviews was the importance of associating with a group of friends at about the same economic level you are because you'll be able to do things with them that you can afford to do. Often a couple's resources dictate what they can do and how much they can spend. You and your spouse need to find your own comfortable level of spending and watch out for the "keeping up with the Joneses" mentality.

Spending can be an area of conflict in a marriage or partnership. If you have different views about spending and conserving, you probably have had numerous discussions during your marriage about one partner's "overspending" and the other's "miserly ways." Hopefully, you have come to terms on this subject. If you haven't, your differences can come back to haunt you in retirement. This is a time that you need to function together to maximize your retirement income to achieve the best result for both of you. Use the questions in the Tool Kit at the end of this chapter to help you clarify each of your views and dialogue about your results.

For those retirees who either plan on having two homes, or those who already have them, there is no getting around it—you are spending more to live this lifestyle. Maintaining two homes is a cost factor you have to be able to afford. Even if you are thrifty and shut off the water and turn down the heat in the winter, you will still have ongoing expenses of upkeep, gardening, security, and utilities. If you bought or plan to buy a second home, attempt to forecast the possible expenses so you have an idea of what the costs will be. You can then decide if you can afford this level of lifestyle in retirement.

If you own two homes you have to carry a lot of overhead. We have been fortunate that the two houses in which we live six months a year have both gone up in value, because the last six years were boom years in the housing market. However, this increase is on paper. We try to keep track of real expenses like house insurances on two homes, homeowner fees, taxes, as well as fixed expenses for upkeep, etc. These expenses are ongoing and generally out of our control. Most of our expenses are of this kind. We don't do a lot of discretionary spending. We don't go abroad on vacation like some of our friends. We go from house to house as both places are vacation destinations. However, we do take small trips when we are in each locale.

Bob G

Spending on Charity

Some couples are financially able to donate to specific causes. You may have been making donations right along during your work years, but in retirement, you begin to look at giving with "new eyes."

During our work years, we were able to contribute to various community organizations, charities, and national fundraising programs. Now that we are retired, we need to be more selective about financial donations. Over the years we have watched illnesses take many of our older family members. We are beginning to think about how these diseases might affect our progeny, if substantial progress isn't made in dealing with them. So, we've decided to earmark our donations to fund research in such diseases as stroke, heart disease and Alzheimer's disease. We don't

*expect any cures during our lifetime. We want to help
future generations.*

Barbara C

You are now a couple on a fixed income and will most
likely be borrowing from savings to give to others. During your
working years you may have contributed to specific charities or
religious organizations. If you wish to continue donating, review
your financial plans with a financial counselor to be sure your
monies will cover your forecasted needs. You will then be able to
identify what discretionary funds you have for gifts to family or
donating to charities.

Spending on Insurance and Medical

Insurance and medical benefits aren't free in retirement. It's
easy to forget that, especially if you've spent years working for
an employer who covered or supplemented your health insurance
and other benefits.

> *We are now on a fixed retirement income from our teach-
> ing careers and are lucky to have medical, dental, and vision
> coverage. Most people don't get these benefits. They rely on
> Medicare to kick in when they are 65 or whatever. Unless
> you retire close to that age, you won't have that coverage. I
> would have had ten years without Medicare coverage by
> the time I would be eligible for it. If I didn't have medical
> insurance, we would have been a deep trouble.*
>
>
>
> *Jo S*
>
>
>
> *Over the years our medical expenses ran approximately
> 40 to 60 percent of our taxable deductibles, even though*

we qualify for Medicare. The fees for Medicare are taken out of our social security check. I believe supplemental health insurance is a must. You have to cover for catastrophic illness. However, health insurance costs seem to go up every year and now exceeds $6,000 per year in our case, which is a big chunk out our yearly budget. Without it we would have been greatly impacted financially a few years ago when I had to have heart bypass surgery. So it is worth having, but we still have to pay out-of-pocket for medications and expensive dental work.

Stephen S

In planning retirement I think it is critical for retirees to understand they need to have long-term health insurance. We would all like to believe that our children will take care of us, but you don't know if they will be in a financial position to do so. Most of our parents didn't have long term insurance and many of us are at an age group that may have to take care of them now.

Joann S

In retirement, health insurance, long term care insurance, and medical costs can take a larger amount of your retirement income and savings. Knowing this may give you incentive to take care of your health in retirement.

His/Her/Their Finances

Your financial roles in marriage may have been established and operating for a long time. In retirement you may see no reason to change, but if you feel a change might be needed, this is a good time to negotiate and take on new responsibilities.

> *I have always paid all the bills since we were first married. Recently I turned over a portion of my bill-paying role to my husband because of taking on additional commitments and lack of available time. Now I just handle the credit account statements. Sharing a good portion of the job has been very liberating.*
>
> *Bonnie B*

Financial roles may be delegated or chosen according to who has the interest in money management, financial experience, and time available to handle financial chores. How the two of you decide to manage your money would best be determined by a cooperative decision between you.

In our situation, my husband has an interest in investments and has taken the lead in bringing up new investment areas and steering our financial ship. However, he and I have our own funds, which we have the discretion to invest or use as each of us sees fit. I believe some of our way of managing money as a couple comes from our experience as entrepreneurs with our own small firms. We both have had a control in how money was used in our businesses. Surprisingly we haven't had differences of opinion on money management since we retired, probably because we have similar views on spending, saving, and investing. We both tend to be somewhat cautious and do our homework.

If you are not the spouse who handles the investments and makes financial decisions, you need to learn now. Some women have said that they didn't have the foggiest idea about the couple's financial matters. When their husbands died, they had to learn all about investing from scratch. They never thought they needed to know about their finances nor how to fix things in the house.

> *Prior to retiring I always had a separate account to handle house and family expenses. Since I am not working very much now, we put a set amount from the general fund into my separate account. I know how much is there and I can blow it all the first week if I want, or I can hoard a bit of it for the next month. I have a choice to spend it or not and it is nice to have money without having to ask for it. I don't spend money foolishly. I usually pay for things like decorating items, wallpaper, patio furniture, or personal items from my account.*
>
> *April P*

April and her husband have set up a separate account she can access without having to request spending money. If the husband was the one who handled the money in the household, a number of women have told me that they felt belittled by having to ask their husband for money in retirement. They felt like they were children asking for their allowance. This may not seem like it could be a sore point in retirement, but discussing who has what responsibility and control over financial matters would best be sorted out before problems arise.

> *I told my husband that since his mother had her own social security checking account that I wanted my own social security money to do with as I pleased. I think I've started*

> *a brouhaha for several couples because the other women in our community now want control of their social security checks. During Christmas I was extravagant with my own money and asked my husband for a thousand dollars. He said, "What?" My friends told me that I have just as much right to the money and could take it out myself. I just felt that I couldn't do it without asking. However, he made such a big fuss, he made me angry. Give me a break.*
>
> Joan T

As the women who are a product of the women's movement retire, they most likely will have different expectations than previous generations as to financial control. They may want to have greater participation in investment and money management in retirement and should at least be informed about investments and how decisions are made in the event they may have to handle finances in their future.

Joining Together Later in Life

Most couples don't plan on having to establish a new personal relationship in their retirement years. But divorces do occur and spouses do die. People remarry. Some couples find it financially advantageous to live together or to keep their separate abodes. They may maintain their single status because of possibly jeopardizing their financial benefits. When you marry in retirement, you haven't planned to retire together, nor have you planned your finances together. With a new, romantic relationship going on you aren't likely to be thinking about something pragmatic such as financial planning.

I think it is tough for couples coming into a relationship in retirement or even when they are in their 40s or 50s. If they live in a community property state and divorce, the partner will get one-half of everything, including your planned retirement funds. When you remarry later in life, you will not have planned your finances for retirement together. You need to find a way to cope with this.

Jo S

When Jo and her husband married in their 50s, they needed to sort out and negotiate their plans for their planned retirements. They had to sit down and figure out how to handle all of the issues in advance of retiring.

Both my husband and I have been married before, so we talked about how we were going to handle our finances. He is retired and I'm not yet retired. We decided to have a mutual community account under both our names to handle household expenses and monthly bills. Then we each have separate checking accounts. My paycheck goes right into my own account and I pay for some groceries and personal purchases from that account. He also buys groceries, plus odds and ends from his account. Since we both have children and grandchildren from a previous marriage we decided that his investments, which he earned before we were married, should go to his children and mine will go to my children. If something happens to one of us, the other will get the house. Down the road when it is sold, the proceeds would be parceled out to all of the children.

Diane B

It was wise for Diane and her husband to set up clear financial guidelines that they can follow. She said that she felt it was important to make these kinds of financial arrangements because she knew of friends who had been burned by not protecting themselves in advance. If you have specific guidelines as to how money is to be distributed, you might want to see a lawyer and be sure your decisions are in writing. Determining how you want to handle your financial savings and investments can be very important and can eliminate difficulties in the event of something happening to one or the other partner. There are all kinds of situations that occur that you don't plan for in your retirement years. That's why it can be important to consider back-up plans.

Back-up funding

One of the big concerns for many retirees is having enough money to see them through their lives. Will they have sufficient funds and insurance to cover possible major expenditures? There is no way to protect against all possible problems. You can try to protect yourself, but there is no way to take all possible events into consideration.

> *We have a motor home in addition to our home and I feel that is our extravagance. So if we get financially strapped, we have a way to pull back. We knew that we could take early retirement without having our house paid for. So we planned to make payments in retirement. I think you have to have a back-up plan. I'm not tied to things, except our artwork, which I enjoy. If things turned against us financially, we could sell the artwork and the house and move*

into a fifth-wheel trailer in a trailer park. We could live more cheaply and still travel, have friends and be part of a community. I think we could be perfectly happy and this gives me a sense of comfort.

Liela S

If we ever get into financially difficult times, my wife and I still retain some rental property we could sell. Right now it gives us a little additional income each month. This way we would still be able to keep our retirement house. The rental provides us with another asset to fall back on before we would need to deplete all of our savings.

Sal B

It is nice to have the security of a back up plan to turn to if your financial picture changes, such as when the stocks went down in 2002. If you have two homes, you can sell one. If you have two cars, you can drop back down to one.

Linda R

Family Finances

Many of today's retirees jokingly talk about spending their children's inheritance. Although they may set aside some money for children or grandchildren, they still plan to spend their savings to lead the life they want in retirement.

One thing June and I have discussed and have always agreed on is that we are not going to save a great big nest egg for our heritage for the kids, because they are all taken care of and they are successful. They can manage on their own.

Duane L

This appeared to be the philosophy of a number of couples who were in their 50s, 60s, and 70s. It reflects a personal achievement philosophy. If I earned it, I have the right to spend it as I choose. This attitude also demonstrates that retirees believe younger generations should earn their own way in life.

When retired parents do want to provide for their children or grandchildren, they often set up a trust account for them.

> *My second husband has set up a trust for his adult girls who have a long-term illness. His sister will administer the trust when he dies. I have also set up a trust for my children. So we feel confident that things will work out well because we have taken both families into account.*
>
> *Deryl C*

If you are considering providing for children or grandchildren during your lifetime, you need to research the best ways of doing this. Many retirees provide gifts to their children or grandchildren as a way of gifting them with some of what would be a future inheritance. The Internal Revenue Service allows you to give a gift of $10,000 a year to one person. If you are able and decide to do this, you might want to provide a caveat that some of the money be saved for a specific purpose such as education, or saving towards their retirement.

If you find yourselves in a situation where you have to care for your parents, you need to research various options for their care, then talk to a financial counselor as to ways of protecting their financial wealth.

> *You have to assess what you can do for your parents and start doing it. Once something happens to your parent like*

falling down, he or she may never come back from the nurs-ing home. Most states have programs that cover nursing home costs after the person has expired all of their assets. If there is a spouse living in the home, they are not thrown out, but the house will go to the state after he or she passes on.

Larry M

The Impact of Change

As we discussed in the chapter I, change is inevitable, ongoing and unstoppable. Events will happen. The stock market decline in 2002-03 affected many investors. None were harder hit than retirees who lost much of their retirement portfolios. Many weren't able to go back into the work place and recoup what they lost. You may think that this kind of event is in the past, but it can happen again.

In the stock market decline many retirees lost as much as half of their retirement portfolios. This was money that they counted on to provide them with the ways and means to have a positive retirement. The retirees I spoke with who had been affected by the stock market incident told me that they learned from it, dealt with their losses, rebounded or found a way to live with the lower income.

My husband is a great planner and had these computer-ized models of what our retirement was to be like. We both retired early while in our 50s and we planned to take four major international trips per year. Every three months we were going to go somewhere and we easily had enough money to do it. We thought of taking a world cruise or live in other countries for periods of time. Then the stock market crash happened which was unplanned and all of our dreams for that kind of travel just vanished. Fortunately, we had traveled a lot before retiring. Since our children were grown up, we just wanted to travel more and be footloose and fancy-free. We have since gone back to work and plan to continue our travels in the future.

Lorraine W

On one of our trips to the northwest, we fell in love with the beauty of the San Juan Islands in Washington and bought a condo as a second home. At the time we made the decision we had the discretionary money to purchase it as a summer home. However, after our net worth was cut in half when the stock market fell a number of years ago, we not only had to sell the condominium but we had to make major changes in our lives. I began to teach elementary school and my wife found a job as a part-time nurse. We decided to sell our California home at a profit and move to Texas where housing costs are a lot lower. Every dark cloud has a silver lining. By doing this we will have a chunk of money so we can continue to have a nice retirement life.

Ken W

Some people didn't lose as much money in the stock market downturn as others because they diversified their investments. They balanced their investments between stocks and bonds and this helped them to survive the downturn in 2002.

Patrick S

Something will always happen. If it's not the stock market, it's something else. Your children may have money trouble and need your assistance. Parents or grandchildren may become seriously ill or have an accident. Pension funds are lost. Investments lose money. Couples divorce and have to split their retirement nest egg.

> *I had retirement money vested with one former employer but in the 1980s our retirement money was involved in a junk bond scandal. I still get letters from whoever is trying to recoup the money. At one point they were going to give us a payout of ten cents on the dollar. I've reconciled myself to the idea that it will be only a few thousand dollars when the time ever comes.*
>
> *April P*

April believed that the people who were retiring at the time of the financial loss really had almost nothing of what they expected to receive. Most likely you've read about similar experiences of lost pension savings.

> *A couple shouldn't have too much money in speculative stock. You need to invest in more secure resources. It's true that since you won't be working, you may live a less costly life style, but you will still need 70 percent of what your income was when you were working.*
> *I believe that when you retire you should have all your resources in place. Plan for the long run. Make your investment decisions based on what you want for your retirement.*
>
> *Judith A*

> *My husband didn't get a job after he retired from the service so we lived on his retirement income. We always lived to*

*the hilt. We joined the country club and played golf. We had
a boat and went any place we wanted to go. Although we
never really had as much money as we wanted, we always
did well on what we had. We had practically no savings. I
kept telling my husband we needed to save more. During
our marriage he took care of the bills. I never knew anything
about what was financially going on with us. After retiring
here I got into stocks and joined an investment club. I would
use the money from my social security check as well as well
as some money my husband put in. That is the only way
we could ever save. Now that we are divorcing, he wants
half of the stock. We had a good life together. Now that we
are apart, it's not going to be that way.*

Jo G

Separating or divorcing as an older adult can be financially
overwhelming and emotionally devastating. Plans for retirement
are turned topsy-turvy. You go back to square one in order
to revise your life plan and how to finance it. It takes time to
recover and to reassess where you are and what you can do.
Because of the emotional turmoil that can accompany this
experience, it is important to have good legal and financial
advice.

*When I divorced I had to be concerned about how I would
financially fend for myself. So in terms of resources, you
have to develop a system that will protect you and lead you
in the right way so that you come out in a win/win situation. I surrounded myself with professionals. One of the
smart things I did within two days of my husband leaving
was that I hired a lawyer.*

Gail K

Reaping the Rewards

If you do handle the financial end of retirement correctly and have the money for the kind of life you want to live, you reap the rewards of a lifetime of saving.

I would have to say that our plans for retirement have worked out about the way we planned and we think we have been very successful. These have been good years and they continue—thanks a lot to John knowing so much about financial issues. He and our broker have done very well, so that we can have a nice home in a nice community. I grew up in a very simple home in a small town. Everyone once in a while I just look around and say wow!

Shirley L

It is an eye opener for me that this kind of pleasant retirement lifestyle can exist, if you plan for it. You really have to be set up to do it. You can't just stop working and then wonder "Where am I going to find the money to do this?" You have to have had to put away some acorns for the winter to be able to live this way. If you have saved, one of the surprises is that when you stop working, money comes to you from different sources. You get your retirement pension funds and you get your social security and you didn't even plan on that. You knew there was social security money out there somewhere, but that is not what you count on for your retirement. You look at your investments for retirement. When my husband was about to retire, he did an analysis of his income and found that he would make just as much not working as he did working. So why work?

Marge G

Many couples expressed how lucky they were to be able to do what they planned in their retirement years. But it is more than luck. It takes positive financial planning as well as proactive life planning.

SUMMARY

Financially planning for retirement can appear to be a difficult and insurmountable task to the uninitiated. However, people who have done their homework are successful and you can be too. The whole point is to start early enough. Today there are all kinds of resources out there to help you. Not only retirement counselors, seminars and workshops, but websites like the AARP and the United States Department of Labor provide you with "how to" information. These sites cover everything from calculating your retirement date to managing your money and investments. You can't start too early to educate yourselves in this area of retirement.

FINANCIAL TOOL KIT

Questions:

Answer these questions individually and then sit down together and dialogue about your answers. Discuss your views on money and what your financial plan will look like.

1. Have you developed a pre-retirement financial plan? What is holding you back from developing one? If you already have a plan and have retired, review your plan in relation to information and guidelines from the financial sources mentioned above. See if you want to make any changes or adjustments.

2. Do you think you will have to change your lifestyle in retirement? If so how?

3. Are you using a budget now? If you do have to live within a budget, how do you each feel about this? What are some actions you and your mate might need to take to better budget your money?

4. What are some forecasted expenses you see for your initial "honeymoon period" of retirement? How long do you think this will last?

5. What roles do you each play in relation to financially managing your money? Do you see these changing or remaining the same in retirement?

6. Do you have back-up financial income or investments you can count on in time of loss or financial difficulties?

7. How much are you now spending on: Benefits? Donations? Children? Grandchildren? Parents? Extended Family? Do you see this changing and if so, how?

8. Are you planning to leave a "nest egg" for family or are you of the mind to utilize your money for the retirement life you both want?

CHAPTER 10 –
DOWN THE ROAD
Changes in Later Years

*Aging is not lost youth but a new stage of opportunity
and strength.*

— *Betty Friedan*

CHALLENGE:

To do the right things and make the best decisions that will help you grow old gracefully and enjoy each stage of life.

Increased longevity, the result of advanced health initiatives, has contributed to people living longer and having more productive lives. However, each of us continues to grow older day by day and there may come a time when we may need to adjust some aspects of our retirement lives and change to a slower lane. This chapter focuses on how you can make the most of the changes that occur in later years so that you can be more prepared to handle what's in store "down the road."

> *In the first half of our lives we were always climbing up the mountain. Now in retirement I think we are beginning to slide down the other side.*
>
> Lorraine W

Sliding down the mountain is what most likely frightens us as we get older. When some people reach their 60s and early 70s, they try to turn back their odometers. They try to look younger, feel younger and act younger than they are. Others appear to be more comfortable with aging and accept it as part of life. No matter what age you are, or how you respond to growing older, each age can be unique if you can appreciate it for what it is.

Although old is a relative term depending upon your own age, most retired people who I've talked to don't think of themselves as old. Retirees, especially pre-boomers, who today are in their late 60s and 70s, may not feel old or act old. They see themselves as "mature adults" who are leading healthy, active, and busy lives doing the things they enjoy. They don't want to be stigmatized by being thrown into an "old" category. However, as we age, our health may start to diminish and we may begin to feel the years "catching up to us." Aging is such a gradual process, that you may not even feel you've passed on from "mature adult" (someone in their 50s, 60s, and early 70s) to what I call "elder adult" (someone in their late 70s, 80s, and older). Rather than the terms "aged" or "old," I've used "mature adult" and "elder adult" to describe people of retirement age because I think these terms show respect for the knowledge, wisdom and growth a person has achieved over a lifetime. This chapter focuses on the issues facing mature adults as they move into the elder status. As in other sections of this book, we'll look at changes in our later years through the lens of activities, quality of life, health, couple relationships, family, friendship, and finances.

Activities

Aging forces us to be more conscious of time. Time appears to fly. Days fly by. Months fly by. Years fly by. If you are in the mature adult or elder stage of life, you might tend to think about the number of years you have left and what you still wish to do with those years. Some of you may have places you still want to see in the world. Others may identify relationships they want to nurture, books they want to read, or experiences they still want to have. At this stage, you may look back at your life and not only wonder where the time went, but wonder what you have to show for that time. If so, this can be a good point to stop and look at your activities and take an assessment of what is important to you and to your life partner.

In her book, *Another Country*, Mary Pipher talks about developing a mnemonic device that helps her make good decisions about the time she spends on activities. Pipher identified five things in her life that she felt she needed to have—respect, relationships, results, relaxation, and realization. If any of the activities or experiences that came her way didn't meet one of these criteria, she didn't spend time on them. This concept provided an epiphany for me a number of years ago as I began to think about my retirement life and was searching for some meaning. Did I have a need to be respected by my spouse, family, and friends? What result was I expecting from projects or activities I was involved in? And, although I valued my relationship with my husband and friends, I found that I needed some self-realization time alone to replenish and reinvigorate myself. You may also want to identify what's important in your life. Do you value these five qualities or can you think of others that are important to you? There is no hierarchy to my need for these things, but being able to identify what is important has helped me to better focus my energy and time where it counts. If you choose to use this concept in your life, it can help you to see how your activities support your personal objectives. You'll find yourself identifying and maintaining some activities that support your identified objective needs, while eliminating other activities that don't add to what you value. Your important objectives may differ from your spouse's because they're based on your personal values, relationships and interests.

If you've been involved in a lot of activities in your mature years of retirement, as you move into your elder years, you might find it more difficult to continue some of the same activities. You may need to search out new ones that are more in line with your evolving abilities. My mother-in-law, who has become less physically mobile in her elder years, became an avid reader. When she couldn't sleep she would read. She not only read books, she read the newspaper and news magazines, which helped her keep up on world affairs and made her an interesting conversationalist. Many elders find reading helps to maintain their mental acuity. According to a study conducted by Dr. Rane-Szostak and Dr. Hertj, elders with financial or physical limitations who read for pleasure, were less lonely than those who didn't read.

One activity that you may already enjoy is using the computer. Many retired men and women spend a large amount of time on their computers checking on the financial condition of their investments, reading news articles, staying in touch with friends, doing research or playing games.

I have a friend whose wife is an invalid and he has to stay pretty close to home. He expands his world by spending time on the computer monitoring the financial market, reading various newspapers, and keeping in touch with friends.

Steve B

Computers and the Internet have opened up the entire world to people who are home bound or have limited mobility. In the years ahead, I anticipate that involvement with computers will continue to grow exponentially, especially with a large aging boomer population in the United States.

In elder adulthood, loss of physical and mental ability not only can reduce activities, but it can also mean a loss of independence. If you always have driven where and when you wanted to go, and the time comes that you no longer can drive yourself, you most likely will feel dispossessed and possibly depressed.

Both of my wife's sisters had to give up their cars and it was a gut wrenching feeling for them. They now have to take community vans where they want to go. They now don't have the freedom to come and go as they please.

John L

Driving is more than just the ability to get in the car and go—it most likely has provided you with a sense of independence and control. Driving means you are functioning as a capable adult. Losing this privilege tends to strip you of your power and freedom of choice. It is a very difficult pill to swallow at any age. I believe that's why so many elders maintain driving as long as they possibly can. I know of several elder women who held on to their cars after they moved into an assisted living residence, even though they rarely drove them.

Quality of Life Issues – Destination

In your younger years the size of your home may have increased over time. Now in your later years, you're most likely moving down to smaller and more manageable living quarters. Life continues to be a progression of changes. If you haven't downsized to a smaller house or condo in your mature adult years, you may do it when you become an elder. Maintaining a large house or the inability to go up and down stairs can influence a decision to move. Since a couple's home is an important part of their life together, this can be one of the difficult aspects associated with downsizing. Moving during your elder years from a family home can be a daunting task. But it can be made more manageable with the help of professionals like Senior Transitions NW, who specialize in helping elders explore later life moves. Not only can you get help with weighing the options of a move, you can get assistance in sorting and organizing your belongings, plus all the details in arranging and coordinating your move. Perhaps caring professionals or family can help you through the transition process.

Many retirees select to go into an independent living situation either in a retirement community, senior condominium, apartment development, or continuing care retirement situation (CCRC). Independent living situations provide residents the greatest versatility and freedom in their later years because they reduce house maintenance, provide security in a seniors-only environment, and provide activities and opportunities to meet people of like interests and economic status. With independent living you maintain your own residence and retirement lifestyle. If you need the help of custodial or medical care, you'll need to bring in these services or move to where the services are provided. The continuing care retirement community option (CCRC) permits retirees to "age in place" because it provides flexible accommodations to meet the elder's changing needs over his or her lifetime. If you select a continuous care facility, you are assured that your health and housing needs will be met as they change over time. However, (CCRC) can be your most expensive long-term-care option because it has a buy-in, or entrance, fee ranging from $20,000 to $400,000 and requires a monthly maintenance fee ranging from $400 to $2,500.

Whether you live in your family home, or in a home or condominium in a retirement community you may find that at some point you or your spouse can no longer be totally self-sufficient. It can be difficult to decide when to move to an assisted living residence, especially if your partner might need assistance and you don't. In this case, hiring additional help in your present home might be the best answer. If you or your spouse can carry on the activities and duties with some help while living in your home, this provides you another alternative for consideration. However, when and if both of you get to a stage that you can't operate in your own home, it might be time to move to an assisted living residence.

> *We've been able to function just fine so far, but I don't know where we will go down the road. Many of our friends have transitioned to one of the country club assisted living places and this is most likely what we will do at some point.*
>
> *Joan T*

Today, many assisted living residences are similar to resorts, having cottages with kitchens and small private apartments with senior designed bathrooms. Several of the assisted living facilities I visited had a number of cottages where couples could reside, in addition to apartments for singles. Although moving from your home can be a sad time, it's not the end of the world. Remember, change means letting go of the known, transitioning through a neutral zone to another way of life. What can help ease the pain of leaving your home is some sort of farewell ritual. Perhaps holding a "goodbye party" for friends and neighbors can help you in your transition. Friends or family could perhaps host a little house-warming party at your new residence. Some people have even had their new residence blessed following the Christian, Jewish, or Buddhist custom.

Generally, assisted living residences offer meals, light housekeeping, laundry, and personal assistance with some daily living activities, including transportation.

> *When it became hard for my mother to cook and shop, she moved to a very nice assisted living apartment in a two-story facility where she received her meals and assistance. Although she was still mobile, she didn't like having to ride the elevator every time she wanted to go out or down for her meals, so she moved to another assisted living residence, which is all on one floor. My mother is now 95, still mentally alert and gets around by riding a small scooter. She still laments not being able to cook for herself, but she has good care in pleasant surroundings.*
>
> *Steve B*

Although assisted living facilities can be pleasant and comfortable places to live, elders may still feel the loss of their home and their daily pattern of life. Steve's mother missed her own Italian cooking. However, there came a time for her when cooking was not only difficult, but dangerous. Initially, you may feel resentment at having to move into an assisted living environment and see it as a loss of self-sufficiency. In some ways it is, but you can also view it as gaining assistance, support and new friends in a new environment. If you have any concerns, talk them over with your family and the assisted living director. Some residences allow you to stay for a trial week in a furnished apartment. Often when you become settled in your new apartment, begin to meet people, make friends and get involved in some of the activities, you begin to see attributes of the new way of life. If, however, you continue to feel sad and depressed, don't just sit there; seek help from a psychologist, your doctor, or your family. Restarting your life in a new place can be an upsetting change, especially if you have recently lost your life partner. At the same time, a change of scene can help you to begin to have new experiences and build new memories in a new environment, while maintaining the old memories in your mind and heart.

One area of concern for families is when one or both elders become increasingly frail and their needs exceed the level of care provided in an assisted living residence. If you or your spouse has a heart attack or stroke, you might be incapacitated temporarily or perhaps permanently and need nursing care. You would then be moved to a skilled nursing facility. Some assisted living facilities are connected or associated with a skilled nursing facility. A manager of one residence said that if residents had medical problems, they could be moved to their skilled nursing facility until recovery and then they could move back into their apartment. If a couple were living in an assisted living residence adjacent or incorporated with a nursing facility, it would be much easier for one spouse to visit the other if they are located close by. This is also a benefit for people living in continuing care retirement communities because it encompasses not only housing for independent living, but assisted living and nursing home accommodations as well.

Sometimes elders experience a gradual erosion of either mental or physical ability. In these cases, it can be difficult to determine just when they should transfer to appropriate facilities for their care. If you become terminally ill, you may need to be in a hospital, nursing home, or be taken care of at home with the assistance of hospice nurses. It isn't easy to talk about later elder years and some of you may not even want to think about this aspect of life. But, if you want some modicum of control over your destiny, you might want to lay out some general plans as to what you want for yourselves.

Health Issues

Through the miracle of modern medicine, mature adults and elders can continue to do more in their later years than ever before due to knee and hip replacements, heart operations, and new medications for a variety of ailments. Today's retirees who are in their 60s, 70s, and 80s are more active and feel better than previous generations of retirees.

> *I am 81 and I have something going every day. I joined a water aerobics class and go on Monday and Wednesday.*

I walk two miles and do floor exercises for ten minutes every morning. I also do tai chi to a senior five-minute tape after I watch a soap opera. My 83-year-old partner and I go ballroom dancing on Tuesday, Thursday, and Saturday nights. I even gave him tango lessons for his birthday one year.

Ruth B

I met Ruth and her partner, AJ, on a travel tour of South America. I was drawn to Ruth because she exuded such a positive and energetic attitude towards life. She and AJ are two of the resilient elders who carry on in spite of problems. They know how to keep busy and focus on their interests. They don't let their aches and pains get them down. As you progress into being an elder adult it will help if you don't let your frustrations get the better of you and gradually begin to accept your limitations. When you move into a slower lane and have reasonable expectations, you won't become as frustrated and disappointed with what you can do or can't do. What you don't need as you age is more stress in your life.

Even though we experience gains and losses in every stage of life, we may feel that as we age in our elder years there are more losses and fewer gains. In the area of physical health, changes do occur and illnesses do happen to us. In our mature adult years we most likely are able to cope with the illnesses or accidents that occur, unless they are serious and debilitating. But in our elder years experiencing a dramatic physical decline can be a frightening thing. We see that our bodies are breaking down. No matter what we do, we can't revitalize this body that has carried us through our lifetime. Generally one physical breakdown appears to happen at a time. Perhaps it may be a loss of muscle power, balance, memory or agility.

> *It's a good thing you don't fall apart all at once. Then what would we do?*
>
> *Mary Ann S*

Not long ago a friend shared with me a parody about her body as a car. "If my body was a car and I had dents and scratches, unfocused headlights, burned fuel inefficiently, and lost traction, I would trade it in for a new model." I think many elders can relate to this as they experience various health issues. When you reach elder status, you begin to experience, think and talk more about health problems that slow you down or put you out of commission. While I was waiting for my husband in the waiting room of a doctor's office, another man in the room proceeded to tell me about all his ailments. I politely listened and felt sorry for him, but this conversation made me realize that most people really don't want to hear about someone's health problems. They don't want to know about such things as: incontinence, chemotherapy, emphysema, dialysis, heart bypass surgeries, hip replacements, and memory loss. Most people want to be around people who have a more positive view of life. That's why it is wise to remember that we don't need to talk about our illness with every person we meet, but that shouldn't stop us from keeping on top of progress in researching cures for specific diseases that occur in our families and discussing inroads with family members and appropriate others.

It takes a lot of emotional, physical and spiritual strength to forge ahead and do things in your elder years. My neighbor Ruth is 87 and has been through a number of illnesses. I admire her for her strength, endurance, and positive attitude towards life. She not only cares for herself, she is the support for her 90-year-old male friend and drives him on errands and to the doctor. She recently invited several of us over for dinner and still likes to do limited entertaining.

Perhaps you are wondering how you will be as you transition into your elder years. If you have had some experience in assisting an ill parent or relative, this experience may have helped you to better understand some of what aging is like. Knowing this, you might be able to assess how you might react in similar circumstances because none of us knows what lies ahead of us. About 16 years ago when my mother was going to have heart surgery, I could see she was scared and worried about the operation. She didn't say much, but I could tell she was very apprehensive. I knew her to be a strong woman who had overcome a lot of adversity in her life. Yet, she seemed very vulnerable. I wanted her to go into the operation with a strong positive attitude, so I helped her to develop some affirmations that she could say to herself. They were words to the effect, "I am strong. I'm invincible. I am woman. I will get through this." She came through the operation very well and as she began to awake, she was saying an affirmation. She said, "I am woman" and the doctor said, "I know." When our family heard this we all laughed together. I keep this experience in my memory as a way I may use to strengthen my own resolve in time of illness.

It is extremely difficult to stay future-oriented after experiencing a life-threatening illness or debilitating disease. It takes fortitude and strong sense of discipline to be able to stay with, not only the physical exercise regimen, but to maintain a positive mental and spiritual outlook. Illness may become a vicious cycle for some elders. It can become a round robin of doctors, hospital, nursing home, and then back to their home. When elders are in pain, they most likely take prescribed medications, which although they may help, also can lead to more physical complications. Some drugs can counteract one another and need to be checked out with the doctor and pharmacist. It's hard to cope and be resilient when you are experiencing pain. If you experience too much chronic pain for a long period of time, you can easily get addicted to the drugs or become cranky and difficult to deal with.

> *I had a situation where I was the caregiver to my father, who was in his late 70s. He had been ill for a number of years and had been in and out of the hospital. Over time he became angry and difficult. He actually screamed and threw a cup at a nurse in the hospital. I know he was frustrated, angry, and depressed about his illness, but it did him no good to lash out at people around him who could help him. We had a heart-to-heart talk and I explained to him that what he was doing was driving away people who could help him.*
>
> *Barbara T*

Pain and depression about illness can cause elders to respond and react out of character. They may rely heavily on medications to solve their physical pain and depressive state. Although medications can help, generally in the elder years, it is difficult to reverse what's happening to your body. Because each of us wants to live our lives to the fullest extent, it can be a difficult to accept the realization that our bodies are aging and life is fleeting.

Couple Relationships

Sometimes the first few years for newlyweds can be a little rocky as you adjust to each other. In elder adulthood, you may have spent many years together and face a future separation. These years also can seem rocky. There is an underlying, unspoken fear that you or your spouse may complete life without the other. This underlying notion sometimes surfaces in a variety of different, subtle ways.

> *I never thought my husband would experience serious illness early in our retirement. Since his heart operation, when I think he is doing too much and overloading his schedule, I can't help but bring it to his attention. But when I do, he gets all huffy and jumps down my throat. All I wanted to do was protect him. I am learning to keep my mouth closed on the subject.*
>
> *Betty B*

Betty's husband may see her concern as over protectiveness. Unconsciously he might be a little afraid to admit his vulnerability, so he reacts brusquely. For her part, she loves her husband and may be acting out of fear of losing him. Sometimes we can be frightened by a loved one's serious illness and become overly concerned not only for them, but also for what the loss may mean to us. Once we understand this, we can come to the realization that we really have to let our partner or spouse make his or her own life decisions. This can be hard to accept for a couple that has been together many years.

In researching this book I talked with a number of women who have husbands quite a bit older than they are. The husband's longevity was in the forefront of their minds. When there is a large difference in age, and the husband is beginning to have serious health problems, many of the wives experienced for the first time a concern about being left alone. Most did not have a plan to deal with this occurrence, but the possibility was in the back of their minds.

> *I'm aware of the possibility that my husband will go first. However, his family members have a long life span. In fact, he may live until he is 90 or something. I didn't think I would have a long life span because my father died when he was 60-something. However, my mother is now 88, so maybe there is a chance of a long life for me too.*
>
> *Susan S*

> *Since my second husband died, I do think about the possibility that my present husband might do the same because he is seven and one-half years older than I am. At night when I can't hear him snoring, I poke him to see if he is alive. I scold myself for doing that, but every once in a while I can't help it. So far we both are in good health and I wonder why I worry. His mother lived until she was 92. When we got married, I said I'm going first this time. I don't want to go through losing a husband again.*
>
> *Darlene L*

Because Darlene has already experienced the loss of one spouse, she is more aware of how such a loss affected her and really doesn't want to experience it again.

> *I have thought about what would happen if my husband dies or is seriously ill. I've seen some of my acquaintances*

*have problems when their husband died. They not only
missed him, they didn't know where anything was. It's important to know where everything is cash, safe deposit box,
trust information, who is to administer the family trust. If
something happens to either my husband or I, we need to
be sure that a son or daughter knows where things are. You
can't just think that someone will take care of it.*

Liela S

Liela highlights for us the necessity of knowing some
practical and important information about financial issues and
end of life issues. The personal loss of a loved one is difficult
enough without the problems being compounded by not knowing
where important papers are, or who to contact, and what
to do.

Death and separation are themes that tend to run through
elder long-term marriages. When a couple has been married
for a long time, losing one's partner may make it difficult to
continue on life's journey alone and these feelings can lead to
depression. Often elders simply don't talk about their feelings
of emotional distress because they don't want to be perceived as
weak and helpless.

*I really see a lot of men and women go into a depressive
mental state when they lose their spouse. They don't have
resources to go on. You need to get away from the depression
that can set in when you are alone. You need to remember
why you get up every morning and think through your situation. You are now single, retirement age, and your children
live far away. Think about what you can do for yourself.*

Jean S

When a couple have been married 50 or more years, their daily lives revolve around each other. It's not uncommon when the husband or wife dies, the other spouse may die shortly afterward or quickly marry again for fear of being alone.

> *I think that when a wife or husband dies shortly after the spouse dies, it's because they never thought of themselves as individuals. In retirement, I think you need to be an individual. I waited for a long time to let the individual inside me come alive. Earlier in life I was assigned the roles of mother, teacher, and wife. In retirement I can choose my role. If you don't take a breath, change, and grow you won't have planned for that critical moment when your spouse dies and you are left alone. Then you'll die too.*
>
> *Jo S*

Jo has taken the time to think through the importance of maintaining her individuality within her second marriage. Often during your earlier life, you may have taken on necessary roles within your marriage and family. Although you may have fulfilled the roles willingly, you may not have chosen the roles. Jo suggests that individual survival may depend on each partner developing personal strength and separate involvements, which can help one, or the other, carry on after the loss of the spouse. As you progress through your elder years, this aspect of personal fortitude and ability can help you through some of the difficulties that might lie ahead.

> *My aunt began showing signs of Alzheimer's disease in her early 70s. At first my uncle took care of her in the home. When it got to be too much for him, he did enter her into a nursing facility. It was hard for him because she is the*

love of his life. Since he visited her daily, he saw she was not being well taken care of and brought her home where he continues to care for her. She hasn't spoken for a long time, but still enjoys being held and loved. He's had some health problems himself of late and it is getting very difficult for him to continue her care.

Patty B

Watching the love of your life deteriorate right before your eyes is indescribable. An illness such as this may weaken the connective relationship, but not the strong bond established by this couple. A person's need for physical affection never really subsides. As babies, being held and touched is important and we might remember that it's important near the end of life as well. There are many things a married couple learns over the years of living together, but accepting deterioration as you age is hard to prepare for. When one partner experiences deterioration sooner than the other, either or both partners may experience loneliness and depression. The care giving spouse can feel alone and isolated due to the other's illness. This is the time he or she needs family and friends as support. If you find yourself in a similar situation and family or friends aren't available, research and join a support group in your community.

My interviews with a number of single retirees who experienced the loss of a spouse, showed me that you can survive a traumatic loss and establish a new life and positive relationships. Some people have remained single and have expanded their friendships through their interest groups, while others have married or have a special relationship with a significant other. Several couples met through a singles group in their community. Two former classmates became reacquainted at a high school reunion and married. Another couple met through a retirement community grief group. Both had lost their spouses and as time passed they became friends and later married. What stood out for me is that these individuals were able to survive their loss and reestablish a positive retirement life.

Family Relationships

Mature adults are usually able to drive all over and visit children, grandchildren, and family members, but when you advance in age, depending upon your health and ability, you may no longer be able to drive long distances. Generally, there comes a time when the family needs to travel to visit you. If you made the decision to live in a place far away from family, this might be the time to think about being closer in case you need family support.

> *When people reach the 75-year threshold they tend to start moving closer to the kids. I think that is the advent of phase three of a three-stage transition of aging. We think of ourselves as going down a ramp. It's a gradual thing.*
>
> *John A*

Having family close by can be advantageous to you when you become an elder. It can also be an advantage to family members because visiting and caring for a relative who lives near you is a whole lot easier than worrying and trying to set up care from a distance.

> *About ten years ago my sister helped my 80-year-old mother move from her home in Arizona to live near her*

and her husband in Oregon. At first my mother lived in a modular home and was reasonably self sufficient with help from my sister. Now my mother is in an assisted living place. Although she gets help daily, my sister still takes her to church, shopping, and to the doctors office.

Joe B

It's important for elders to have as much connection as possible with their families and friends. This gives them something to look forward to and appreciate each day. To attend church, go shopping, go to the park, or out for a coffee or an ice cream cone can be important outings for someone living in a facility where the routine can become so repetitive that you don't know what day it is.

A number of years after my father died, my mother relocated to be near my sister and her family. She is now situated within a reasonable driving distance from her children, grandchildren, and great-grandchildren. They visit her there and she sees the great-grandchildren more than she ever had living in another state. The great-grandchildren have even gotten to know and love her.

Peter B

Elders don't necessarily want money or gifts; they enjoy time with those they love. They want to have children, grandchildren, and other relatives visit them. Visits provide a distraction from what would be a monotonous daily routine. Think about it. If you were living alone or in a facility, wouldn't you welcome more frequent visits, even if they were of short duration?

Friendships

If you are lucky enough to have stayed in the same town or area where you presently live, you and your spouse may have been able to keep friends over many years. However, as you and they age, friends may not be able to see each other because of illness or death, and may disappear from your life. If you have moved to a retirement community, you hopefully have made friends with other mature adults and it is wise to nurture these friendships. These will often be the people who will be your friends and support group in later life. You will all grow old together. When family can't be there, hopefully you will have friends to help you, visit you, or support you through what could be a trying time in your life.

As we discussed in chapter 8, on friendship, it is wise as a couple to have couple friends and individual friends. Often when a spouse dies, the other partner has her or his friends there for support.

> *After my husband passed away many of our couple friends remained as friends even though I was now alone. I believe that if they are not friends with you after your husband dies, it's better not to have them as friends at all."*
>
> *Lee S*

People have told me about sad experiences when the husband died, their couple friends no longer remained friends with the surviving wife. In a couples' retirement community, it does happen that a couple may no longer spend time with the single spouse, for whatever reason. Sometimes friends may shy away because the loss of a friend may not only make them feel sad, but it awakens in them the sense of their own vulnerability. However, if you can put yourself in the shoes of the lone spouse and look at the situation from his or her perspective, you may realize the importance of extending your friendship.

As you age, you may not physically be able to go out to see friends or they may not be able to see you. A friend doesn't always have to be visiting face to face. You can keep in touch with friends by letter, e-mail, or by telephone. By calling a few times a week, just to say hello, you not only meet your own social needs, you can make a friend happy too. Although social relationships tend to be important when you are young, they have been shown to be even more important for elders because they may not be able to go out and make new friends. Often a retirement community or assisted living facility will have established a "buddy system" where residents monitor neighbors that may be ill, frail, or live alone. Keeping in touch or being aware of a phone not answered, newspapers not being collected, or mail not picked up is important to note when living around vulnerable elders. Recently I came across a creative, unobtrusive idea that kept me informed about a friend's operation and recovery. Each day her husband recorded an update on her condition on their outgoing phone message. Friends could call, get the update, pass it onto our group, and leave a message for her during her recovery period.

An assisted living facility can offer you the opportunity of making friends and establishing a social network without going out of the building. Based on what I have observed, you can be as active or inactive as you want. You might select an assisted living facility that has a resident group of similar age and economic level. As more and more boomers age, I believe facilities will expand and will become more generally defined by age, ability, interests and need for assistance. It might be a carryover from retirement communities, where people of the same generation and interests tend to gravitate to each other.

> *When I went to review the assisted living facility under consideration, the manager placed my daughter and I with a group of residents for lunch. This gave me an opportunity to meet and talk with residents. After I decided on the facility, they've arranged for me to sit at a table with several of the same ladies and they have became my mentors.*
>
> Marion B

Developing and maintaining friends younger than you can also be beneficial. Not only will they most likely live longer than you, they can help you to continue to expand your horizons.

> *I was having trouble with my computer and I went to the local computer club to find someone to help me. A young man in his 40s came out to the house and we have since become friends. He doesn't want to be paid and so I repay him by giving him a home-cooked dinner. He will be getting married soon and I am invited to the wedding.*
>
> Lenora R

Lenora is 80 years young. She likes modern conveniences and tries to use them. She said. "There is always something new to learn." Lenora exemplifies the old adage, "You're never to old to learn." She's open to making friends of all ages and because of her positive attitude, they want to connect with her.

Financial

Several issues come up in the financial area as mature adults reach their later years and become elders. One is that as you age, you generally are not able to do as many activities or travel as much as you may have earlier in your retirement. Also, you may not need as many clothes or other sports or hobby equipment, so your expenses for these kinds of items may go down.

> *As you get older, you probably don't need as much income because you won't be doing as much. One of my uncles once said, "When you are young enough to do things, you don't have the money to do it and you have all these other commitments. When you have the money, you are too old to do it. Life is sort of reversed."*
>
> *Larry M*

However, some of your other costs will increase. Your medication bills may very well go up. Dentist bills can also increase. You'll need supplemental medical insurance and depending upon your health care coverage, medical bills may rise.

> *When I was a kid, I felt that I would be very lucky to live to 75. My gosh, I have relatives that are in their 90s. There is longevity in my family. So, my wife and I have to start thinking about how we will be cared for in our later years. This is like retrofitting—I suppose we should have done something different when we started retirement. If I am going to be here when I am 90 I need to be thriftier in spending.*
>
> *John L*

Since retirees are living longer, it's more likely that some of you will spend your elder years not only in a retirement community, but will make use of assisted living residences and possibly nursing homes as well. If you decide on an excellent assisted living facility, this too can be a costly item in your elder years. However, if you choose to stay in your own home you'll still have the additional cost of support help. So in your later years it can be important to have a financial advisor you trust or family member who is financially knowledgeable to help you determine what you can afford given your financial means.

Later Life Decisions

In your mature adult years, it is wise to prepare the proper forms such as living wills, advanced care directives, etc. Recently my husband and I went through the process of reviewing and updating these forms and I can understand why some people put it off. Often we don't want to think about how in later life, our health may diminish and we'll need directives to guide our care providers as to what we wish. It's hard to anticipate what illness might affect us or what medical decisions our spouse or family may need to make, since later in life we may experience multiple medical problems. In some cases, medical treatments may offer minimal benefits and, in fact may cause more pain and suffering. Those will be times that you or your family may have to weigh possible benefits against possible burdens. These can be complex and trying times for you, your spouse, and your family. I understand most retirees in their mature adult stage may not even want to think about issues of declining health and survival decisions. When and if you are ready to read more about the hard choices you might have to make for yourself or your family may need to make, I would encourage you to read books like *Hard Choices for Loving People*, written by Hank Dun, a chaplain with the Hospice of Northern Virginia, and *The 36 Hour Day* by Nancy L. Mace and Peter V. Rabins.

Understanding your transitory nature and what will happen in the future can make each day you do live more precious and important. As she discusses in *Another Country* Mary Pipher found that resilient elders held strong spiritual beliefs, which helped them rise above their own egos. Getting in touch with your inner self and your spiritual nature can help you to be resilient in meeting the adversity you may face in your elder years. You may want to read over the sections on mental and spiritual health in chapter 4.

Some elders are even thinking ahead enough to plan their own funeral arrangements. They figure that someone has to make the choices and why not make them in advance so their family won't have to. In this way they can have the kind of ending or celebration of life that they would like to have. They may list whether they want cremation or a burial, the kind of service, and location site for burial or where to have ashes strewn. Often Advanced Care Directives address some of these issues. If you decide to do this, be sure to explain in writing your wishes and be sure that every family member has a copy. Many individuals have written out their wishes and even described the kind of service, music, prayers, and special requests they might have. You can obtain more information by checking the Funeral Consumers Alliance or AARP. (www.funerals.org or AARP)

SUMMARY

At this point you might be thinking, there seem to be all these losses later in life, where are the gains? Gains are in the eye of the beholder. Each of you most likely will view your elder years in the same way you approached other stages of your life. If you view life optimistically, you will believe each stage of life has something to offer. Yes, the gains may be fewer, but with a positive attitude of acceptance of what you can enjoy and appreciate such as a beautiful sunset, a tasty bakery treat, a phone call from a grandchild, or a moment spent with a loved one, you'll be able carry on each day. Elder couples realize that life is fragile and that each day is precious and should be appreciated. They understand the power of practicing gratitude.

LATER YEARS TOOL KIT

Questions:

You and your mate can answer these questions for yourselves and then sit down together and discuss your answers. After you come up with possible actions you want to take, share your decisions with your children to get their thoughts and concerns.

1. Have you thought about your elder years and what they may hold for you and your spouse?

2. What are the five most important things you believe you need when you move into later life? What can you do to focus your time appropriately on these objectives?

3. What would be your first choice about where to live in later life? Do you think you will be able to afford it? Is it something you both agree on?

4. If you were left alone later in life, where would you choose to live? Have you thought of how you would carry on if you find yourself single in later life?

5. What do you know about each other's medical information, financial information, insurance information and how things function in the home? Do you have an Advanced Care Directive completed and on file with your doctor, hospital, with family members?

6. Do you know where all the important papers are located and can you or your spouse access them if one or both of you are ill or die?

7. Review these questions yearly in later life to be sure you both feel the same way with regard to what you want.

LATER LIFE RESOURCES

Books, magazines, and web sites offer a wealth of useful information that can help you with your planning for later life. Here are just a few to start you in your own roadmap research and planning:

Alzheimer's Organization – www.alz.org/index.asp

Advanced Directives & End-of-Life-Care – www.caringinfo. org

Community Directories
- Listings of local assisted living facilities, residential care, Alzheimer's care, nursing care and rehabilitation
- Community Programs and Services - counseling, financial assistance, senior centers, or referrals

Continuing Care Retirement Communities – www.helpguide. org/elder/continuing_care_retirement_communities.htm

Funeral Help – www.funerals.org

Geriatric Care Management – www.caremanager.org

-Information and advocacy in medical, psychological, residential, social, legal and financial areas
-Geriatric Care Manager helps with home care planning, independent living plans, assisted living planning

Hospice — www.familyhospice.com.
www.nationalhospicefoundation.org

Local Social Service Agencies and Community Centers
- Meals on wheels, community lunches, transportation program, daily welfare telephone calls

"Making Important Decisions" information/workbook for family & friends related to illness of death — Gkolsky@msn.com

Medical Alarms Systems www.rescuealert.com, www.alert-I.com, www.lifelinesys.com

National Caregiver resources - AgeNet — www.agenet.com

National Geriatrics Society — www.americangeriatrics.org/links/

Senior Health Net — www.NIHSeniorHealth.gov

Senior Transitions NW — (206) 264-4400 - Help for people leaving a lifelong home

Solutions for Better Aging — www.caregivers.com

Substance Abuse — Geriatric Mental Health Foundation — www.gmhfonline.org

CHAPTER II –
REAR VIEW MIRROR
History, Legacy, Advice

Beautiful young people are acts of nature, but
beautiful old people are works of art.

— *Eleanor Roosevelt*

CHALLENGE:

To review and learn from your own history and use the information to live the rest of your life in a positive way.

LOOKING IN THE REAR VIEW MIRROR

At some point in our retirement years, couples (and individuals) tend to look back on their life's journey, where they have been and how they have lived their lives. Some people look back with nostalgia and perhaps long for happier days gone by. Other people see the past as a time when they made mistakes, learned from them and grew to what they are today. Still others might look at a past that they would like to leave behind and make a fresh start in the last one-third of their lives. Whatever your motivation, looking in the rear view mirror to the past can help you determine how you want to live the years you have left. You can learn from your own history, whether you want to enhance the future or change it. This chapter shares retirees' views on life, along with ideas for ways of passing on your history, values and ethics to a younger generation. Autobiographies, memoirs, journals, and ethical wills are discussed. This chapter also includes words of wisdom from couples recently retired, as well as from seasoned retirees.

When you reach your elder years, you might have a frightening sense that you are closer to the end than the beginning. The gnawing thought that you may have a limited number of years left in your life can be frightening and depressing, especially if you see yourself spending them alone, without your partner. As you age, time may appear to slip away more rapidly, and it may be hard to see how the years you are living are still relevant. Looking back on your life can provide you with the knowledge and fortitude to fully live the time you still have. The past may be prologue, but you are still living your life and writing your future epilogue.

> *Getting old is complex. It is much more difficult to be old than it was to be young. It's not because of the physical problems. It's because of the demands on you. As older adults, we are supposed to be wiser. We are supposed to be settled. We are supposed to have truths and values that sustain us. We aren't supposed to be afraid. I don't think we are ready for that fact. I'm often frightened. Maybe some of us didn't build a psychological resource to pull ourselves up from the bootstraps so to speak.*
>
> *Jo S*

Almost everyone has been frightened about something during his or her lifetime. When we're able to learn from fear rather than react to it we can use this difficult emotion for the wisdom it holds. You can actually use fear to help you survive and advance through your elder years. By looking back and learning from moments of challenge and fear, you can better understand yourself and hopefully help to enhance your later years.

Looking Back on Where You've Been

Think about this reflection on your life as an exploration. What will help you explore your past life? What will help you to remember? Many people use family photo albums, movies, and videos to jog their memories. Playing music tapes or CDs from the time you want to access can also bring back memories. You want to access your own life history and create a catalogue of information about you. Exploring your life events can be a way to get to know your self better. You may identify forgotten personal attributes from the past that can help and re-enforce you in the present.

Native American storytellers used a method by which they would identify life's milestones. They would take a length of leather twine and tie beads at specific locations on the twine to designate specific events in their lives. When the storyteller fingered along the twine he or she would be reminded of a specific event and shares the story with younger people. Using today's methods on paper or the computer, you might make a timeline of your life and place various events along that timeline that were important or had a landmark influence on your life. Some events and experiences may stand out more than others because they occurred during a time of change. Such events as starting school, connecting with a favorite teacher, selling something for a school project, or winning a speaking contest could qualify as markers on your early childhood time line. Often the experiences you had and the important people in your life had a primary role in forming your character. They contributed to shaping you into the person you are today.

> *Although I don't use the term elder, I think we have the wisdom of experience that I know that young people want to have, even though we are older and it may not be cool. I notice the youngest of my grandchildren will ask me what I think about something or what I did as a little girl. She'll ask about what happened to my mother and father. This gives me the opportunity to then share what I think about and what I value.*
>
> *Diane H*

You have a lifetime of accomplishments, experiences, and information in your memory bank that you can share with family members. If you need to shake up that memory of yours, take time to go through old scrapbooks, high school or college yearbooks, etc. Read over diaries, or journals that you may have kept earlier in life. These can remind you of what went on in the days gone by and make them vividly come alive for you. They can help you to remember the stories and events in your life that you might want to share with loved ones.

Ways of Sharing Background and History

Although reflecting on your life can be a reward in itself, if you wish to share your experiences and insights with your children, grandchildren, and great-grandchildren you can write an autobiography. Many retirees turn to writing their memoirs or autobiographies. In order to do this, they have to look back on their own personal history, as well as their history as a couple. Often the autobiographies consist of their recollections of events in their lives, people who influenced them, turning points they experienced and lessons they may have learned.

> *Because I felt that it was important to save my family history and family recipes for future generations, I put together a Sicilian Family Heritage Cookbook. I used my mother and grandmother's recipes along with my own variations of some of the Italian dishes. I also collected recipes from aunts and uncles, cousins, in-laws, and grown children. I asked that a wedding picture of the couple and a story of how they met accompany each recipe. When I put it all together I had a history of the family and the town where my Sicilian family began. The project was fun to do and has been popular with family and even friends who have asked for copies of the book.*
>
> Steve B

Steve shared some of his family background in a unique way by sharing recipes and couple's stories. He was wise enough to do it early in his retirement, which allowed him to obtain information and recipes from some of his family who have since passed away. You might want to think about beginning to collect information for a family history project while your parents and relatives are still able to share stories with you. Some people who have done this have used audiotape and even videotape. Others take notes because the person being interviewed is uncomfortable speaking into a recording device. If you have a small audio recording device unobtrusively placed, then the interviewee can forget about it and just talk with you "one-on-one." In fact, you might think about telling your own story on tape rather than, or in addition to, writing an autobiography. There are many ways to collect historical information. Our two grandsons recently interviewed their great-grandmother about her life and experiences for a Cub Scout project. They each wrote about and drew pictures of some of the events she told them about. One picture showed the sinking of the Titanic in the year she was born. She was so happy when they shared their booklets with her. It made her day!

If you begin to have a sense that you may pass through this life without leaving a footprint, this can be the time to write your story—the positive events, the mistakes you've made, and the problems you encountered. Don't be afraid to share the highlights of your life, it won't be bragging. You'll just be telling your story. In addition, writing about your mistakes, especially if you learned from them, can provide schooling to others. You might be helping someone in your family to face a similar situation in the future. Reading about an ancestor's talents and gifts gives relatives a way to see their own abilities. Your story provides a mirror for readers, who are related, a way to know themselves better too. A grandchild might relate his or her talent for debate as coming from you, because you won a speaking award in the seventh grade.

As you can see from Steve's idea for a family cookbook, you can portray your story in different formats. If you decide to write your autobiography or memoir you might want to take a particular approach or focus as to what is important to you. Some people write their story chronologically, while others might write about the experiences that helped them develop and grow. Still others look back at the turning points in their lives and write from that perspective.

> *At the seniors center I enjoy the Memoirs Group. We have worked on our life's history. I kept a journal since I went to college and that helped me write about my experiences. I focused my biography on experiences and turning points in my life. I had breast cancer back in 1978 and that is the year my sister died of the same thing. I had to live with the problem and accept what is to be. I just turned it over to God and I am still alive today. I've been able to lead a full life and I want my children, grandchildren and great-grandchildren to know my story.*
>
> *Dorothy N*

Autobiographies often focus on one life. It might be interesting to write a couple's autobiography of your lives together from when you first met to the present day. The focus could be on special days you both shared, turning points in your marriage, or perhaps the different places you lived and what you have seen together. By sifting through old photos, old letters or watching home movies/videotapes, you can relive your shared memories. About twelve years ago one of our sons asked me if I saved our family Christmas letters. When I said yes, he suggested that I might put them together in a book for the family. So, a month before Christmas, I searched through boxes to find the letters and pictures, copied them and put them in a book for each of our children. What I thought would be an easy project did take more time than I expected, but it was worth it. Now we have a chronological history of our family from the time my husband and I married to the most recent holiday. Each year I take time to reminisce, read each of the letters, look at the pictures, and nostalgically remember family times. I think our children and grandchildren appreciate the book and I hope others who come after will too.

Many people have saved letters or cards from loved ones and these can also be memory reminders of specific events or occasions. These might even be of interest to children or grandchildren if you want to share them.

> *I always date my letters to friends and recently one of my friends sent back some of the letters I wrote to her a long time ago. I've started a box of letters and when my two granddaughters come to visit me, they love to read those letters. The letters tell about my childhood and some letters talk about life with my brothers and sisters. The girls come over and they ask to read the letters.*
>
> Marilyn T

> *Forty-six years ago when my husband and I were first engaged, we were separated for six months by three thousand miles, until shortly before our wedding. We were young and didn't have the money to fly back and forth, nor did we have the money to spend on long phone conversations. We used our letters to converse with each other. I saved those letters along with any letters and poems he wrote for me since that time. I plan on sharing some of these letters with our grandchildren some day.*
>
> Barbara B

Reviewing letters, memorabilia, mementos, and awards can all bring back memories as to how the events and times shaped your life. Reading them with your spouse or with children or grandchildren helps to make the past come alive.

Many retirees are becoming interested in studying their genealogy. Retirement communities and senior centers sponsor genealogy seminars, clubs, and groups. There are even Family History Fairs to help you learn how to research and find your ancestors. I went to one sponsored by the Church of the Latter Day Saints. The computer and Internet sites, such as Ancestry. com, have opened up many avenues to check out family history and genealogy today. Often people will travel to the country of their heritage to research records and possibly look up distant family relatives.

> *Going way back in my family there were a lot of pioneering people who were willing to leave everything they had and go to a new place. Our son looked up my genealogy and it goes clear back to when the Vikings conquered France. Then William the Conqueror came over to England. They were people who were willing to fight for what they wanted. Now we know from whom we evolved and will pass this on to the younger generation.*
>
> *John L*

Learning and writing about your relatives, your family and your life can help you to clarify who you are, as well as provide your family with knowledge of your life's history. Some individuals have gone so far as to use a short version of their life history in writing their own future obituary. They felt they were the only ones, who knew their history and what they wanted shared with others. What better way to help your family in a time of sorrow, but by providing them with a drafted obituary, and a list of friends and acquaintances they should contact after you pass away.

Personal Reflections

You may want to record your thoughts about your past and present life in a journal. It can provide you with a way to express yourself and how you feel about life. You'll be putting down your personal history on paper. I always write in a travel journal on every trip I've taken as an adult. Years later I can review my entries and identify what I saw and how I felt at the time. You can also write in your journal around the time of your birthday each year so that you can express how you feel and what you are thinking at each age. Before I write in my birthday journal, I usually go back and read some of the previous entries I've made in recent years. Then, I'll find a quiet place where I can sit and I write down my thoughts at whatever age I am celebrating. It's been an interesting exercise over these retirement years and I've learned more about my self, and how to understand and accept changes and events that occur with each year of age.

Whether you call the book you write in a journal or a diary, it is an expression of yourself on paper. You can tell about what happened that particular day, how you felt about it and what came of it. Some diaries come with thoughts for the day printed in them. You can even add your own "thought or highlight for the day." You might think that you have nothing to write about in a diary or journal because you don't feel like you are doing much in retirement. This doesn't have to be true because your book can be what you want to share from deep within you. If you have read the book *The Diary of Anne Frank* you know that she chronicled her daily life, while hiding with her family and others in an attic apartment in Holland during World War II. You might think that this young Jewish girl had little to write about, as she couldn't go anywhere or see anything outside that attic. But her diary has become a classic because it shared what was on the mind of a twelve year old, how she spent each day, and how she felt about what occurred that day. It was her way of expressing her feelings, dreams and hopes for the future not only for herself, but also, eventually, for the world.

Passing on Your Legacy

Retirement isn't only a time to assess who you are. It can also be a time to review what "footprints" you've left on this earth. Have you thought about what kind of footprint or legacy you'll leave? How will someone know that you were here? Some people are financially able to fund scholarships, or leave a donation or a large sum to some charity, school, or philanthropy. Others may leave their financial wealth to family members. However, we all may not be able to make financial donations or leave a large estate, but that doesn't mean we can't leave a legacy.

Edward Curtis, a photographer of Native American culture, believed that as each generation passes it means the loss of some tradition or knowledge. That's why he gathered information about the Native American culture for the benefit of future generations. How can you pass on your knowledge, culture and traditions? Is there a time, a place or a way you can do this, so that your younger relatives will have the benefit of learning about you and your story? If you live near and spend a lot of time with children and grandchildren, you can transfer this knowledge through daily conversations and stories. However, if you don't see them that often, or you're not a good storyteller, you might need to find another way.

One way is to share your wealth of knowledge, values, love, and insights in a legacy letter or ethical will. The ethical will derives from medieval times when it was a custom to write a letter to your descendants to pass on your guidelines for living an ethical life. It is a loving, caring letter that expresses your feelings and transmits your non-material assets to your family members. You can actually write several different letters to children, grandchildren, great-grandchildren and other family members. The theme of the letter can focus on your life history, what you value, lessons learned in life, or your love and wishes for those addressed in your letter. You might want to share the influences you have had in your life. Some people use an ethical will to give a personal context to their financial wills in order to explain the decisions they made. Some ethical wills define why you want to donate a portion of your estate to philanthropy. An ethical will is a "work in progress" because it can be filed on your computer and be added on to or changed over time. An ethical will can be one of the most personally valuable things you can leave your family members.

WORDS OF WISDOM FROM RETIREES

When the retirees who contributed their comments for this book were asked to look in their rear view mirror—at their experiences and share relevant advice, concerns and counsel for other retirees, they provided the following "words of wisdom."

I've organized their comments into sections that correspond to the subjects in this book.

Change and Flexibility

You have to be willing to face change, organize yourself, and have a goal. Maintain a mindset of getting both feet out of the ocean and when you get to the right age, jump into retirement. Make yourself a part of retirement and it will become part of you. JE

When you first retire don't make too many changes at once. Don't be in a rush. Be patient and expect the unexpected. Changes can happen in any part of your life, whether it is health, living environment, family or financial. It is all going to happen. RH

Look at change as a new adventure instead of getting all crazy about it. You are going on an adventure and enjoy the ride. MF

You have to be prepared for all kinds of changes and adjust accordingly. RH

Don't be afraid to make changes along the way. Don't just let things happen. JS

Focus or Goals

Get some idea of what you want to accomplish in the next 10 to 20 years—personally and together. Both of your plans are equally important and need to coincide. RS

Intentionally create a life where things aren't the same day after day. You have to create an interesting life for yourself. Discover new possibilities each day. SS

You not only have to have personal goals, but also couple goals—things you would like to do together and accomplish together. Identify them and both of you stick with it. It's too easy to forget that and get off on your own individual program. RS

Encourage your own identity in retirement. Follow your bliss or passion to make you happy. JD

You have to have a good idea of what you want to accomplish. Do you want to give to the community? Do you want to be more available for family? Have more recreation? Plan ahead. JAF

Planning

A positive retirement doesn't just happen. It takes a certain amount of planning, a certain amount of work. JE

One of the problems in retirement is that you can't prepare for the unexpected. Don't write your plans in cement. Don't think that just because you said you were going to do this and the other thing, that's the way it will happen. Be flexible. Be willing to change your mind. NE

When planning retirement I think the best thing is to talk to people who are retired and to your peers and friends to find out what they are doing. FS

You have to have a game plan. You can't go at retirement blindly. I also don't think you can afford to make a lot of huge mistakes. JS

Transitioning

The main advice I would give is to retire sooner than later. I think people wait too long. They want to be extremely sure that they can retire without financial problems. If anything I wish I had retired sooner. BG

Go to a retirement workshop and take the time to reassess who you are and what you want now. Don't just walk out of the door at work and then ask, "Now what do I do?" You need to assess your own strengths, weaknesses and abilities. Figure out who you are and what you want. PS

Remember that if you retire early, you most likely will have about 25 or 30 years left in your life. Have a good idea about what you want to do with the rest of your life. BAB

Activities

Think about the things you like that bring you joy and find ways you can continue to experience those things. I like working with kids and am signed up as a substitute teacher and I tutor children. LS

If you have the physical ability to keep doing what you are doing, do it! Those are the things that count. You don't just say you are tired, sit back, and drink a beer and watch television. That is fine when you re 95 and can't do other things. LM

I always said to my husband that there's going to be a day when we can't travel and we are going to sit in our rocking chairs and remember. That day came a lot sooner than I expected it to. So I encourage new retirees to travel and do things in their early retirement years while they physically can. JAF

Do the things early on in your retirement that you didn't have time for while you were working. You can always cut back your spending after three years or so. If you wait, you may not have a chance to do what you want. LMM

Give careful thought to what you are going to do in retirement. See if the recreational activities are enough to sustain you day in and day out. You might have to search for new opportunities. LMF

Don't waste time on things you don't care to do but feel you have to do. Life is too short. CC

My number one advice is both the husband and wife have to retire to something—whether it is art, music, golf, tennis, volunteering or whatever. JS

Quality of Life

Research, research, research where you are going to live and make sure it's got what you both want. Try out a place before you make a definitive move. Evaluate what life there will be like. GK

Don't make any real fast decisions about where you are going to locate. Take your time to be sure that it is where you both want to be. You both have to be happy with the decision. JM

Keep active and enjoy your freedom. When you take slow walks and smell the flowers, you have time to think about a problem, and the answers will just come to you. Use the time in retirement to think and enjoy being alive. DM

You have to map out a lifestyle. What kind of roles will you have? How do you want to spend your time? Talk about such little things as having breakfast together or going off to do something on your own. KW

Health & Illness

I'd say be sure to plan for healthcare. Health issues are very important in retirement. RS

When you are living with a person that is terminally ill, you have to let go of the denial because it's really happening. You may have to go forward and keep a smile on your face and maintain your sense of humor and baby-step through the change. MF

The key thing is to have a medical plan. Long-term care insurance is important too because your finances could be wiped out with one long illness. FS

Continue to learn about new things, new places, and new ideas. It's been shown that learning new tasks and doing them in a different way can slow aging of the brain. BAB

Couple Relationships

I think it helps if you both want the same things in retirement and discuss it ahead of time. You can't just let it happen because you may not necessarily get what you want and then both people will end up in trouble. JS

Think about how you and your spouse spend your weekends now and multiply by seven. It's a big shock to go into retirement. I think if you can do it gradually, it's better for both of you. JAF

I'd say that when a problem arises in your marriage, get some counseling. You might find out you may be wrong. You need somebody that sees both sides. JG

Do things that you both are interested in, but give each other space. You've got to have space for yourself. JGF

Sharing responsibilities in the home is important in retirement. Men should be able to fix their own lunch and share household chores, so they both can do activities outside the home. JL

Both men and women need to be aware of each others' household responsibilities and how to do them. BAB

A lot of our success in retirement is because we did talk about it before. So I'd say do a lot of communicating about what he and she likes and wants. DL

Find time each week to have a date night with your mate. Whether you go out to dinner, attend a concert, walk on the beach or sit in your hot tub and enjoy a glass of wine, you will be maintaining your relationship. MN

Family Relationships

Spend time with your family when they are available. Don't get so busy with your retirement life that you don't allow for family time. You can schedule it in. BA

Find ways to connect and keep in touch with your family members—children, grandchildren, and great-grandchildren. BS

If you want to see your children and grandchildren more often, take into consideration how far you live away from them. If you are only an hour or two away, you might drive there or they may come out to see you more often. SB

Friendships

Don't use precious time on people who are marginal in your life. There are a lot of people who walk through your life and you wonder why they came? They don't add to your life and perhaps actually take away something. Spend time with people that really mean something to you and you can enjoy. CC

I would say to a woman or a man, to be secure with yourself and your abilities to survive. Make sure you have a network of friends and family to insure your survival and success. Having friends who you can talk to is like therapy because you can verbalize what's in your head. MB

You have to have a sense of humor; you have to laugh. Work at making friends, talk to good friends on an ongoing basis. Stretch yourself to meet new people if you move to a new location. JD

Financial Issues

I think you have to start financially planning for retirement early on. You especially have to look into all kinds of health plans such as long term care planning and maintaining good insurance. CT

Start thinking about retirement 20 years ahead of time. Talk about what the two of you want to do and then figure out how much it is going to cost in future dollars. If you can't swing it, downgrade your plans and be just as happy. SB

Start putting retirement money aside early on in your work life. Money is the coin of the realm when you are older. If you want to have a good time when you are young you can do it on a shoestring, but when you are older you'd rather *sleep in a hotel bed than on the ground in a sleeping bag at a campsite. Your body just can't take it. MG*

Change in life can be positive as well as negative. You may find yourself with more money than you knew you had for retirement, but more often it will be less and you need to adjust your lifestyle accordingly. RH

Make sure you have enough money put away to sustain a lifestyle that you want and have become accustomed to. Have the major things like home basically paid for. You can't depend on social security, you need other income sources. FS

Later Years

Maintain your sense of humor and continue to educate yourself. Life is slower as you get older. Don't sweat the small stuff. After you have been married for many years, every year gets easier. You don't have the tumultuous changes in your life. RB

When you retire, you have to think ahead as to what you can get involved in. You just don't turn the light switch off and say I am in the dark. Don't turn the light switch off; just keep turning it down. JA

Think and plan ahead as to what you might do if you can't live totally on your own. Don't assume that everything is automatically going to be hunky dory the rest of your life. That's living in a dream world. DL

General

> *Enjoy retirement. You only come through once. If you play your cards right, once is enough. JA*

> *As long as you set your life in order and you have things provided for, you should enjoy what you have. JAF*

> *Don't give up your dreams, but be brutally honest with yourself about who you are. I think we are creatures of habit and we go back to our comfort zone. We might have the best of intentions to try new things in retirement, but often we return to what we know and loved in other times and places we lived. LW*

> *I believe that satisfaction, gratitude, and acceptance in retirement are necessities. Be satisfied with your personal achievements and good fortune. Make the best of it. RB*

SUMMARY

Looking in the rear view mirror can help you to assess your life—its accomplishments, losses, growth, and development. You can take the knowledge you learned and the abilities you gained to help you through the later adult years. At a recent church service I heard the reverend say that we are the authors of our own lives. The word author derives from the word authority. You and your spouse do have the authority to live your lives the best you can. Now is the time to commit to making your retirement life and that of your spouse or partner the best it can be.

REAR VIEW MIRROR TOOL KIT

Questions:

Take a sheet of paper and answer these questions and discuss your answers with your spouse or partner.

1. Have I done all the things I wanted to do? What are they?

2. Looking in the rear view mirror is there anything I need to do to change a relationship, behavior, or personal trait?

3. As I move toward the later years of my life, am I living the best that I can for myself? My spouse? My children? My grandchildren?

4. What can I do to improve or change my interactions with those I love and care about?

5. What do I want to leave my spouse and family with?

6. What would I want said about me? What do I want to be remembered for?

7. How do I make these post retirement years take me to the ending I want?

CHAPTER 12 –
ROADMAP TO RETIREMENT
Personal Roadmap Guidelines

*People tend to spend more time planning their
vacation than they do their retirement.*

— *Stan B*

CHALLENGE:

To develop a roadmap that will be detailed enough to meet
your needs as a couple in retirement.

Whether you are in the process of planning retirement,
already retired, or see retirement in your future, mapping out
your retirement plans can make a difference. Given that many
of you have retired or are retiring earlier, and the life expectancy
in the United States is increasing, you may have many years in
retirement—perhaps one-third of your lives. A roadmap for
envisioning how you and your spouse or life partner hope to
live these years is critical. Even if you are already retired, such a
roadmap can help you to achieve your goals for retirement.

YOUR ROADMAP

A roadmap is a personally crafted working plan. This plan should answer: who, what, when, where, why, and how you plan to accomplish your retirement transition and life goals. Some of your plans may be very comprehensive and others may end up being very general in nature. This will vary with each couple because of differences in personal style, interests, and needs, as well as your proximity to retirement age. The further you are from retirement age, the more general your plan may be. The challenge is to develop a plan that not only meets both of your needs, but is flexible enough to be changed as you continue in your retirement years.

If you have answered the Tool Kit Questions in each chapter, you are ready to follow this outline and develop your own strategic roadmap. Don't be concerned if your initial plans are quite general, because as you go over them and rework your ideas you'll be able to clarify the nebulous areas. As in planning a vacation trip, it's important to begin outlining your planned retirement journey. You can then review your roadmap during your planning years and into your retirement years to verify that you are on course, or change your plans if necessary. If you're already in retirement, use the roadmap to guide you in making the right decisions that can make your retirement experience even better. The following roadmap guidelines provide you with the general points to follow through pre and post retirement. Customize the roadmap based on what you and your partner decide.

Forecasting Your Retirement

Fifteen to ten years before

Vision and Plans

- Sit down together to vision your preferred future.
  Where will you live?
  What will it be like?
  Do either of you want to continue working?
  Talk about what each of you wants in your retirement life—to achieve a specific personal dream, more together time, closer family ties? If your goals are different, begin to explore ways you each can begin to compromise. Both of your goals are equally important and need to coincide

Transition

- Read over Chapter 2, the "Braking Away" transition chapter in this book.
  Read other articles and books about retirement, transitioning from employment—careers, or possible second careers and volunteer opportunities.
  Get a better idea of what other retirees have experienced and what they think about retiring, transitioning, or working.

Financial

- Read over Chapter 9, the financial chapter in this book.

- Assess whether you have sufficient funds for making your dreams come true. Calculate the retirement funds you'll have available from pension plans, profit-sharing plans, savings plans.

Then, calculate how much you anticipate spending yearly in retirement. Do you need to save more, work longer? Do you need to find additional means to increase your retirement nest egg?

- Define what you can do over the next ten years to financially move you closer to meeting your retirement goals.

Health and Wellness

- Read over Chapter 4, the chapter about health and wellness in this book

- List the ways you are maintaining (or will maintain) your health, exercise and eat healthy

- Research Your Illness Probability - Assess genetic illnesses that run in your family and learn more about them

- Obtain appropriate yearly physical exams and dental exams.

Goals and Objectives

- Begin to outline a plan for achieving both of your future dreams.

- Once you've identified your dreams and assessed your financial status, you can plan your goals and objectives for your retirement.

Pre-retirement

Ten to five years before

Education

- Attend a pre-retirement workshop or seminar in your city or community.

- Gain knowledge about the latest government information, financial retirement plans.

- Talk with retirement experts and other pre-retirees.

- Continue reading new articles and material on retirement issues. Investigate on-line sites such as www.civicventures. org/nextchapter - directed at baby boomers and adults already in their 60s, 70s and beyond, who are interested in exploring life options, civic engagement, and continued learning.

- Join AARP if you are eligible. Read educational material on retirement and research online topics of interest to you.

Vision and Plans

- Review and refine your vision plan for retirement and clarify or refine your ideas about retirement.

- Assess how you and your spouse's ideas intersect, or differ, and attempt to coordinate your plans.

- If you have differing plans for leaving your work, what can you do to better coordinate or coalesce your plans?

Financial

- Review your financial status and your available funds from the various savings plans, pension plans, investment accounts to assess your progress towards what you think you will require in retirement.

- If you plan on selling your home and purchasing elsewhere in or out of the country, begin research.

- Check out the real estate markets in given areas, real estate tax rates, as well as state income taxes.

- Be aware of real estate market fluctuations because they can have a bearing on when to sell, when to buy, and when to move.

Health and Wellness

- Develop plans and ideas to maintain your physical, mental, emotional and spiritual health. What can you do now to maintain good health?

Five years before retirement
Transition

- Identify what you've derived from your job or employment and how you can channel your energies into preparing for or evolving yourself in the area(s) in which you have an interest, whether it's working in a second career, volunteering, or retiring to follow leisure pursuits.

- If you haven't already done so, check out on-line resources and retirement ideas, such as: Civic Ventures-Next Chapter projects, and University Programs on life and career transition.

Preparation

- Decide what you can begin to do over the next five years to prepare yourselves for retirement.

Planning

- Make your plans for a future of working or when and how you both plan to retire.

- Set a tentative date if you plan to retire.

- Estimate your life expectancy based on life expectancy tables, family health information and your present health and that of your spouse.

Financial

- Estimate income sources from social security, investments, 40I(K), IRA, etc. given the number of years you expect to live.

- Assess where you are financially in relation to your forecasted needs and retirement goals.

- If you need more money, change your savings habits or determine if you can work for a longer period of time to save more, or work part-time in retirement.

Quality of Life and Location

- If you are thinking of moving to a new location, visit or spend time vacationing in the locations that hold your interest.

- Talk to people there to see what they do and how they feel about living there.

- Determine what it might cost to live in an area of interest and if you can afford this lifestyle on your retirement income.

- If you plan on moving to a new community, narrow your options.

- If you are considering two locations, you may want to purchase the second location while you are still working.

- Investigate the kinds of retirement choices that you identified as something in which you both or each of you was interested such as retirement community, two locations, travel, etc.

Activities

- Prepare yourself either by reading about your interests, developing skills in a specific sport or hobby, or begin participating in your field of interest.

Health and Wellness

- Define how you can prepare yourselves mentally, physically, emotionally and spiritually for retirement.

- Review your present health and life insurance plans to assess coverage and gain knowledge about possible future insurance needs.

- Continue maintaining good health habits and establish a routine for health check-ups, mammograms, prostate exams, etc.

Closing in on Retirement

Two years before

Transition

- If you or your spouse plan on continuing to work, talk about how this affects your plans and discuss possible ways you can handle this scenario.

- Attend transition workshops and continue to read and share with each other — internet information, articles and books on establishing the "next chapter" of your lives.

Financial

- Assess your financial condition in relation to your goals set in your earlier planning.

- If something has happened beyond your control that has impacted your retirement funding, you may still be able to delay your retirement plans or make some other plans to work part-time in retirement.

Health and Wellness

- If you move to a new community or decide to spend time in two communities, research appropriate physicians, dentists, pharmacy etc. in both communities so that when you do move, you have accessible healthcare where you live.

- Research health plans you might need after retiring and obtain health insurance or supplemental health insurance if you qualify for Medicare.

Activities

- What activities do you plan to do together and what areas do you anticipate pursuing your own interests?

Couple Relationship

- Decide on the amount of individuality and duality you both want in your retirement life. Review how you both feel about the result of this decision and make adjustments or changes accordingly.

- Identify how you see your roles in your retirement marriage and negotiate possible new roles.

- What are your plans to maintain open, honest and effective communication with each other?

- What method or rules will you use to resolve differences and conflict in order to find a compromise that each of you will perceive as fair?

- Together determine the importance of intimacy in your marriage and how you will deal with the possible evolving changes as you age.

- Will dialoguing (introduced in Chapter 6) be a method you both continue to use to help you maintain a healthy marriage?

Family

- Talk with each other about the kind of relationship you plan to maintain with children, grandchildren, and other relatives.

- Talk to your children about what retirement plans the two of you have made and how you hope to maintain your relationship with them.

Friendship

- Discuss with each other the meaning of friendship in your later years and determine how you plan to change or maintain your friend relationships—singly and together as a couple.

In Retirement

Track Progress

- Review your personal retirement roadmap areas to see how you are doing.

- Identify the kinds of changes the two of you may still need to make.

- If a change is needed, don't be afraid to make it.

- Sit down to review and define your various alternatives and make the change.

- Then follow up to check if you made the right change and adjust it if it's not working, or change again if you need to.

Health and Wellness

- Continue to actively work to maintain your health, mental, emotional and spiritual health

- Verify that you have sufficient medical insurance coverage to cover catastrophic illness.

- Continue to maintain your knowledge of health and illness issues, learn and maintain CPR and other life saving skills if you are comfortable in doing so.

- As you experience some of the bumps in the road— health issues, care giving and changes in later years, review chapters 4, 5 and 6 in this book, and update yourself on the areas important to you.

- Keep abreast of the most recent health information online or in print.

- Make sure your family members know your wishes in regard to care if you become seriously ill.

- Obtain and complete an Advanced Directive stating your wishes in case of serious illness.

Personal

- Be sure you keep all your important papers and information updated and available to family or your attorney.

- Although you both may have your own responsibilities, share with each other what these tasks involve and how to do them.

Couple Relationship

- Be aware that maintaining your couple relationship continues to be an important factor in how much you enjoy your retirement years.

- Continue to carve out meaningful, personal couple time with each other.

Family

- Assess every so often how you are maintaining your contacts and relationships with family, and if you both are satisfied with the way it's going.

Friends

- Assess every so often how you are maintaining your contacts and relationships with friends and if you both are satisfied with the way it's going.

Vision and Planning

- Look for ways you can make this time in your life even better.

- Continue to review your roadmap every few years to see if you're on course.

- Make any changes or additions that can help both of you continue to have a positive life experience.

This roadmap guideline can help you to start laying out your own needs and wants as a couple. Feel free to make additions or personalize it to your specific situation. It is meant to be a working document, which provides you with ideas and thoughts about your own retirement plans and considerations. You might want to store your roadmap in your computer so you can adjust, change, and add to it as you and your spouse come up with new areas you want to cover. This roadmap doesn't have to be a humongous piece of work. Just put down the information that will help guide the two of you. The point to remember is that you both are sharing your ideas and have begun to author a roadmap for your retirement lives.

SUMMARY

Retirement doesn't need to be a static time of life. It's a time that can be one of the best periods in your life if you plan and set an intention to lead it the best that you can. To do this, you may sometimes need to do more than adapt to changes; you may need to proactively initiate change. My hope is that after reading this book, you are empowered to make the changes you need to as you grow and develop through your mature and elder years together and traverse the various lanes of retirement life.

References

Change

Bridges, William, Transitions: Making Sense of Life's Changes. Reading, Massachusetts: Addison-Wesley Publishing Company, 1980.

Goleman, Daniel, Emotional Intelligence. New York-Toronto-London-Sydney-Auckland: Bantam Books, 1995.

Marshak, Robert J. Ph.D., "The Tao of Change," OD Practitioner, Summer, 1994.

Planning and Transitioning

Bauer-Maglin, Nan and Radosh, Alice, Editors, Women Confronting Retirement: A Nontraditional Guide. New Brunswick, NJ: Rutgers University Press, 2003.

Cort-Van Arsdale, Diana and Newman, Phyllis, Transitions: A Woman's Guide to Successful Retirement. New York, NY: Harper Collins Publishers, 1991.

Merriman, Paul A., "Planning for retirement is as much about spending time wisely as saving money," Alaska Airlines Magazine, February, 2000, p. 83.

"Not Retiring," The Desert Sun, March 14, 2007, sec. E, P. EI.

Rich, Phil; Sampson, Dorothy Madway; and Fetherling, Dale S., The Healing Journey Through Retirement: Your Journal of Transition and Transformation. New York-Chichester-Weinheim-Brisbane-Singapore-Toronto: John Wiley & Sons, Inc., 2000.

Health – Physical, Mental, Emotional, Spiritual

Chopra, Deepak, M.D., Ageless Body, Timeless Mind. New York, NY: Harmony Books, 1993.

Corrigan, Patricia, "Exercise Your Brain," The Desert Sun, April 17, 2003, sec. F, p. FI

Ellis, Albert, Ph.D. and Harper, Robert A., Ph.D., A New Guide to Rational Living. No. Hollywood, California: Wilshire Book Company, 1975.

Katz, Lawrence C., Ph.D. and Rubin, Manning, Keep your Brain Alive. Workman Publishing Company, Inc., 1999. (www.neurobics.com)

Morley, John, M. D., "The Total Brain Workout," St. Louis Post Dispatch, 3/24/03

Morris, Desmond, "Growing Old Means Growing Up," Future, The Hoechst Magazine, March, 1998. p. 12-14.

Orlock, Carol, The End of Aging: How Medical Science is Changing our Concept of Old Age. New York, NY: Birch Lane Press, 1995.

Preidt, Robert, "Health Tip: Brain Exercises," Forbes.com.

Rowe, John W., M.D. and Kahn, Robert L., Ph.D., Successful Aging, New York, NY: Pantheon Books, 1998.

"Keeping Fit," StayWellNews, Community Resources for California's Seniors, California Department of Aging, Volume II, p. I.

General and Financial

Busacker, John M., "On Purpose: What's your life-Worth?" A Journal About Taking Charge of your Life/Work. Vol. 9 No. 2, 2005

Dychtwald, Ken, Ph.D. and Kadlec, Daniel J., The Power Years. Hoboken, NJ: John Wiley & Sons, 2005.

Keating, Peter, "Retire Early," Smart Money — The Wall Street Journal Magazine, April, 2007, pp 57-72 (p. 60).

Warren, Rick, The Purpose Driven Life. Grand Rapids, MI: Zondervan, 2002.

Couples

Post, Peter, Essential Manners for Couples. New York, New York:Harper-Collins Publishers, pp 151-152, 13-16, resolving disagreements P25-26.

Bilodeau, M.S., Lorrainne, Responding to Anger – A Workbook. Center City, MN-Hadelden, 2001.

Hendrix, Harville, Ph.D. and Hunt, Helen, M.A., The Couples Companion: Meditations and Exercises for Getting the Love You Want. New York, NY: Pocket Books, a Division of Simon & Shuster, Inc., 1994.

Schlessinger, Dr. Laura, The Proper Care & Feeding of Marriage. New York, NY: Harper-Collins Publishers, 2007.

Later Years

Baines, Marry K., M.D., Ethical Wills: Putting Your Values on Paper, Lifelong Books, 2006.

Dun, Hank, Hard Choices for Loving People, Hospice of Northern Virginia. (www.hospicenet.org/html/choices.html)

Mace, Nancy L. and Rabins, Peter V., The 36 Hour Day: A Family Guide to Caring for Persons with Alzheimer Disease, Related Dementing Illnesses, and Memory Loss in Later Life. Baltimore, Maryland: The Johns Hopkins University Press Book, 1999.

Pipher, Mary, Ph.D., Another Country: Navigating the Emotional Terrain of our Elders. New York, NY: Riverhead Books, A Member of Penguin Putnam Inc., 1999.

Rane-Szostak, Donna and Hearth, Kaye Ann, "Pleasure reading, other activities, and loneliness in later life," Journal of Adolescent & Adult Literacy, 39:2, October, 1995.

Turnbull, Susan B., The Wealth of Your Life: A Step-by-Step Guide for Creating Your Ethical Will. Wenham, MA: Benedict Press, 2005.

Made in the USA
Middletown, DE
05 November 2022